ALONE

Also by Admiral Richard E. Byrd

Little America

Skyward

ALONE

RICHARD E. BYRD

Macdonald
Queen Anne Press

A **Macdonald** BOOK

© Richard E. Byrd 1938, renewed by Marie A. Byrd 1966

This edition first published in the USA in 1986 by Jeremy P. Tarcher, Inc.,
9110 Sunset Blvd., Los Angeles, California 90069

First published in Great Britain in 1987 by
Queen Anne Press, a division of
Macdonald & Co (Publishers) Ltd
3rd Floor
Greater London House
Hampstead Road
London NW1 7QX

A BPCC plc Company

Jacket photographs — Front: Four By Five
                     Back: Bettman Archives

British Library Cataloguing in Publication Data

Byrd, Richard E.
   Alone.
   1. Antarctic regions ——— Discovery and
   exploration
   I. Title
   919.8'9043   G860

   ISBN 0-356-14053-9

Reproduced, printed and bound in Great Britain
by Hazell, Watson & Viney Limited
Member of the BPCC Group
Aylesbury, Bucks

CONTENTS

PREFACE

THIS book is the account of a personal experience—so personal that for four years I could not bring myself to write it. It is different from anything else I have ever written. My other books have been factual, impersonal narratives of my expeditions and flights. This book, on the other hand, is the story of an experience which was in considerable part subjective. I very nearly died before it was over. And, since my sufferings bulked so large in it and since a man's instinct is to keep such things to himself, I did not see how I could write about Advance Base and still escape making an unseemly show of my feelings. Also, I was a long time recovering from the effects of my stay at Latitude 80° 08′ South, and the whole business was so intimate in memory that I doubted that I could approach it with the proper detachment.

But in this decision my friends would not let me be. Wherever I went, they asked me questions. And finally, in December, 1937, some of my closest friends, whom I happened to be with one evening in New York, persuaded me to write the book while the facts were vivid in my mind. I agreed, but with reluctance.

I foresaw that a number of difficulties would rise to plague me once I started to write. For one thing, I knew that it could not be other than harrowing to relive again some of the bitter moments of Advance Base; and, for another, I appreciated that I should be obliged to discuss matters of personal moment in a way that would be distasteful. But, encouraged by the enthusiasm of my friends and the urgings of my publishers, I shut out the doubts and agreed to go ahead.

As the writing progressed, my earlier misgivings were confirmed. Indeed, there were times when I was on the verge of giving up the book entirely, and would have done so had there been any honorable way out. For there were aspects of this situation which I would rather not mention at all, since they involve that queer business called self-respect. Nevertheless, I finished what I started out to do, and this book represents the simple truth about myself and my affairs during that time.

The original intention was to use my diary, which was very detailed and voluminous, as the prime ingredient in the book; but I soon discovered that it was almost impossible to maintain an intelligible sequence and proportion by relying on the diary alone, since it was inescapably full of repetitious matter, cryptic references to things meaningful only to myself, and random jottings; besides, there were many very personal things directed to my family which I did not wish to include. In consequence, though I have used considerable sections and many excerpts, I have used them only where I felt they were illuminating. No particular effort has been made in the text to indicate whether the entry for a particular day is complete or only an excerpt lifted bodily from the diary; I did not want to clutter up the book with bibliographical apparatus. However, the diary, as well as numerous notes which I made on my meterological forms, the calendar, and loose sheets of paper, have been an excellent means of refreshing my memory.

Now, this book is called *Alone;* but obviously no one man could have done what I did without the loyal and sympathetic support of many other men. That support was one of the fine things of the whole experience; and it was especially manifested after my return from Advance Base, when the fifty-five men at Little America did everything possible to lighten the burden of leadership. One debt which I am happy to acknowledge in this connection is to my old shipmate, George Noville, the Executive Officer, who cared for me unsparingly until we reached New Zealand.

R. E. B.

Boston, Massachusetts,
    October, 1938.

1933: THE IDEA

Bolling advance weather base, which I manned alone during the Antarctic winter night of 1934, was planted in the dark immensity of the Ross Ice Barrier, on a line between Little America and the South Pole. It was the first inland station ever occupied in the world's southernmost continent. My decision to winter there was harder, perhaps, than even some of the men at Little America appreciated. For the original plan had been to staff the base with several men; but, as we shall presently see, this had proved impossible. In consequence, I had to choose whether to give up the Base entirely—and the scientific mission with it—or to man it by myself. I could not bring myself to give it up.

This much should be understood from the beginning: that above everything else, and beyond the solid worth of weather and auroral observations in the hitherto unoccupied interior of Antarctica and my interest in these studies, I really wanted to go for the experience's sake. So the motive was in part personal. Aside from the meteorological and auroral work, I had no important purposes.

There was nothing of that sort. Nothing whatever, except one man's desire to know that kind of experience to the full, to be by himself for a while and to taste peace and quiet and solitude long enough to find out how good they really are.

It was all that simple. And it is something, I believe, that people beset by the complexities of modern life will understand instinctively. We are caught up in the winds that blow every which way. And in the hullabaloo the thinking man is driven to ponder where he is being blown and to long desperately for some quiet place where he can reason undisturbed and take inventory. It may be that I exaggerate the need for occasional sanctuary, but I do not think so—at least speaking for myself, since it has always taken me longer than the average person to think things out. By that I do not mean to imply that, before I went to Advance Base, my private life had not been extraordinarily happy; actually it had been happier than I had had right to expect. Nevertheless, a crowding confusion had pushed in. For fourteen years or so various expeditions, one succeeding the other, had occupied my time and thoughts, to the exclusion of nearly everything else. In 1919 it was the Navy's transatlantic flight; in 1925, Greenland; in 1926, the North Pole; in 1927, the Atlantic Ocean; 1928-30, the South Pole; and 1933-35, the Antarctic again. In between there was no rest. An expedition was hardly finished before I was engaged in putting a new one together; and meanwhile I was lecturing from one end of the country to the other in order to make a living and pay off the debts of the completed expedition, or else scurrying around to solicit money and supplies for a new one.

You might think that a man whose life carries him into remote places would have no special need for quietude. Whoever thinks that has little knowledge of expeditions. Most of the time they move in fearful congestion and uproar, and always under the lash of time. Nor will they ever be different, so long as explorers are not rich men and so long as exploration itself deals with uncertainties. No doubt the world thinks it is a fine thing to reach one pole, or both poles, for that matter. Thousands of men have devoted the best part of their lifetimes to reaching one pole or the other, and a good many have died on the way. But among the handful who have actually attained Latitude 90°, whether North or South, I doubt that even one found the sight of the pole itself particularly inspiring. For there is little enough to see: at one end of the earth a mathematical spot in the center of a vast and empty ocean, and at the other end an equally imaginary spot in the middle of a vast and windy plateau. It's not getting to the pole that counts. It's what you learn of scientific value on the way. Plus the fact that you get there and back without being killed.

Now, I had been to both poles. In prospect this had promised to be a satisfying achievement. And in a large sense it had been—principally because the poles had been the means of enabling me to enlist public support for the full-scale scientific program which was my real interest. The books of clippings which my family kept up grew fat, and most of them said good things. These were among the tangibles of success, at least in my profession; these, plus goodwill, were the visible assets, although I should point out that the wisest among us, like conservative accountants, seldom carry the latter item in excess of $1.

But for me there was little sense of true achievement. Rather, when I finished the stocktaking, I was conscious of a certain aimlessness. This feeling centered on small but increasingly lamentable omissions. For example, books. There was no end to the books that I was forever promising myself to read; but, when it came to reading them, I seemed never to have the time or the patience. With music, too, it was the same way; the love for it—and I suppose the indefinable need—was also there, but not the will or opportunity to interrupt for it more than momentarily the routine which most of us come to cherish as existence.

This was true of other matters: new ideas, new concepts, and new developments about which I knew little or nothing. It seemed a restricted way to live. One might ask: Why not try to bring these things into daily existence? Must you go off and bury yourself in the middle of polar cold and darkness just to be alone? After all, a stranger walking down Fifth Avenue can be just as lonely as a traveler wandering in the desert. All of which I grant, but with the contention that no man can hope to be completely free who lingers within reach of familiar habits and urgencies. Least of all a man in my position, who must go to the public for support and render a perpetual accounting of his stewardship. Now, it is undeniably true that our civilization has evolved a marvelous system for safeguarding individual privacy; but those of us who must live in the limelight are outside its protection.

Now, I wanted something more than just privacy in the geographical sense. I wanted to sink roots into some replenishing philosophy. And so it occurred to me, as the situation surrounding Advance Base evolved, that here was the opportunity. Out there on the South Polar barrier, in cold and darkness as complete as that of the Pleistocene, I should have time to catch up, to study and think and listen to the phonograph; and, for maybe seven months, remote from all but the simplest distractions, I should be able to live exactly as I chose, obedient to no necessities but those imposed by wind and night and cold, and to no man's laws but my own.

That was the way I saw it. There may have been more than that. At this distance I cannot be sure; but, perhaps, the desire was also in my mind to try a more rigorous existence than any I had known. Much of my adult life had been spent in aviation. The man who flies achieves his destiny sitting down. Conflict, when it rises between the ship and the medium, comes to him indirectly, softened and stepped down by the mechanical advantage of the controls; when the conflict reaches the ultimate decision, the whole business is transacted one way or another in a matter of hours, even minutes and seconds. Where I was going, I should be physically and spiritually on my own. Where Advance Base was finally planted, conditions are not very different from what they were when the first men came groping out of the twilight of the last Ice Age.

That risks were involved, all of us knew; but none, so

ALONE

far as we could foresee, that were too great. Otherwise, as leader of a big polar expedition, and subject to all the responsibilities implicit in command, I could not have gone. That I miscalculated is proved by the fact that I nearly lost my life. Yet, I do not regret going. For I read my books—if not as many as I had counted on reading; and listened to my phonograph records—even when they seemed only to intensify my suffering; and meditated—though not always as cheerfully as I had hoped. All this was good, and it is mine. What I had not counted on was discovering how closely a man could come to dying and still not die, or want to die. That, too, was mine; and it also is to the good. For that experience resolved proportions and relationships for me as nothing else could have done; and it is surprising, approaching the final enlightenment, how little one really has to know or feel sure about.

*   *   *

Now, I have started out in this vein because a misunderstanding arose in some quarters concerning my reasons for occupying Advance Base alone. Indeed, some people disputed my right to do what I did. What people think about you is not supposed to matter much, so long as you yourself know where the truth lies; but I have found out, as have others who move in and out of newspaper headlines, that on occasion it can matter a good deal. For once you enter the world of headlines you learn there is not one truth but two: the one which you know from the facts; and the one which the public, or at any rate a highly imaginative part of the public, acquires by osmosis. It isn't

8

often that the one person centrally involved ever hears
about the second kind; his friends see to that. Nevertheless,
I happen to be privy to several of the gospel truths cir-
culated about Advance Base. God knows, there may be
others, but these could hardly be improved upon. One
is that I was exiled by my own men. Another is that I
went out there to do some quiet but serious drinking. In
the past such tales would have shocked me; most certainly
they would have made me mad. But not now.

The one criticism that might have given me pause was
disposed of by my friend, Charles J. V. Murphy, a member
of the expedition. Before leaving for Advance Base I asked
him to look out for my affairs in collaboration with the
Second-in-Command, Dr. Thomas C. Poulter. My an-
nouncement that I would occupy Advance Base alone was
not wirelessed to the United States until I was actually
established there. It said simply that I was going because
I wanted to go. My friends received the news with different
emotions. Radio messages poured into Little America during the next forty-eight hours. Most of them were from
men whose judgment I value. Considering the little that
they had to go on, I must say that they were surpassingly
fair. And yet, for every message of approval, there were
three of puzzlement or forthright disapproval. I was urged
—virtually ordered—to reconsider. My going off, they said,
must end in disaster, almost certainly for myself and probably for the fifty-five men presumed to be left leaderless at
Little America. The head of a great geographical institu-
tion warned that, if anything went wrong at Little America
during my absence, my disgrace would be worse than that

9

of Nobile, whose crime lay in leaving his shattered dirigible before all of his men were taken off. A banker friend said flatly that the whole idea was a reckless whim and that any shame in withdrawing would be more than offset by the escape from the consequences which must flow from my decision, if persisted in.

All of these messages were addressed directly to me, but they went to Charlie Murphy. He was in a tough spot. The winter night was coming on, the cold was deepening, and I know that he himself was troubled on my account. He knew how close was my friendship with these men in America. To each man he replied that I was where I was for a deliberate and useful purpose; that the tractors were on their way from Advance Base back to Little America and a return trip would expose other men to considerable risks; that in his opinion I was irrevocably resolved on my course; and that, because my psychological burdens were already heavy enough, he did not propose to add to them by informing me over the radio that my friends were in a panic. Therefore the messages were being filed at Little America for my return in October. Then it was March. And six months of darkness and cold would meanwhile intervene.

But of all this, of course, I had not even a hint. I am glad this was so; for I was human enough not to want to be misunderstood, at least by my friends—I wasn't big enough for that. In his radio conversations with me at the time Murphy was always cheerful; he never mentioned what had happened. And, for that matter, I never asked him what my friends thought, for the reason that I didn't want to know. I suspected, of course, that there would be criticism; but I couldn't do anything about that; my bridges were burned behind me. Whether I could have been persuaded to turn back if Murphy had passed those messages on is a matter I shall not undertake to answer. It would be stupid to do so. Hindsight has a way of inventing different compensations and motives. My only purpose in bringing the matter up now is to illustrate some of the misunderstandings that attended the manning of Advance Base and the different pulls that rise inevitably to deter the man who tries something out of the ordinary.

* * *

Advance Base was no reckless whim. It was the outcome of four years of planning. The original idea came out of my first expedition to the Antarctic, and was an indirect by-product of my interest in polar meteorology. Of all the different branches of science served by a soundly constituted polar expedition (on the last we served twenty-two branches) none to the popular mind has a more practical value than meteorology. The farmer whose livelihood comes from crops, the people whose stomachs are kept full by these crops, the speculators who gamble in them, the industrialist whose factories depend upon the farmer's purchasing power, the sailor on the seas—all these and others, even to the casual holiday tourist, have a vital stake in weather. But few of them appreciate the extent to which the poles enter into their local schemes.

Most of us have a schoolboy's understanding of the theory of simple circulation: a cold current of air flowing

11

inexhaustibly from the poles to the equator, a counter current of warm air returning poleward above it; and the two together creating the endlessly renewed interchange which is the breathing of the globe. The extent to which the poles influence the weather is still a subject for speculation. Some authorities go so far as to say that each pole is the true weather maker in its respective hemisphere. This latter belief has been formulated in Bjerknes' theory of the polar front, which undertakes to explain atmospheric circulation in terms of the effects produced by the interaction of masses of polar-cooled air, the so-called polar fronts, with the masses of warm equatorial air into which they intrude.

Although a knowledge of polar meteorology is indispensable for enlightened long-range forecasting, we really know very little about it. And, because of the need for more information about the general laws of circulation, the first concern of an expedition leader is to see that his meteorological department is strongly staffed. This obligation has been earnestly met by most expeditions. The results, nevertheless, have been meager; for Antarctica has been under scientific investigation for less than half a century; and, so far as weather data are concerned, the bulk of the knowledge is represented by the work of perhaps a dozen well-found expeditions.

For a continent having an estimated area of 4,500,000 square miles, this is not much of a showing. Or so it seemed to me. In the course of my first Antarctic expedition, I was struck by the thought that the most valuable source of meteorological data was still left untouched. What data existed had for the most part been collected at fixed bases on the Antarctic coast or on islands adjacent to the coast; by ships exploring contiguous waters; and by field parties poorly equipped for research making fast summer dashes inland. Meteorologically, the interior of Antarctica was a blank. No fixed stations had ever been advanced inland; no winter observations had ever been made beyond the coast; and the fragmentary data collected by sledging parties covered only the comparatively mild summer months. Yet, inland, beyond the moderating influence of the seas which surround the continent, was the coldest cold on the face of the earth. It was there one must look for typical continental conditions. And it was there that I proposed to plant Advance Base. There, where weather is manufactured. The data accumulated by a station like Advance Base when correlated with data gathered simultaneously at Little America, ought to throw a highly revealing light on the facts of atmospheric phenomena in high southern latitudes. Why should a civilization as technologically alert as ours continue to tolerate a situation that allows ruinous storms, kindled long before at remote storm centers, to break without adequate warning upon the civilized parts of the world? Only recently Mr. Willis R. Gregg, chief of the United States Weather Bureau, predicted the establishment in the polar regions of robot observers which would flash data by wireless to stations in lower latitudes. That way, meteorologists could watch conditions as they develop in the main amphitheaters of meteorological action, and plot their charts accordingly.

I rather wish I had thought of that myself, because Advance Base was intended to be the pilot station for a polarwide system of similar outposts, except that it was to be manned by flesh and blood instead of a mechanical brain untroubled by cold and darkness and memory. Our original plan was decidedly a daring one. In the preliminary discussions with Bill Haines, then, as on the second expedition, my Senior Meteorologist, I never pretended that the idea was more than speculative. In other words—great stuff, if we could do it. Where we finally decided to aim for was the foot of the Queen Maud Mountains. Even with that, we realized that we were probably over-reaching ourselves. It meant hauling tons of supplies some 400 miles across the crevasse-ridden Ross Ice Barrier and relying upon tractors whose capacities on Barrier surface would have to be determined by guess and by God.

In all aspects, particularly the psychological, the risks surrounding the project were very real. Whoever should elect to inhabit such a spot must reconcile themselves to enduring the bitterest temperatures in nature, a long night as black as that on the dark side of the moon, and an isolation which no power on earth could lift for at least six months. Now, against cold the explorer has simple but ample defenses. Against the accidents which are the most serious risks of isolation he has inbred resourcefulness and ingenuity. But against darkness, nothing much but his own dignity.

In the kind of station we had in mind the normal risks of a polar base would be intensified a thousand fold. The difficulties would be great. The amount of supplies that could be advanced would be small, and, therefore, only very few men could occupy it. The men would be jammed together at arm's length in a tiny shack buried in the snow. Wind and cold would keep them from ever leaving it for more than a few hours a day. Change in the sense that we know it, without which life is scarcely tolerable, would be nonexistent. The party would be dedicated to an iron routine. The day would be the repeated pattern of the hour; the week, the repeated pattern of the day; and one would scarcely be distinguishable from the other, even as an interval in time. Where there is no growth or change outside, men are driven deeper and deeper inside themselves for materials of replenishment. And on these hidden levels of self-replenishment, which might be called the pay levels of philosophy, would depend the ability of any group of men to outlast such an ordeal and not come to hate each other.

My idea was that three men—preferably two weather observers and a radio operator—should man the Base. The difficulties of hauling supplies into the Antarctic interior made three the maximum; and the risks, especially those of a psychological order, argued forcefully against less than three. Three is a classic number. Three men would balance each other like the legs of a tripod. With three men as compared to two, the chances for temperamental harmony seemed infinitely increased, since, in the nature of human relations, one man would constantly be present in the stabilizing role of a neutral judge, a court of appeal. Instead of hearing one voice everlastingly and seeing one face and being confronted with one pattern of habits and idiosyncrasies, a man would have two aspects and personalities constantly facing him.

Under such conditions it doesn't take two men long to find each other out. And, inevitably, this is what they do, whether they will it or not, if only because once the simple tasks of the day are finished there is little else to do but take each other's measure. Not deliberately. Not maliciously. But the time comes when one has nothing left to reveal to the other; when even his unformed thoughts can be anticipated, his pet ideas become a meaningless drool, and the way he blows out a pressure lamp or drops his boots on the floor or eats his food becomes a rasping annoyance. And this could happen between the best of friends. Men who have lived in the Canadian bush know well what happens to trappers paired off this way; and, mindful of these facts, I resolved from the beginning not to have Advance Base a two-man project.

Even at Little America I knew of bunkmates who quit speaking because each suspected the other of inching his gear into the other's allotted space; and I knew of one who could not eat unless he could find a place in the mess hall out of sight of the Fletcherist who solemnly chewed his food twenty-eight times before swallowing. In a polar camp little things like that have the power to drive even disciplined men to the edge of insanity. During my first winter at Little America I walked for hours with a man who was on the verge of murder or suicide over imaginary persecutions by another man who had been his devoted friend. For there is no escape anywhere. You are hemmed in on every side by your own inadequacies and the crowding pressures of your associates. The ones who survive with a measure of happiness are those who can live profoundly off their intellectual resources, as hibernating animals live off their fat. Occupied by three men of this sort, Advance Base should not be too difficult a place. So I reasoned, in all events.

* * *

During the months that followed the return of the first expedition the idea was continually challenging my imagination. Since the idea wouldn't down, I made a serious study of the practical possibilities. Well in advance of the mobilization of the second expedition late in 1933, four of us started working on the Base. One man was Victor Czegka, a Warrant Officer assigned to me by the Marine Corps. Another was Paul Siple. Both had served on the first expedition and knew the problems to be overcome. Czegka's job was to design the shack which would be the Base, and Siple's was to study and collect the essential materials required for it. The actual building of the shack was done by Ivor Tinglof, a cabinetmaker, in a Boston loft. And when the *Jacob Ruppert*, flagship of my second expedition, put out from Boston in October, 1933, she carried secreted in the hold the cunningly contrived knockdown sections of a three-man shack. In the hold, also, were four tractors, which would be available for lugging the Base into the interior.

Except for Haines, the builders, and myself, nobody else aboard had more than a dim suspicion of what that shack was for. I had said little about it, experience having taught me that the polar regions sooner or later will chasten the best-laid plans. While I had a number of men under consideration for the base, including several whose quality I knew well from the first stay at Little America, I had actually decided on none. The 15,000-mile sea voyage (by the course we had set) would provide ample opportunity to study and weigh the candidates. As for myself, time and circumstances would decide. At first I rather thought I had no right to put my own name in nomination. Having whipped an expedition together in the midst of the depression, naturally I owed a whale of a lot of money; I was in command of two ships, four airplanes, and a hundred men; so the chances of my being able to drop responsibilities did not look promising. On the other hand, it was hard to see how a leader could ask three other men to volunteer for a risk he was not prepared to take himself.

*　*　*

Of the long voyage to Little America I shall not attempt to write. It has been adequately described, I think, in *Discovery*, my general account of the expedition. After a sortie into the ice-strewn and fog-bound seas off the still-undiscovered coasts to the eastward of Little America, we finally steamed into the Bay of Whales on January 17, 1934. There we had our first glimpse of the appalling ice conditions that were to have a profound bearing upon all our proposed operations. Although masses of loose, broken ice jammed the spacious entrance to the bay, we were able to push the ship to within three miles of Little America. Three miles, that is, as the skua gull flies. But in

between, following the eastern shore of the bay, was a
mile-wide belt of pressure ice, with wave upon wave of
upheaved and broken ice, shot thought with deep crevasses,
pits, and open water leads with bottom 350 fathoms down.
Unless you have seen pressure, you cannot imagine what
it is like. The belt which blocked us off from Little America made me think of a hurricane-whipped sea petrified at
the height of the blow. It was forty feet from the crests of
some of the waves to the troughs. If that were all, the situation might not have been half bad. But the tides and
currents were ceaselessly working on the bottom of the
ice. You could hear it groaning and heaving in a dozen
different places; and a spot that would offer safe transit one
day would be a gaping crevasse by the next. After survey-
ing the region, both by airplane and with exploring parties
on skis, we came to the gloomy conclusion that not even
the dog teams, much less the tractors, could safely pass
through to Little America. Indeed, we were on the verge
of abandoning Little America entirely and building a new
base on the west shore of the Bay of Whales when a skiing
party returned with the news that they had charted a
passage through, though it was a good seven miles long
and full of potential hazards.

That passage we took, dreading the alternative of building a new main base on the other side of the bay. Misery
Trail was the name we gave it; and the name was an
understatement. For two whole months, twenty-four hours
a day, we flogged between the ships and Little America,
shifting the passage to meet the rapidly altering ice conditions, throwing bridges across the worst crevasses, while

the sea pounded the ice at our backs. Some days the midnight sun, making its unhurried round of the sky, was with us all the time; then it was warm enough for the men to strip to the waist, while the dogs, of which we had 150. suffered from the heat and floundered waist deep in snow turned soft. But most of the time it was not like that at all. The blizzards came shouting in, filling the air with drift, and blinding the tractor drivers and the sledgers, who felt their way along the range flags marking the transit. Almost always there was fog, the pale, mischievous fog of the Bay of Whales, which is like no other fog I have ever seen; almost milky in consistency, but turning the snow and atmosphere into a flat plane where all proportions are horribly twisted, and imparting to a traveler the queer feeling that he is treading the bottom of a heaving ocean.

But of Misery Trail I shall write no more. How we hauled 650 tons of supplies into Little America has been described at length in *Discovery*, though you may read the chapters without ever feeling the utter exhaustion that claimed us, an exhaustion so deep that it sent men stumbling on errands they could not remember when they reached their objectives and reddened their eyes with sleeplessness and numbed their bodies against cold and dropped them in their tracks from exhaustion. Anyhow, after a long time, the ships went away; then one midnight the sun popped for an instant below the horizon and each night thereafter set a little bit earlier; then the caches on the trail were empty; then Little America was being rebuilt and reoccupied; and for the first time in what seemed a thousand years I was able to give thought to the matter of Advance Base. By then it was almost too late. March had come, the winter was close upon us, the unbroken night was scarcely six weeks away, and I was surrounded by men whose strength had been sapped almost to the limit.

*　　*　　*

All this time the Advance Base shack, transported with the utmost care through the pressure, had been standing in the center of Little America. Paul Siple had taken possession to test out the ventilating and heating equipment. Now that I had time for serious reconsideration, it did not take long to reach one conclusion, which was that, wherever we did finally succeed in planting the base, it would not be at the foot of the Queen Mauds or anywhere near it. First, time was running against us. Here it was March, with the temperature dropping through the minus 20's, 30's, and even 40's; in March your Antarctic field parties are normally swinging toward home, racing the oncoming night. Secondly, the four tractors which we were relying upon to advance the base had been driven almost to wrack and ruin on Misery Trail, and a thoroughgoing overhaul was in order before the fleet could be sent out on the Barrier. Dogs were of no use to us in this journey. The pick of the pack had gone with Captain Innes-Taylor on a base-laying journey for next season's southern operations; but, even if the remaining dogs had been in good shape, they still could not have transported unaided the seven tons of material and stores needed for the base.

Airplanes might have been used as freighters, but that idea went by the board when the Fokker crashed on a test hop and was washed out completely. That left us with two planes capable of carrying any sort of load—the twin-engined Condor and a single-engined Pilgrim. I wouldn't use the Condor; if anything happened to her, our entire exploration program might be ruined. The Pilgrim I tried to use for relaying lighter loads, but, after emergency rations and equipment had been stowed aboard for the flight crew and a safe margin of gas included, the pay load was too slight to be of much use. Even so, I might have used the ship for what she was worth, had not the weather turned bad; the crew, returning from an experimental flight, got lost in a fog, very narrowly missing a crash; and it took a whole day to find them. After that experience I determined not to risk any more men in the air, nor the one airplane available for reserve duties.

Therefore, if Advance Base was to be advanced a foot beyond Little America, it would have to be by tractors. How far the tractors could push would depend in turn on how quickly Demas was able to complete the over-hauling of the engines and the caterpillar mechanisms, besides rebuilding one machine which had been partially destroyed by fire. I, for one, was not particularly optimistic as to the outcome. Three of these machines were 10-20 Citroëns, acquired in France; the runs over Misery Trail had demonstrated that they were definitely underpowered for day-in and day-out Barrier travel. The fourth was a 20-40 Cletrac, made in the United States. All were short; all, particularly the six-ton Cletrac, were heavy, which shortcomings made them vulnerable to crevasses.

So the trip was a gamble, no matter how I looked at it. This was the first serious attempt to operate automotive equipment in the Antarctic; the risks were the inevitable risks of pioneering. No one could tell how well the engines would function in temperatures down to 60° below zero or how the caterpillar treads would work on a snow surface which cold granulates to the fineness of sand or whether the machines could penetrate crevassed areas. If the fleet made a southing of 200 miles, it would be performing a miracle, I decided. And I was ready to settle for 150 miles —less, if necessary, so long as the journey could be made without undue hardships for the men.

Yet, we were not allowed to prepare in peace. When I recall the events that preceded the start, I wonder that we came off with as little lasting damage as we did. Young John Dyer, Chief Radio Engineer, plunged forty-five feet from the top of an antenna pole, with no worse hurt than a barked shin. Rawson, the Navigator, had to be operated on for a streptococcus throat infection. Then Pelter, the Aerial Photographer, came down with appendicitis; this meant another hasty operation under conditions made melodramatic by the doctor's unwitting act. Knocking over a lamp, he set fire to the cache in which all the surgical instruments were stored; all hands were wildly mustered to save the instruments and a dozen sleeping men who were in danger of being trapped in the adjoining shack. And this happened just a day or so after the Fokker had crashed in full view of the camp, and four men, stunned but otherwise unhurt, had crawled out from the wreckage.

Breaking rapidly one on top of the other, these incidents, any one of which might have been fatal, rasped nerves already drawn taut by the exhausting demands of Misery Trail. We were ready to find anything under the bed. In this mood we jumped one day to the grim conclusion that Little America was on the verge of breaking loose from the Antarctic Continent and drifting into the Ross Sea as a calving iceberg.

Little America is actually a city on a raft. The 300-foot thickness of ice on which it rests is pocketed in the coastal reach of the Ross Ice Barrier, whose sheer cliffs in places rise to 150 feet above sea level. Partly floating free, partly resting on deep submarine reefs and shoals, and elsewhere riding over the land, this gigantic Barrier fronts the ocean for 400 miles and also extends inland clear to the foot of the Queen Maud Mountains. It is not fixed in the sense that land is fixed. It is, in effect, an enormous glacier, wide enough to blanket the Atlantic seaboard States, and, like a glacier, it is forever creeping toward the sea. Propelled from behind by the massive rivers of ice pouring down through the mountain passes from the polar plateau, the coastal edges tend to bulge out over the sea, until the sheer weight of the projecting shelf or the violent pressures of tide and storm cause great strips to break off.

In this way the vast fleets of icebergs which patrol the ocean approaches to Antarctica are created. We had seen

these products of continental disintegration. In the course
of the voyage through the Devil's Graveyard, far to the
north and east of Little America, we had counted no less
than 8,000 bergs in a single day, some of them twenty
miles long. I don't think that any of us will ever forget
what it was like in the Devil's Graveyard: the sunless
corridors of waste waters; the fog that sometimes thinned
but never lifted; the crash of the gales, and occasionally
over that uproar the heavier sound of bergs capsizing in
the storm; and everywhere those stricken fleets of ice,
bigger by far than all the navies in the world, wandering
hopelessly through a smoking gloom. Through this ambush the ship groped and side-stepped like a lost creature,
harried by enemies her lookouts rarely saw full view, but
only as dark and monstrous shadows sliding through the
fog. The engine-room telegraph bells never stopped ringing; and months after some of us would start out of a
sound sleep, braced for the impact which we could not
forever expect to avoid. With the spell of that region upon
us, the realization that Little America might itself be
destined to join the ghost fleets to the north was enough
to shake us out of our weariness; for Little America was
barely three-quarters of a mile from the water's edge.

Ever since our arrival in January, the new, or bay, ice
in the Bay of Whales had been breaking up with unprec-
edented speed. Toward the end of February, when from
experience we had reason to expect a freeze, the pace of
the break-up quickened instead. The pressure ice started
to go; and with it went the ice cementing which held that

stretch of Barrier in position. Huge cracks opened up all around Little America. Each day they gaped a little wider. At night, when everything was quiet, one could sometimes feel the floor of one's shack heave gently from the swell pulsing against the ice basement hundreds of feet underneath. Fierce storms in the ocean to the north were apparently responsible. The waves continually smashing against the coast were breaking up the old ice and the new ice as fast as it formed. With Dr. Poulter, Senior Scientist, I took a long trip in a tractor along the Barrier crest to the north and east. The sound of the seas sixty feet below us was like thunder; and at least once, when the car was stopped, we heard far off the tremendous *whoosh* of a huge stretch of Barrier giving way.

We were worried, make no mistake about that. We were worried because we honestly didn't know what was coming, and couldn't stop it if it did come. So I did an extraordinary thing. I summoned the entire winter party into the mess hall, where I laid before them the facts, inviting every man to have his say on the steps, if any, which we should take. The outcome was a decision to continue as we were on the assumption that Little America would last; but at the same time to move approximately one-third of our stores to high Barrier, a mile or so to the southeast. If Little America did go out, we should then have a handy place to scramble to, with enough supplies cached to carry us through a winter. And if it didn't go out, there wouldn't be too much stuff to haul back. So for a couple of days we forgot everything else to haul gasoline, coal, food, clothing, and other gear to Retreat Camp. To hurry it up, I had Demas' tractors hauled out of the repair shop and pressed into service.

All this had a bearing upon the fate of Advance Base. Time was lost that could not be redeemed, and the energies of the men were depleted by that much more. The pity is that it seemed like so much labor lost. No sooner were we done than the seas abated, the outrush of the ice ceased, and the freeze-up set in almost at once.

Wearily the tractor men returned to their preparations. At midnight on February 15th, by the light of gasoline flares, the Advance Base shack was dismantled; and the sections were piled on two tractor sledges. Next afternoon, the four tractors moved out of Little America in echelon; trundling behind each was a string of sledges loaded down with food and fuel and meteorological gear and books and clothes and tools and all the other countless things required to defend existence in a place which offers nothing to man but air to breathe. Ahead of them ran a 178-mile life line through the heart of the Barrier, which had been flagged and scouted by Innes-Taylor's Southern Party, then making ready for the turn-around and homeward journey.

Nine men made up the party, including Siple and Tinglof, the carpenter who had built the hut in Boston. June and Demas were in joint command. Both were optimistic—I was not. Watching the column creep up the long white slope to the south, I was conscious only of misgivings. Although the sledges were loaded to the gunwales, a careful inventory of the supplies that were leaving showed

27

that they were insufficient for three men and that, unless a second round trip could be made before the winter night, our plans for manning the Base would have to be drastically changed. But before committing myself to any decision I would wait and see.

MARCH: THE DECISION

THEREAFTER FROM THE TRACTOR FLEET CAME AN ALMOST
continuous stream of radio reports, mostly discouraging.
Vexed by cold and drift and blizzards, and reduced to low
gear on loose, newly fallen snow, the machines made slow
going of it. About twenty-four miles south of Little
America two cars narrowly escaped disaster in an unsus-
pected crevassed region; and about fifty miles out in a
bowl-like depression named the Valley of Crevasses the
party was compelled to take a long detour eastward to
avoid blind crevasses whose roofs had been strong enough
to pass Innes-Taylor's dog teams, but not the heavily
loaded machines. On this jog, sixty-seven miles out of
Little America, the Cletrac gave out entirely: a crankshaft
pin, made brittle by the cold, sheared off; and, the necessary repairs being beyond the party's resources, the machine was abandoned. With it was lost 50 per cent of the
party's carrying capacity. Redistributing the loads as best
they could, June and Demas pushed south in the other
three tractors. Any chance of an extended southing was
gone. The three surviving Citroëns, June advised, had all

developed mechanical trouble of one sort or another. The generators—even the spares—were worn out, the radiators were leaking, the anti-freeze solution had been lost, the drivers were cramming snow down the radiators to keep going, and one car was without headlights.

More vividly than the terse radio bulletins described, I knew what the men were up against. The sledgers, at Little America, hating the break with tradition, sneered at tractor travel as "limousine exploring." But, so far as discomforts went, there was little to choose between the two ways of travel. You could go faster and haul more in a tractor, and certainly you could do your exploring sitting down. But tractoring had its own punishing hardships, not the least of which was waiting exasperating hours for the blow torches to thaw out the lubricants in the crankcase, rear end, and the transmission, which the cold congealed to a rubbery toughness after the engine stopped. And sucking frozen condensation from the gas lines. And melting snow in the food cookers to make water for radiators that leaked like sieves. And leaving the flesh of your fingers on metal parts too delicate to be handled with clumsy mittens. And sitting as if trapped in a moving cabin, waiting for the awful lurch, and the *whroom* of slithering tons of snow to warn you that a crevasse roof was letting go under the treads.

Even a demanding leadership can ask only so much of flesh and blood. The evening of March 21st, the tractor party reported that it was at a depot put down by Innes-Taylor's Southern Party 123 miles by trail from Little America. Almost at the same time Innes-Taylor wheeled in from the south, with just one day's dog rations on the sledges and a story of bitter cold and blizzards. That, I decided, was far enough. Let Advance Base be planted alongside this depot at Latitude 80° 08′ South, Longitude 163° 57′ West, just a hairsbreadth off the Little America meridian. The distance was sufficient, the meteorologists decided, to permit satisfactory correlations. June was instructed to retrace his tracks and pick up the remnants of the Cletrac's load in the morning. The temperature where he was dropped meanwhile to 52° below zero.

That night, between the hours June arrived at, and went from, Latitude 80° 08′ South, I made my decision. Advance Base would be occupied and, inevitably, by one man. With the tractors crippled and the sun due to quit us in less than a month, neither the means nor the time remained to stock it for three men as planned. The alternative of two men I again rejected for the same reasons I had rejected it before: that is, on the logic of temperamental harmony. The truth is that I myself did not dare to go as one of a two-man team. The other man might turn out badly, as indeed might I, in his eyes. Hating or being hated by a man whom you couldn't avoid would be a degrading experience leaving the mark of Cain in the heart. Feeling as strongly as I did, I certainly couldn't very well ask two other men to do what I wouldn't risk myself. It had to be one man, and that one myself, if for no other reason than that here again I could not bring myself to ask a subordinate to take the job.

The idea of letting Advance Base go by default was never seriously entertained. The expedition had planned too long and endured too much on its account for me to give up so easily, even though we had failed to push the base as far south as the meteorologists might have wished. Moreover, as I said at the outset, I was anxious for the opportunity to go. This was an experience I hungered for, as soon as I grasped the possibilities. But apart from that, I was better equipped, perhaps, than anyone else in camp to handle the job. The Base was my scheme. I had wet-nursed it from birth; and nearly everything about the shack, from the insulation to the double-action trapdoor, represented some pet notion. From Dyer, who had instructed me in radio, I had picked up enough primer information to enable me to keep in touch with the main base; and Haines had taught me how to take care of the meteorological instruments, which were mostly automatic, anyway.

As for the practical matters of existence, I felt that my service as an explorer had made me self-reliant. I don't claim that, like Thoreau, when he retired to his lonely hut at Walden, I was all prepared to build a house, lay a chimney, survey a field, and manufacture pencils. The fact is that I was not nearly as handy as I had imagined; but, for all my clumsiness, there were one or two improvisations at Advance Base that would have done credit to that scholarly experimenter and even to that inspired artificer Robinson Crusoe.

I was up all night rearranging my affairs. It was not as easy as I pretended. My break with the interlocking conveniences and practices of normal life would be clean and sharp and irrevocable. I had moments of heart-sinking

doubt, particularly when I visualized what might happen
to my family if I should fail. And this alone gave me pause.
As to the moral aspects of my leaving fifty-five men leaderless at Little America, that did not trouble me a bit. My
officers had a comprehensive idea of what was expected
of them during my absence. We talked almost steadily from
midnight to dawn. In charge, with the title of Second-in-
Command, I put Dr. Poulter, the Senior Scientist. He is
a physical giant of a man. Though attuned to the quiet of
the university campus, he had the practical judgment and
intellectual balance which are indispensable for the leadership of men who like to call themselves men of action—
as if by that they put themselves beyond the penalties of
rashness.

Poulter would have under him a hard-bitten crew who
were well able to take care of themselves. Misery Trail had
toughened and schooled the new men as no other experience could have done; with them was a hard core of
veterans of my other expeditions. Haines, the Third-in-
Command, was serving on his third polar expedition, as
was Demas. Noville, the executive officer, had served under
D'Annunzio during the war, had been a Superintendent
of the Air Mail, and had been with me on the North Pole
affair and the transatlantic flight. June, whom I appointed
Chief of Staff, had flown with me across the South Pole.
Bowlin, the SecondPilot, had been in the Navy sixteen years.
Innes-Taylor had dueled with Zeppelins in London's war-
time skies, and trekked the Yukon for the Royal Canadian
Police. Siple, who was a scientist and trail party leader, and
Petersen, who was a first-rate photographer, radio man,

and skier, had proved their worth on the previous expedition. Von der Wall, another Navy man, knew what it was like to be torpedoed in the Atlantic Ocean, and Bob Young, another veteran as well as a retired British naval rating, had fought in the Battle of Jutland. And Rawson, though the youngest of the lot, knew what it was all about from four voyages into the Arctic. There were these and others like them.

To these men I could entrust the winter destinies of Little America without fear. For one thing, the winter night is ordinarily tranquil. No parties are in the field; the men are fully occupied in making preparations for the spring campaigns; and, secure from the blizzards and cold, life finds new and easy ruts underground. Moreover, I expected to keep in fairly close touch with them by radio. Hence, except for some special instructions to Poulter, I did not feel it necessary to draft a complicated set of regulations. My last general order to the camp, which was primarily intended to announce the line of command, covered less than three typewritten pages. It was a simple appeal to work industriously, conserve supplies, abide by the safety rules, and respect discipline. In conclusion, I said: "Every man in this camp has a right to be treated fairly and squarely, and the officers are requested to hold this fact in mind. In a sense our status is primitive ... We have no class distinctions as in civilization. What a man is back home does not count at Little America. He who may have failed back there has his chance to make good here; and he will not be judged by the position he holds so much as by the way he plays the game and does his job, however humble it may be. . . ."

* * *

This order I finished on the morning of March 22nd, just before I flew to Advance Base. I did not have time to post it. Somebody read it to the men after I left. Noville, who had shared his quarters with me, helped me pack a few personal things—several dozen books, a sextant, a couple of fine chronometers, a fine and rather elegant fur flying suit that a friend had given, a shaving kit, my own set of phonograph records, and various odds and ends. There was no ceremony about it whatever, if only because Byrd expeditions never stand on ceremony. The cook shouted cheerily, "Remember, Admiral, no class distinctions at Advance Base!"

Bowlin and Bailey were fretting in the Pilgrim. Although hot oil had just been poured into the engine, it chilled rapidly; the temperature was 43° below zero and dropping. I remember glancing at my wrist watch as we left the ground. The time was 10:35 A.M. (180th meridian time). Bowlin, as if sympathizing with my mood, made a banking turn around Little America before squaring away for the south. I took in every detail. If I had created anything tangible and unique in life, it was this sprawling, smoke-spewing, half-buried city called Little America, pocketed within the eastern heights of the Bay of Whales. It heartened me just to look at the place. The job of reoccupation was nearly finished, and I need have no further worries on that score.

35

A quick glance to the north confirmed what I already knew: that the Ross Sea was frozen to the horizon, and any danger to Little America from further disintegration of the Barrier had passed. Beyond Amundsen Arm, where the Bay of Whales curves in behind, and to the south of, Little America, we picked up the tractor tracks, the crimp marks of the caterpillar treads standing out clearly on the white, virginal flesh of the Barrier. Every third of a mile was an orange trail flag; and every twenty-five miles was a tall snow beacon, surmounted by a big orange banner on a bamboo pole, with a line of burgee and pennant flags running to the west and east. These were depots in which Innes-Taylor had cached rations for the main spring journeys: the markers—the Antarctic equivalent of roadside stands and route signs—on the Advance Base road. Sixty-seven miles out, Bowlin dropped low over the foundered Cletrac. Demas and Hill, who were still slaving over the engine, crawled out from under a canvas apron and waved a greeting. Not long afterwards a dark speck on the horizon resolved itself into a cluster of tents—Advance Base.

Where Advance Base lay, the Ross Ice Barrier was as flat as the Kansas Plains. Snow rolled on forever to meet the sky in a round of unbroken horizon. Here was the spaciousness of the desert; the spaciousness, you might say, of the raw materials of creation. Against it the huddled clump of tents, tractors, dogs, and men was just a pinprick in infinity. Although this was all familiar stuff to me, it was not until then that I had an intimation of what I was in for. On the verge of starting a dangerous task, I suppose that even the most unimaginative man must know that in-

stant of premonition when the last unresolved forebodings
come swimming out of nowhere. Whatever it was, I dis-
missed it before the skis touched. Innes-Taylor and Siple
were coming forward to meet me; and Bowlin was impatient to be off, lest the cold stop his engine. Fifteen
minutes later the plane was in the air. The vapor from the
exhaust trailed behind like an enormous banner, which
hung long after the plane had vanished into the lusterless,
low-swinging sun.

"How's the shack coming?" I asked Siple.

"Slowly," he said. And, looking at him and at the other
men who came up to say hello, I saw that their faces were
yellowed by frostbites, and the cracked lips within the
parka hoods wore mirthless grins.

"Everybody all right?" I asked.

"Everybody but Black," Innes-Taylor said. "He's got a
bum knee. But, if it's all right with you and if we can get
this shack up fast, I'd like to get my party out of here in
a day or two."

"We'll see," I said. I knew, without being told, what was
in Innes-Taylor's mind. He and his three men—Paine,
Ronne, and Black—had been on the trail over three weeks,
enduring temperatures exceeding 50° below zero. I gathered that they had had a rough time of it, largely on
account of defective zippers on the sleeping bags. Ice had
gathered in the bags. To sleep more than a few minutes
at a time was almost impossible; and lying still meant
freezing to death. Hence, as the party still faced a five-day
journey back to Little America, I promised Innes-Taylor
that I would not hold him any longer than was absolutely

37

necessary. Not alone for the men's own sakes, but also out of consideration for the dogs, of which he had two dozen tethered around his tents.

June, with six men and two tractors, was somewhere on the trail, making for the Cletrac. So eight of us were available for the preliminary work on the base—Innes-Taylor's party, myself, and Siple, Tinglof, and Petersen from the tractor group. A pit fifteen feet long, eleven wide, and eight deep—big enough to take the shack bodily—had already been dug before I arrived. Sunk in the snow this wise, the shack would be out of reach of the wind and the drift, which mounts with the speed of a tide around any upraised object.

Luckily for us, the shack had been designed for quick assembly. Tinglof and Siple were laying the floor sections when I took charge. Putting up the walls was a simple matter of heaving the numbered sections into the right places and bolting or spiking them together. Afraid that a blizzard might strike during the night and fill up the pit, we worked like hell. That afternoon the temperature sagged through the minus 50's, and our breaths made a continuous fog in the pit. We watched each other's faces for the dead-white patches of frostbite. "A blossom on your nose, Petersen," somebody would say. Petersen, until then unaware of the danger, would mold the flesh with his finger tips, his fingers stinging the instant they left the warmth of the gloves; then the blood would come surging back into the affected spot with stabs of pain. "Jesus," he would say. Then back to work.

Hard as we pushed, the shack was still unroofed when

the night rushed down from the South Pole at 5 o'clock. By then the temperature was 61° below zero. We worked on by the light of pressure lanterns and the heat of primus stoves. Then the lights died when the kerosene froze; and a flashlight, the battery frozen, went out in my hand, leaving us in darkness. Tinglof stumbled and fumbled in the caches until he found two gasoline blow torches which June had left behind; by their feeble glow and with the heat from the flame near our legs, we carried on.

It was verging on cruelty to drive so hard, but we had to have shelter before we could sleep. Tinglof's mittens were filled with ice; when he bared his hand to tip in a spike, I saw that the skin was covered with puffy yellow blisters. It was the same with Siple, who was putting the stove together. Before the bolts would turn, he had to close his mittens over the metal to take the frost out; his hands became swollen lumps, and again and again I saw him, biting his lips against the pain, slip them under his parka to snatch at the body's heat. Paine's face and helmet looked like a solid lump of ice. Ronne's lips were cracked and bloodied. All of us were coughing, not from colds but from the superchilled air that tortured the lungs as we breathed more deeply from exertion.

No exaggeration, it was brutal work. I climbed out of the pit to fetch a piece of meteorological equipment from one of the caches. While I was ransacking the pile, my nose and cheeks froze. I stood up a moment, kneading the flesh. A ghastly blue reflection showed over the excavation, and the way smoke from the torches and freezing breaths spiraled up through the unsteady light made me think of that terrible frozen pit in the *Divine Comedy*, which leads down past Lucifer to the lost souls. A low moan came out of the darkness. I reached into the chest pocket of my parka for the flashlight. Nothing happened when I flipped the switch; the batteries were still frozen. But ringing me were dozens of anxious eyes, glittering with ravenous light and framed within the restive shadows of the wolf dogs. My heart really bled; for they had to sit and wait, spaced out on the steel tethering line. But I could do nothing for them, except promise myself to start Innes-Taylor north just as soon as I could.

The single door of the shack was made to face west—for no reason at all, so far as I can remember, except that after the pit was sunk, the hut simply had to face west to fit. The pit was dug overly wide to accommodate what I was pleased to call my "veranda," created by projecting the roof some two feet past the wall on the west side. This would give me access to a tunnel system and to a trapdoor set in one corner of the projection and reached by a ladder. If I do say so myself, the hatch was a clever double-action arrangement. You could open it by pushing up; or, if the drift was packed too tightly overhead, you could pull it down by removing two pegs. "Look, Admiral," Czegka had exclaimed, when he first demonstrated the door. "Push him up. Push him down. No danger, now, of being buried alive in a big blizzard."

It was nearly 1 o'clock in the morning and 63° below zero when we were done with securing the roof. The job was infernally complicated as a result of several sections' having been warped in transit from Little America.

The door, which had been made to shut tight on bevels, just as on an ice box, now couldn't be made to latch at all. (Nor did I ever succeed in closing it entirely during the seven months I occupied Advance Base.) I was worried, too, over finding that we had blundered in calculating the depth of the pit. Instead of being flush with the surface, the roof stuck up a good two feet above it. That would make for troublesome drift. The mistake was past remedy, however; so I let it pass. Siple had the stove rigged up and burning; and, though it would be a long time before the chill would go out of the shack, we all went below to enjoy the little warmth it gave off. None too soon, at that. Innes-Taylor remarked casually that he thought one of his feet was frozen. And indeed it was, as we saw as soon as he peeled off his mukluks (boots). I tried warming the foot with my hands and working the flesh gently, but without effect. That superstitious business of massaging the skin with snow isn't done in the Antarctic. At sixty below, snow takes on a hard, crystalline structure; you might as well use sandpaper. What we tried in this case was a method familiar to all polar travelers. Paine, I think it was, unbuttoned his shirt, and let Innes-Taylor slip the foot against the warmth of his stomach. He held it there fifteen or twenty minutes, until the circulation revived with a pounding pain that brought sweat to Innes-Taylor's forehead.

* * *

That night, after Innes-Taylor, Paine, and Ronne had repaired to their own tents, which were pitched just a few

yards from the roof of the shack, five of us stretched out
our sleeping bags on the Advance Base floor. The instant
the fire went out the cold settled with the force of a blow.
"You'll freeze to death in this dungeon," Petersen remarked cheerfully from his bag. But, having lived in the
shack at Little America, I knew otherwise; it would be comfortable enough as soon as the frost went out of the walls.
The shack was as tidily built as a watch. Although enclos-
ing over 800 cubic feet of space, it weighed only 1,500
pounds; the hut and everything about it had been kept
as light as possible to make for easier transportation.
Fine white pine stiffened the frame and flooring, but the
rest was mostly shell. The walls were only four inches
thick. A three-ply veneer, one-eighth inch thick and composed of a layer of wood between two strips of cardboard,
sheathed the outer and inner walls. Loosely wadded in the
hollow between was insulation of kapok, which resembles
raw cotton. Tacked to the inside walls was a green fireproof canvas fabric. The ceiling and the upper walls were
a bright aluminum, to reflect light and heat. Czegka had
remembered everything. And that night, sleeping for the
first time at Advance Base, I had reason to think well of
what he and Tinglof had created.

Next morning we were roused by the *beep-beep* of the
tractor horns; June and Demas were back with the
Cletrac's load. Considering the night they had spent on
the open Barrier, the crew were in an astonishingly cheerful mood.

"It's amazing," young Dick Hill observed, "the way

these jallopies keep moving. Even when they're falling apart."

"He means," Skinner interrupted, "the way you can get 'em started after they've stopped. Every time the engine dies, you think it's the finish. But if you tinker long enough, damned if they don't turn over again."

Although spoken in jest, the news was disturbing. The return trip to Little America would be difficult enough at best; and, considering the present killing temperatures, the chance that mechanical breakdowns might maroon some 20 per cent of the expedition's personnel on the trail was one I found hard to accept. I had only to look at the men to visualize what they had been through. They were like scarecrows, the way the torn windproofs, caked with frozen oil, fluttered about their legs. Their hands were eloquent, Demas' and Hill's particularly. The flesh had been burned and shriveled by the frost in the metal which they were forever handling; the nails had turned black and were rotting away; and blood was oozing from sodden blisters.

June and Demas, however, were reassuring. "I'm not worried," Demas said. "With a break, we'll have all three cars in Little America twenty-four hours after leaving here." If anything did go wrong, plenty of help was available at Little America; and, anyhow, Innes-Taylor's party would be bringing up the rear. Nevertheless, the situation was not to my taste; for at that season in the Antarctic the line between safety and a major mishap is hair-thin. "It's too damn cold for men to be on the trail," I said. "I want all of you out of here within forty-eight hours."

Actually only one big job remained to be done: cutting out and stocking two supply tunnels, one for fuel, the other for food and miscellaneous stores. The tunnels were laid out in parallel, running west from the opposite ends of the veranda. With fourteen men to help, the job didn't take long. They were each about thirty-five feet long, about three feet wide, and deep enough for me to walk erect. The food tunnel was to the south. To make this we mined out a subterranean passage, leaving a vaulted roofing of snow about two and a half feet thick. Here provision boxes were stacked in recesses along both walls, one box on top of the other, with the marked sides facing out so that I should be able to tell the contents at a glance. At the far end we dug a hole for a toilet, which was distinguished, in Petersen's phrase, for "the open plumbing." Into the other tunnel went the drums of fuel, which were rolled into alcoves let into the sides. As soon as the drums were underground, we roofed this tunnel with coarse paper laid across wooden slats, and anchored with snow blocks. The rest of the supplies were dumped through the hatch into the veranda.

As the stuff dropped underground, Siple and I made a rough check. The variety of things was really amazing: 350 candles, 10 boxes of meta tablets, 3 flashlights, and 30 batteries, 425 boxes of matches (safety and wax), 2 kerosene lanterns, a 300-candle-power gasoline pressure lantern, 2 sleeping bags (one fur and one eiderdown), 2 primus stoves. Also, a single folding chair with an air-cushion which the tractor men generously donated, 9 fire bombs and a Pyrene fire extinguisher, 3 aluminum buckets, 2 wash basins, 2 mirrors, a calendar, a small fireproof rug,

2 candle holders, 2 whisk brooms (for brushing snow off my clothes), 3 dozen pencils, a 5-gallon can stuffed with toilet paper, 400 paper napkins, a box of thumbtacks, and one of rubber bands. Also, 2 reams of writing paper, 3 boxes of soap and laundry chips, a thermos jug, 2 decks of playing cards, 4 yards of oilcloth, pieces of asbestos, 2 packets of tooth picks. Altogether, the food supplies comprised approximately 360 pounds of meat, 792 pounds of vegetables, 73 pounds of soup, 176 pounds of canned fruit, 90 pounds of dried fruit, 56 pounds of desserts, and half a ton of various staples, including cereals. There were these things, and a good deal more besides.

While the rest of us were hurriedly stocking the tunnels and shack, Waite was rigging the radio antenna, which was about two hundred feet long and strung on four fifteen-foot bamboo poles. He finished in midafternoon; then he installed the transmitter and receiver. With Siple's help I personally set up the meteorological equipment, of which there was a great deal. "My God," remarked Dustin, pausing in fascination, "that's going to a lot of trouble to find out what my feet keep telling me: that it's a damn cold place."

The end of the second day—March 23rd—saw Advance Base just about ready to take over its job as the world's southernmost weather station. That night we had a farewell banquet for Innes-Taylor's party, which was scheduled to head north in the morning. And, because this was made to seem a gala occasion, my guests managed to talk me out of the choicest delicacies in my larder—a turkey and a couple of chickens which Corey, the supply officer, had contributed out of the goodness of his heart, thinking I might like to celebrate one or two holidays. The meat was rigid as armor plate with frost, but the hard-boiled tractor men were prepared to deal with that: they thawed it out with blow torches. Elected chef by acclamation, Innes-Taylor presided over five primus stoves. Nine men sat cross-legged on the floor; and five, who couldn't find room to sit, ate standing up. Judging by the belching of the dog drivers, the meal must have been a satisfying change from the soupy *hoosh* which they had lived on for nearly a month. "It's just having something sticking to your ribs that makes the difference," Paine remarked. "And for my third helping I'll take the neck, Captain, if that isn't your dirty thumb that I see."

*   *   *

The dinner, as it turned out, was premature. During the night an easterly came rustling through the cold; and, when we awakened, it was making into a blizzard. You couldn't see fifty yards, and the wind's edge, at 28° below, was sharp as a knife's. Because travel was out of the question, Innes-Taylor decided to stay another day. That night, as the night before, ten men slept in my shack. Tinglof was stretched out under a table; Black was curled up behind the stove; Waite was sprawled under my bunk; June went to sleep sitting up in a corner; and the others, laid out like mummies in the sleeping bags, covered the floor from one wall to the other. I shall never forget that night. My guests set up such a racket of snoring that I was finally driven out of the shack. So I went topside to see how the sledgers were faring.

The blizzard was slackening, but the wind was still high, and my flashlight made only a blotch of light in the thick drift. But off to one side I could hear the sides of the tents cracking like wet sails in a gale; and I groped in that direction until I came to the tents. Paine was muttering something in his sleep, and Innes-Taylor moaned and twisted away from the beam of light as it fell across his eyes; but Ronne was sleeping the full sleep of a good Norwegian. As I was drawing tight the pucker thong closing the sleevelike entrance, something brought me erect. It was a sound breaking taut and vibrant over the voice of the wind. Then it swelled again, keyed to the gale, but richer and compounded of many voices. The dogs, of course.

I floundered until I found them—three teams in parallel files, each spaced out on a tethering cable between gee poles rammed deep into the crust. The dogs fell quiet when I came through the smother. Perhaps the knowledge that human beings were still about reassured them. As I went down the tethering lines, playing the flashlight, I found each dog curled in a tight ball, with his back to the wind, his muzzle tucked against his belly, and the drift making a wall around him. It did not seem the part of mercy to keep them on the Barrier this late in the season. Yet, wait they must until the weather improved. A lull came in the wind; and for an instant, as the drive of the drift slackened, I saw clear sky swarming with stars directly overhead. Yes, the weather might be mending. In that case, the Southern Party would be homeward bound in the morning.

Maybe Paine's great leader, Jack, guessed that, too. For he heaved suddenly to his feet, shook the snow off his back; and then I heard the indescribable wandering cry of the husky. In an instant all twenty-four were up and joining in; they filled the Barrier with a melancholy wail that was not the melancholy of sadness but rather of hunger and lust. Yes, indeed, there would be a run to the sledges on the morrow.

Sunday the 25th came on clear, still, and cold. "Well, she's certainly covered now," Tinglof reported after peering from the hatch. A foot of drift lay over the roof, and little light came through the three skylights set in the ceiling. The thermometers stood at 48° below, and Waite said, "They lie in their tongues." Innes-Taylor finally got off; and later in the day Demas, Hill, and Skinner left in one of the Citroëns to make a last effort to salvage the Cletrac, leaving June, Siple, Waite, Petersen, Black, and Dustin, with two tractors, still at Advance Base. They lingered only long enough to make everything shipshape. Waite finished his test radio contacts with Little America; Siple was through tinkering with the stove; the meteorological equipment was already spinning out its tale of wind and cold; and finally, Monday noon, in the middle of lunch, June remarked quizzically, "Well, we've done just about everything that needs doing, and a lot of things, I suspect, that needed no doing at all; so I guess it's time to shove off." As simply as that he disposed of a problem in polar

48

etiquette for which the rest of us could not find the right meaningless phrase.

Directly after the noon stand-up meal, the tractor crews made ready to leave. The temperature was 64° below zero. Both cars were half buried in drift, and we were a long time digging them out. Even with blow torches playing on the crankcases and canvas aprons draped around the chassis to hold in the heat, it was two hours before the engines would turn over. The party made a false start at 5 o'clock, only to come limping back two hours later. I was underground when I heard the sound of the treads reverberating through the snow. It gave me a nasty turn because I was desperately anxious to have them on their way to Little America. But, when they returned to the shack and told what had happened, I understood that they had made the wisest choice. Three or four miles out the radiator froze in June's car, and in unscrewing the cap he scalded one hand in the geyser that spouted up and froze the other trying to nurse it. So he decided to return and give his hand a chance to heal in the warmth of the shack. The party stayed all night, sleeping in their clothes. The engines never stopped running, and Waite and Dustin were up all night to tend to them. "If you let them stop," Demas snapped, "you may be here all winter." I didn't bother to go to sleep, but wandered around with the two men on night watch.

Wednesday the 28th, at high noon, the cars put out again; this time they did not come back. In some respects the departure had been as casual as speeding the departing week-end guests. Whatever of importance required saying had been said long before. The one afterthought that had bothered me after quitting Little America was the possibility that I might not have been emphatic enough in my instruction that no rescue efforts were to be made on my behalf in the event of radio failure. This order I impressed again upon the Advance Base party. "I don't know much about radio," I said. "The chances are that I shall lose communication for short periods, maybe for good. Don't let that worry you. No matter what happens, remember that I'm a lot better off in this shack than you are apt to be on the Barrier, and I give you a hard-and-fast order not to come for me until a month after the sun returns. I've got an abiding respect for the Barrier, and I don't want any act of mine to put you in jeopardy from it during the winter darkness." And to make sure that there was no mistaking my earnestness, I repeated the gist of this before they started out afresh.

Siple and Waite lingered behind after the others had boarded the tractors. If they meant to say something, they never got it out. An impatient voice snapped, "For Christ's sake, get going"; and first Siple, then Waite, after mumbling an unintelligible amenity, hurried off.

I stood at the trapdoor and watched the two Citroëns move away. Their red hoods and rounded canvas superstructures made a jaunty picture. June headed due north into the noon sun, so big and swollen, and so low in the sky, that it could well have passed for a setting sun. In the cold air (the temperature was 50° below zero) the exhaust vapor puffed up like a smoke screen, which a gentle northerly wind fanned out until much of the eastern horizon was obscured. I went below, intending to busy myself with the wind-speed records; but the errand was a piece of self-deception which I could not quite bring off. For perhaps the only moment in my adult life I was conscious of being utterly at loose ends. The shack, which had seemed bright and cheery, now was neither. And, obeying an impulse which I had no time to be ashamed of, I rushed up the hatch ladder. Just why, I don't know even now; perhaps for a last look at something alive and moving. Although the cars were by then some distance away, I could still hear the *beep-beep* of the horns and the clatter of the treads, so clearly do sounds carry in that crystal air.

I watched until the noise died out; until the receding specks had dropped for good behind a roll in the Barrier; until only the vanishing exhalations of the vapor remained.

With that the things of the world shrank to nothing. In the southern sky, opposite the waning sun, the night, already settled over the pole, was pushing forth a bulging shadow, blue-black and threatening as a storm sky. Did I see in it the first nervous movements of the aurora australis? I couldn't be sure. A frozen nose and cheeks sent me below before I had time to find out. But, as I slid down the ladder, I *was* sure of something else, which gave me a bad turn; and that was that in helping the tractor men stow the sledges I had fallen and wrenched my shoulder. The right one was hurting like the devil.

* * *

In the shack I stood for a long minute, rubbing the shoulder. Bad business, I reproached myself. Here you're

51

starting the biggest job of your life, and yet, you've blundered and crippled yourself. For things were in an awful
mess. The tunnels were a jumble of boxes and fuel drums,
and I should be weeks putting them straight. Doubtless
they looked shipshape to the tractor men. Hardened to the
fearful disorder of their vehicles, they did their house
cleaning by booting anything offensive out of the way. So
long as there was room to squat, they were content. Well,
I couldn't live that way at Advance Base. But only one
pair of shoulders was available for all the lifting and moving and shoveling; and they were 50 per cent out of commission.

I couldn't just sit and mope. Using one arm as best I
could, I started to clean up my own Augean Stable. Ab-
sorbed in the task, I forgot the ache in the shoulder. The
hours melted away; it was past midnight before I thought
of stopping. I paused only long enough to brew a pot of
tea and to munch a few crackers. Although I had little to
show for the day's work, I could at last move around in the
tunnels without tripping over duffel bags, food tins,
and bundles of bamboo marker poles. Tomorrow I would
commence unpacking the books and racking the medical
stores in a handy place. Later on, I would put the food
and fuel tunnels in order. The main responsibility, after
all, was the meteorological instruments, which, so far, were
running smoothly. Every hour I took time out to inspect
them, a practice I wanted to become a habit. Already I
was regarding them with the warm, covert look reserved
for good companions.

The day's work done, I took the luxury of a meditative

52

inventory; and what I saw was good. The means of a secure and profound existence were all handy, in a world I could span in four strides going one way and in three strides going the other. It was not a bright world. The storm lantern hanging from a nail over my bunk burned dimly; and the gasoline pressure lamp, suspended from the ceiling, seemed to concentrate its brilliance all in one patch, making the shadows seem all the darker. But the dimness was rather to my liking. It gave depth to the room, and, somehow, made my possessions seem bigger.

My bunk, fastened to the north wall, was about three feet off the floor, with the head flush against the eastern wall. At the foot of the bunk, on a small table, was the register, a glass-enclosed mechanism of revolving drum and pens which automatically recorded wind direction and velocity as reported by the wind vane and anemometer cups to which it was electrically connected. The dry cells powering the pens and driving the drum were racked underneath. Across the room, in the southeast corner, was a triangular shelf holding the main combination radio transmitter and receiver, with a key fastened near the edge. The transmitter was a neatly constructed, 50-watt, self-excited oscillator which Dyer had assembled himself, and which was powered by a 350-watt, gasoline-driven generator weighing only 35 pounds. The receiver was a superheterodyne of standard make. Above this shelf was a smaller one holding the emergency radio equipment, consisting of two 10-watt transmitters powered by hand-cranked generators, plus two small battery receivers, each good for about a hundred hours. These were stand-by equipment. And above this shelf was a still smaller shelf holding spare parts for the radio.

The east wall, between the head of the bunk and the radio corner, was all shelves—six, to be exact. The lower ones were stocked with food, tools, books, and other odds and ends. On the top shelves were instruments and chronometers, all placed high and some wrapped in cotton. On the south wall my windproofs, fur mukluks, parka, and pants hung drying from tenpenny nails. Pushed against the middle of the same wall was a food box on which was a portable victrola in a battered green case. The table was also the family board. On the floor in the southwest corner was a box which I called the ice box, since anything put into it would stay frozen. Among other things it then contained were two Virginia hams which my mother had sent me.

The stove was a foot or so out from the west wall, about midway between the door and the triple register. It was an ordinary two-lid, coal-burning caboose stove, except that this one had been converted into an oil-burner by fitting a round burner over the grate and rigging a three-gallon gravity tank to feed it. It burned Stoddard solvent, ranking midway between kerosene and gasoline among the petroleum distillates. A liquid fuel was chosen instead of coal because coal was too bulky to haul. From the stove the stack went straight up to within two feet of the ceiling, where it bent and ran along the wall before passing through a vent above the foot of the bunk. By carrying the pipe across the room this way, we thought we were providing the equivalent of a radiator; but the scheme was a clumsy makeshift. Two or three pipe sections were lost on the trail, somewhere between Little America and Advance Base; and, the only reserve sections being of a different size, we had used empty five-gallon tins as joints, cut open at the ends to fit. Ingenious as they were, the connections were scarcely air tight. This crude, inoffensive-looking heating plant held for me the power of life and death. Innocent in every rude line, it would nearly kill me a few months hence. And the time would come when I should wonder how I could have been such a fool as not to see what was in plain sight for me to see.

The heating and ventilation of the shack had been a problem from the first. At Little America, where we had given the shack a six weeks' "trial run," both Charlie Murphy and Siple had complained about being made ill by the fumes while they occupied it. This was a warning, since the shack, then above ground, was much better ventilated than it would be underground. Glad for having detected that "bug" in time, I had had the machinist make a new burner. During the month I had lived in the shack at Little America it had worked fine. Yet, Petersen, the second night at Advance Base, had had a headache and had felt nauseated when he stayed too long inside. But, as nobody else had complained of feeling funny, I had decided that his sickness probably had come from an upset stomach. True, a queer, sickish, oil smell—the smell peculiar to any oil stove—was always in the air; and now it was somewhat more noticeable as a result of fumes seeping from the ill-fitting pipe joints. But Siple and I were pretty certain that the ventilation system would

55

eliminate any danger from these fumes. The intake system consisted of a U-shaped pipe, of which one arm stood about three and a half feet above the shack roof. This arm came down outside the west wall, passed under the shack, and rose through a vent in the floor. The inside arm of the U, which was enclosed in a square wooden insulating pillar, rose straight in the middle of the room and opened within a foot or so of the ceiling. The idea was that the cold air, flowing into the shack under gravity, would mix with the warm air at the ceiling and circulate naturally. Otherwise it would lie stagnant on the floor. A three-and-a-half-inch galvanized pipe, cut into the roof, disposed of spent air. I had rather wanted to enlarge this exhaust hole, but didn't dare, remembering that the suction effect of a gale always pulls air out of a shack, and probably would pull the noxious fumes from the stove directly into the room as well.

If this setup held the seeds of misfortune, they were not in evidence during my first day alone. On the contrary, I thought the pipe was drawing well. When I put my hand over the end, I could feel a steady flow pouring from it.

* * *

About 1 o'clock in the morning, just before turning in, I went topside for a look around. The night was spacious and fine. Numberless stars crowded the sky. I had never seen so many. You had only to reach up and fill your hands with the bright pebbles. Earlier, a monstrous red moon had climbed into the northern quadrant, but it was gone by then. The stars were everywhere. A sailor's sky, I thought, commanded by the Southern Cross and the wheeling constellations of Hydrus, Orion, and Triangulum drifting ever so slowly. It was a lovely motion to watch. And all this was mine: the stars, the constellations, even the earth as it turned on its axis. If great inward peace and exhilaration can exist together, then this, I decided my first night alone, was what should possess the senses.

No, it wasn't going to be half bad. A man had no need of the world here—certainly not the world of commonplace manners and accustomed security. The Barrier, austere as platinum, was world enough; and onto it I had trespassed but little. The only things of mine that showed were the radio antenna, the twelve-foot anemometer pole surmounted by the silver weather vane, and the aluminum wind cups, the beehive instrument shelter for the thermometers and recording barograph, and the ventilator pipes and stove-pipe sticking above the shack roof. Without taking more than a few steps, I could touch them all; and a traveler on a darkish night might pass at twenty yards and miss them entirely. Yet, wasn't this really enough? It occurred to me then that half the confusion in the world comes from not knowing how little we need.

That night, anyway, I had no consciousness of missing conventional sounds and stirrings. I was as methodical as any family man following his ordinary routine. I turned off the valve in the stove and put out the fire. Then I undressed, draping my clothes over a chair. I remember cussing inwardly when my bare feet touched the floor, and certainly I stepped lively in crossing the shack to open the door for ventilation and in leaping into the sleep-

57

ing bag before the inflowing cold blast overtook me. The
bag at first was cold, as it always was, from accumulated
body moisture. And, while I waited for it to warm up to
a tolerable temperature and massaged the protesting
shoulder and felt around to make sure that I hadn't forgotten the flashlight in case I had to get up, my mind was
wondering whether my family was all right and about the
things I'd do in the morning. But, most of all, it kept
dropping back to the tractor crew somewhere between
me and Little America, and I couldn't help reproaching
myself for having kept them so long.

Out of these rambling notions sprang an awful thought.
Although I had been through all the gear, I couldn't recall
seeing either the cook book or the alarm clock. "Good
God!" I exclaimed, and the explosive echo of the words,
the first spoken aloud since the tractors had left, almost
brought me out of the bunk. In all the planning, the
scrutinizing of every detail, the checking and the double
checking, could we have forgotten these two common but
indispensable tools? Telling the time was no problem. I
had three chronometers, plus a wrist watch. What worried
me was getting up in the morning for the 8 o'clock weather
observations, now that the winter night was coming, and
the twenty-four hours of the day would all be nearly the
same. As for the cook book, I could do without it; yes,
indeed. *But maybe not.* Although I upended my memory,
I couldn't remember ever attempting anything more
elaborate than ham and eggs over the kitchen range, or
a steak over a camp fire, or pemmican *hoosh* on the trail.
A civilized man, a city-dweller used to servants, an ex-

plorer accustomed to a camp cook at least—or what passed for one—I might have to choose between starving to death or slowly going mad on a diet of cereal and canned corned beef. Thank heaven, there was no lack of can openers. Corey had included at least a dozen, and they were scattered among the stores to avoid any chance of their being all lost at once.

So why, I asked myself, weary the mind with small reproaches? Sufficient unto the day was the evil. The assets, after all, were many. Remembering the toilet some thirty-five feet down the food tunnel, I drew comfort from the fact that my kidneys were sound.

APRIL I: THE GOD OF 2.5

DURING THE FOUR AND A HALF MONTHS I OCCUPIED
Advance Base alone, I kept a fairly complete diary. Nearly
every night, before turning in, I sat down and wrote a
thoroughgoing account of the day's doings. Yet, I have
been surprised and puzzled, on reading the entries four
years later, to find that not more of the emotions and circumstances which I have always associated with the first
few days alone were actually committed to paper. For,
afterwards, it seemed that I was never busier. Although I
was up mornings before 8 o'clock and rarely went to bed
before midnight, the days weren't half long enough for
me to accomplish the things I set out to do. A fagged mind
in the midst of a task has little patience with autobio-
graphical trifles. As witness:

March 29

   . . . Last night, when I finished writing, I noticed a
dark patch spreading over the floor from under the
stove. A bad leak had opened up in the fuel line. Worried about the fire risk, I shut off the stove and searched

all through my gear for a spare line. I couldn't find one, which annoyed me; but I finally succeeded in stopping the leak with adhesive tape borrowed from the medical chest. Result: I was up until 4 o'clock this morning, most of the time damned cold, what with the fire out and the temperature at 58° below zero. The cold metal stripped the flesh from three fingers of one hand.

(Later) This being the twenty-second anniversary of the death of Captain Robert Falcon Scott, I have been reading again his immortal diary. He died on this same Barrier, at approximately the same latitude as that of Advance Base. I admire him as I admire few other men; better than most, perhaps, I can appreciate what he went through. . . .

March 30

There will be no peace until I know that the tractor party has reached Little America safely. I blame myself for having kept them here so long. Well, the radio schedule two days hence will tell the story. I've been principally occupied with putting the tunnels to rights, and not succeeding very well on account of my shoulder, which maddens me not so much from pain as from its uselessness. A fearful amount of lifting remains to be done. So far, I've managed with one hand by using my hip as a fulcrum. . . .

March 31

. . . It's been a deuce of a job to wake up without an alarm clock. And this is puzzling, because I've always been able to fix in my mind the time at which I should awaken, and wake up at that time, almost to the minute. I was born with that gift, and it has stood me in good stead when I dash around the country on lecture tours, leaping from hotels to trains on split-second schedules. But now the gift has simply vanished, perhaps because I am putting too much pressure on it. At night, in the sleeping bag, I whisper to myself: Seven-thirty. Seven-thirty. That's the time you must get up. Seven-thirty. But I've been missing it cleanly—yesterday by nearly an hour, and this morning by half an hour.

I was not long in discovering one thing: that, if anything was eventually to regularize the rhythm by which I should live at Advance Base, it would not be the weather so much as the weather instruments themselves. I had eight in continuous operation. One was the register, already described, which kept a continuous record of wind velocities and directions. The electrical circuit, connecting with the weather vane and wind cups on the anemometer pole topside, was powered by nine dry cell batteries; and the brass drum with the recording sheet was turned by a clockwork mechanism which I had to wind daily. The sheet was lined at intervals corresponding to five minutes in time; and between these lines two pens, one representing the speed of the wind and the other its direction, wrote steadily from noon of one day to noon of the next.

Two other instruments were thermographs, which recorded temperature changes. The so-called inside thermograph was a fairly new invention, whose unique virtue was that it could be housed inside the shack. A metal tube filled with alcohol projected through the roof, and the expansions and contractions of the liquid in the tube drove a pen up and down over a rotating sheet set in a clock-faced dial hanging from the wall, just over the emergency radio set. The sheet, marked with twenty-four spokes for the hours and with concentric circles for the degrees of temperature, made one rotation in twenty-four hours; it would record accurately down to 85° below zero. The outside thermograph was a compact little mechanism which served the same function, except that it stood in the instrument shelter topside and the sheets needed changing only once a week.

Besides these instruments, I had a barograph to record atmospheric pressure, which was kept in a leather case in the food tunnel. Plus a hygrometer employing a human hair, for measuring humidity (not very reliable, though, at cold temperatures). Plus a minimum thermometer, which measured the lowest temperature. In it was a tiny pin which was dropped by the contraction of alcohol in the column. Alcohol was used instead of mercury because mercury freezes at −38° whereas, pure grain alcohol will still flow at −179°. This instrument was useful as a check on the thermographs. It was kept in the instrument shelter, a boxlike structure set on four legs, which stood shoulder high, close to the hatch. The sides were overlapping slats spaced an inch apart to allow air to circulate freely and yet keep out drift.

If I had had any illusions as to being master in my own house, they were soon dispelled. The instruments were masters, not I; and the fact that I knew none too much about them only intensified my humility. There was scarcely an hour in the living day of which a part was not devoted to them or observations connected with them.

Every morning at 8 o'clock sharp—and again at 8 o'clock in the evening—I had to climb topside and note the minimum temperature reading, after which I would shake the thermometer hard to put the pin back into the fluid. Then, standing five minutes or so at the hatch, I would consult the sky, the horizon, and the Barrier, noting on a piece of scratch paper the percentage of cloudiness, the mistiness or clarity, the amount of drift, the direction and speed of the wind (a visual check on the register), and anything particularly interesting about the weather. All of these data were dutifully entered on Form No. 1083, U. S. Weather Bureau.

Every day, between 12 o'clock and 1 o'clock, I changed the recording sheets on the register and the inside thermograph. The pens and the pads supplying them always needed inking, and the thermograph clock had to be wound. Mondays I performed the same service for the outside thermograph and the barograph.

*   *   *

April came in on Easter Sunday. It came in blowing and snowing, bringing a southeaster which laced the air with drift but shot the temperature up from − 48° to − 25° before the day was done. Not a pleasant day, but decidedly on the warmish side, after March's cold. In the morning at 10 o'clock, I attempted the first radio contact with

Little America. Considering my inexperience, the fact that it was successful—at least in that I managed to make myself understood—set me up enormously. For, if any contingency truly disturbed me, it was the chance of my losing radio contact with Little America. Not on my account, but on the expedition's account generally. In spite of the orders I had given and the promises made to respect them, I knew in my own heart that both might be ignored if Little America was out of touch with me for long. And, if Little America chose to act, an appalling tragedy might easily result. Realizing how much depended upon my ability to hold communication, I was oppressed by the thought I might fail through sheer ignorance. Dyer had shown me how to make repairs, and Waite had coached me in operating the set; but, whenever I looked at the complications of tubes, switches, and coils, my heart misgave me. I scarcely knew the Morse code. Fortunately Little America could talk to me by radio telephone. So I wasn't obliged to decipher hot outpourings of dots and dashes from skillful operators. But reply I must in dots and dashes, and that I doubted I could do.

Two hours before the schedule I made ready. The gasoline-driven generator which powered the transmitter stood in an alcove, about halfway down the food tunnel, from which a six-inch ventilator pipe went through to the surface. Of course, it couldn't be run in the shack on account of the fumes. To drive the chill out of the metal I brought the engine indoors and put it on the chair, close to the stove. There the engine stood for an hour and a half, dripping with moisture. Then I filled the tank with a mixture of gasoline and lubricating oil, hurried the engine back to the alcove and tried to start it before the metal chilled. I cranked it after the fashion of an outboard motor, using a cord with a wooden handle at one end and a knot at the other. The knot slipped into a notch in the small flywheel; and, after taking a couple of turns around the wheel, I'd pull hard, spinning the engine. That morning it started off on the first spin. By then it was nearly 10 o'clock, and I had to leg it back into the hut to meet the schedule on time.

The receiver was tuned for 100 meters. The tubes glowed when I threw the switch, and the dial readings showed that everything was as it should be. I waited five minutes or so for the tubes to warm up. Precisely at 10 o'clock, as I clamped on the headphones, I heard Dyer's clear, modulated voice saying: "KFZ calling KFY. This is KFZ calling KFY. Will you please come in?" Excited, as nervous as a student pilot on his first solo hop, I cut in the transmitter and keyed: "OK, KFZ. All well. How are trail parties?" Or at least that was what I tried to spell out. The dot-dash equivalents were as confusing and unfamiliar as Arabic, and in the middle of a sentence I forgot completely what I was supposed to be sending.

Nevertheless, Charlie Murphy came on a moment later with the news that both the Advance Base crew and Innes-Taylor's party were safely at Little America. "All hands are well," he continued. After a few more remarks I heard him say, "Is everything all right with you?"

I was encouraged to make a more elaborate answer.

"Great, working hard. Wind here thirty miles. Snowing. Think blow coming."

Murphy chuckled, "I think John got most of that. No snow here as yet, but an easterly is making with lots of drift."

The contact lasted only twenty minutes. The schedule days were confirmed: Sundays, Tuesdays, and Thursdays, at 10 o'clock, with daily emergency schedules to take effect at the same hour whenever my regular schedule was missed. Just before we signed off, Charlie said, "Dyer rates you D minus on your debut, but I think you deserve better than that."

To this I retorted, "Yes, world's finest radio operator south of Lat. 80°."

That night I wrote in my diary: ". . . The fact that the tractor party and Innes-Taylor's party are safely at Little America has raised my spirits to a new high. This is wonderful news. For the first time, after the months of struggle and anxiety, Little America is at last buttoned up for the winter, and so am I. If we both obey our common sense, nothing untoward need happen. I am free to take stock of my own situation and to make the most of the experience that is to be mine. I realize at this moment more than ever before how much I have been wanting something like this. I must confess feeling a tremendous exhilaration."

Now I could relax temporarily and suffer the blow to come on. Monday the 2nd, the wind blew some more, after backing into the east. Tuesday it hiked into the north and blew a little harder. The bottom dropped out of the barometer. Utterly fascinated, I followed the purple trace as it sank on the barograph. In the space of sixteen hours the pressure dropped two-thirds of an inch. About 5:30 o'clock in the afternoon the trace ran right off the bottom of the sheet. The outside barometer finally fell to 27.82 inches. At home a reading of that order would have presaged a hurricane more violent than the great Florida blow. All the portents of an earth-rending uproar were in the air. The wind rasped on the roof. The clacking of the anemometer cups settled into a hum. Drift sifted down through the intake ventilator, making a cold heap on the floor. When I went topside for the last observation, I could scarcely lift the trapdoor against the wind's push; and the drift funneled down the hole with force enough to take the breath away.

But the barometric portent, as so often it is in high latitudes, was a mumbling lie. Consulting the wind record next morning, I found that the velocity had not risen over thirty-five miles per hour during the night. Wednesday the 4th was still windy, but the barometer rose again. That day I found the roof of the fuel tunnel caving under the accumulating weight of drift. The roofing canvas was bulging between the supporting planks, and two planks had already given way. Fearful that the whole tunnel might cave in and that, with my crippled arm, I should never be able to dig it out before the next blizzard, I shored it up as best I could with boxes and two-by-four timbers. The cold following the quieting of the gale would in time anneal the new, light snowflakes into a hard bridge over the tunnel; but to hasten the process I spent hours melting snow on the stove, carrying the water topside,

and pouring it over the weak spots. The temperature was
6° above zero, which should have seemed positively warm,
compared to the — 60° weather I had become acclimatized
to in March. The wind, however, cut to the bone; and my
nose and cheeks were raw from frostbite. I went without
hot food, preferring to use the stove continuously for melting snow; that night I slipped into the bunk an exhausted
man.

April 5

This morning, when I awakened, I could tell by the
sound that the wind had dropped, though drift was still
sifting through the outlet ventilator and past the stovepipe. I dressed rapidly and hurried up the ladder to
take the 8 A.M. "ob." But, when I heaved with my good
shoulder against the trapdoor, it refused to give. Half-
asleep and stiff with cold, I continued to push as hard
as I could. Still the panel would not budge. Remembering then the thick, double-action feature, I yanked out
the restraining pegs and tried pulling down. This didn't
work, either. Even when I kicked loose from the ladder
and swung out, clinging to the handle with my left hand,
the door did not stir. This was serious. I let go and
dropped in a heap to the veranda floor, and the thought
broke through my numbed senses: You're caught now.
You're really caught, double-action and all.

With the flashlight, which I usually carried suspended
from a cord looped around my neck, I located a long
two-by-four under a jumble of gear in the veranda.
Using my good arm to drive and the other to balance,

69

I manipulated the timber as a vertical battering ram. Fifteen or twenty minutes of hard pounding served to crack the door a little; and, by bracing myself on the ladder and throwing the strength of my back against the panel, I finally succeeded in wedging an opening wide enough to wiggle through. Once on the surface, I quickly found the cause of the trouble. The day before, while I was working in the food tunnel, the shack door had been open a long time. The warm air had evidently softened the snow around the hatch; and, after the warmth was cut off, this melted margin had solidified into hard ice, which had wedged the door shut.

However, ice was not alone to blame. A full two and a half feet of drift lay packed over the trapdoor. This accumulation, I noticed, had built up behind the ventilator pipe and instrument shelter, which, in an easterly gale, stood to windward with respect to the trapdoor. Moreover, I observed further that the shack's not having been sunk quite enough, was causing a thick shell of hard snow to come over the roof. Since the trapdoor was on the west side of the shack, it had naturally caught the brunt of the drift, which always fans out to leeward of any upraised object in the pattern of a ship's wake.

* * *

All that day, when not otherwise occupied with my observations, I hacked and dug and sawed at the offending mound, endeavoring to level off the surface round the shack. The day came off fine, but the spent wind still tossed up clouds of drift, and I did not want to go through another experience like yesterday's. The failure of my pet door had impressed me with the necessity of having an alternative hatch, against similar emergencies. Indeed, I had already planned such a one, had, in fact, worked on it intermittently during the blizzard.

My idea was to breach a hole in the west-pointing food tunnel and mine at right angles to it a new south-pointing passageway. The direction was selected after careful study. From experience with Antarctic weather I knew that the prevailing winds are easterly; the easterlies are the strong, snow-making, drift-making winds. Since I was powerless to prevent the drift from building up in the lee of the stovepipe and ventilator pipes, instrument shelter, and the shack itself, and, therefore, over the food and fuel tunnels, the logical move was to drive a third tunnel out of the drift zone. Even this would not give complete security as a norther or a souther might come along presently and build up new drift ridges at right angles to those already cast up. The drift ridges seem to feed and fatten on each other. Queerly, there is little actual increment from snow-fall. Most of it blows away; yet, if the Empire State Building were standing in the Antarctic, it would eventually be smothered in drift.

I started the tunnel about midway down the food tunnel, directly opposite the recess in which the radio engine sat. It was to be from thirty to thirty-five feet long, about six feet high, and four feet wide. I proposed to carry it two or three feet below the surface, and, at the far end, to hole out a little shaft which would come within a foot of the surface. This thin shell could then be punctured whenever the other exit was blocked off. However, a foot a day, I decided, would be all I could do. "Even a foot means hard work," my diary observes, "because I can use only my left arm. I saw the blocks out, then carry them to the hatch, where I hoist them to the surface, load them aboard a small man-hauling sledge, and haul them some distance to leeward."

Unless you know something about the character of Antarctic snow, the reference to sawing it out in blocks may be puzzling. Except that it has been fused by cold, rather than heat, the Barrier snow is like a kind of sandstone. It is hard and brittle. You can't make snowballs with it. When you rub it tiny icelike globules shred off. The color is the whitest white you ever saw; it has none of the smoothness and transparency of ice. After cold has coalesced the crystals of newly fallen snow, you can walk over it and not leave an impress. At times skis will slide helplessly as on slick glacier ice. You can't shovel that kind of snow. A shovel rings when it strikes as it might against rock. I used a two-foot hand saw. With this I cut out blocks, which could be pried clear with a shovel, leaving nice straight lines and debris easy to handle.

As a matter of fact, the escape tunnel was no wasted effort against a distant contingency. It became my water supply. All I had to do was to saw the blocks to a size suitable for the water bucket, and stack them in the veranda like cordwood. Yet, melting snow was an unmitigated nuisance; I loathed it. Two gallons of snow yielded barely two quarts of water after several hours on the stove. The water bucket was almost never off the stove; and, while it was there, little room was available for anything else. I came to hate its soot-blackened, dented sides; its greedy, ever-gaping maw; and once, when it careened to the floor and spilled all the water accumulated for supper, I cheerfully booted the bucket across the shack. Stooping to retrieve it, I caught my reflection in the shaving mirror. I was actually grinning.

April 6

I am sleeping fairly well, which is a blessing. But I still can't seem to wake up when I want to—missed by three quarters of an hour this morning—which is a nuisance. I don't know why I've lost the faculty; I'll have to regain it somehow. When the long night comes, I shall have no light to awaken me.

I'm keeping the skylights cleared of snow to enjoy what little daylight remains. But all three are frosted over most of the time. When the temperature at the ceiling passes freezing, the frost melts; and the drip-drip-drip makes little ice stalagmites on the floor, which is always cold. I've proved, with a thermometer, that when I'm sitting down the temperature at the level of my feet is anywhere from 10° to 30° colder than at my head. . . .

April 7

The six months' day is slowly dying, and the darkness is descending very gently. Even at midday the sun is only several times its diameter above the horizon. It is

73

cold and dull. At its brightest it scarcely gives light enough to throw a shadow. A funereal gloom hangs in the twilight sky. This is the period between life and death. This is the way the world will look to the last man when it dies.

April 8

Were it not for my lame shoulder and the difficulties caused by the weather instruments (which were designed for a warmer place), I should be making much better progress in preparing myself for the oncoming darkness. Unpredictable things, small but often annoying, make continuous demands upon my time. For example, I find that even when there is no drift, the three-and-one-half inch outlet ventilator fills every three or four days with ice (or rather with what looks like névé, which is between snow and ice). It's due, I think, to condensation. Anyhow, I've got to watch that. Good ventilation I must have at any cost. The pipe being held in place by friction, I just pull it out of the hole, carry it below, and lay it on the stove to thaw. The icy stuff won't pound out. It has to be melted.

Just to complicate matters, the same trouble is developing in the topside end of the stovepipe. Around dinner time (or whenever the stove is running hot) the ice melts, and the water runs through a hole in the elbow. Luckily, the register, which stands directly underneath, has a glass top; otherwise it would have been out of commission long ago. I have tied a can under the elbow to catch the water. Nevertheless, I'm rather worried about the blockage in the pipe; unless the fumes from the stove escape to the surface, I shall have trouble. . . .

*　*　*

Thus the first part of April hurried like a man on an errand. I was occupied with all kinds of small projects. Aside from the Escape Tunnel, the hardest task was putting the food and fuel tunnels to rights. These two parallel corridors, it will be remembered, ran out from the veranda and were separated by a three-foot wall of snow. Both were dark as dungeons; whenever I worked in them it was by the light of a storm lantern or flashlight. In the artificial light, though, they acquired a breathless radiance. The ice crystals, which were thickening on the canvas roofing, glistened like candelabra; and the walls glowed with a sharp, blue nakedness.

In the fuel tunnel were four fifty-gallon kerosene drums, weighing about five hundred pounds each, which we set in individual recesses. Besides this, I had 360 gallons of Stoddard solvent for the stove, which came in handy twelve-gallon drums weighing about ninety pounds each. In addition I had about ninety gallons of gasoline for the radio generator, in two large drums at the far end of the tunnel. Except for the fact that the drums all stood upright so as to prevent leakage from the bungs, the place used to remind me sometimes of a French wine cellar, especially the shadows cast by my figure as I moved about in front of the lantern.

75

The food tunnel, which opened directly in front of the door, was a different sort of place. There the walls were formed by the boxes of foodstuffs themselves. Wanting something, I simply had to pry open the sides with a chisel and take out whatever I needed, leaving the empty box as a permanent wall. What disturbed me was the haphazard manner in which the boxes had been stowed. Here and there the walls were bulging out; the beans were hopelessly mixed with the canned meats, tomato juice, and boxes of odds and ends; and the roof was caving in. All this offended my growing sense of neatness. During my spare time I set about rearranging the whole setup.

I didn't try to rush the job. If the polar regions have taught me anything, it is patience. I rarely spent more than an hour on any one job, preferring to shift to something else. In that way I was able to show a little progress each day on all the important jobs, and at the same time keep from becoming bored with any one. This was a way of bringing variety into an existence which would be basically monotonous.

*   *   *

Not that the materials for variety were ever lacking to a mind capable of forgetting what civilization was like. The sheer rigorousness of the Barrier took care of that. At times I felt as if I were the last survivor of an Ice Age, striving to hold on with the flimsy tools bequeathed by an easy-going, temperate world. Cold does queer things. At 50° below zero a flashlight dies out in your hand. At − 55° kerosene will freeze, and the flame will dry up on the wick. At — 60° rubber turns brittle. One day, I remember, the antenna wire snapped in my hands when I tried to bend it to make a new connection. Below — 60° cold will find the last microscopic touch of oil in an instrument and stop it dead. If there is the slightest breeze, you can hear your breath freeze as it floats away, making a sound like that of Chinese firecrackers. As does the morning dew, rime coats every exposed object. And if you work too hard and breathe too deeply, your lungs will sometimes feel as if they were on fire.

Cold—even April's relatively moderate cold—gave me plenty to think about. The novocaine in my medical kit froze and shattered the glass tubes. So did the chemicals in the fire bombs. Two cases of tomato juice shattered their bottles. Whenever I brought canned food inside the shack I had to let it stand all day near the stove to thaw. On very cold days the kerosene and Stoddard solvent flowed like cylinder oil; I dug a deep hole in the tunnel floor for my can to lengthen the drop in the rubber hose which I used as a syphon. Frost was forever collecting on the electrical contact points of the wind vane and wind cups. Some days I climbed the twelve-foot anemometer pole two and three times to clean them. It was a bitter job, especially on blustery nights. With my legs twined around the slender pole, my arms flung over the cleats, and my free hands trying to scrape the contact point clean with a knife and at the same time hold a flashlight to see, I qualified for the world's coldest flagpole sitter. I seldom came down from that pole without a frozen finger, toe, nose, or cheek.

The shack was always freezingly cold in the morning. I slept with the door open. When I arose the inside temperature (depending upon the surface weather) might be anywhere from 10° to 40° below zero. Frost coated the sleeping bag where my breath had condensed during the night; my socks and boots, when I picked them up, were so stiff with frozen sweat that I first had to work them between my hands. A pair of silk gloves hung from a nail over the bunk, where I could grab them the first thing. Yet, even with their protection, my fingers would sting and burn from the touch of the lamp and stove as I lighted them. The old flesh had sloughed off the tips, and the new flesh for a while was insufferably tender. So I had my troubles. Some came from my own inadequacies. At first I had a devil of a time with the weather instruments. The traces became horribly blotched, the pens stuck, and the instruments themselves stopped without rhyme or reason. But, one way or another, I usually managed to contrive a cure. I learned how to thin the ink with glycerine to keep it from freezing, and how to cut the oil in the instruments with gasoline and rub the delicate parts with graphite, which wasn't affected so much by the cold.

Yet, in playing Admirable Crichton to myself, I was far from distinguished. Many of my Advance Base concoctions wouldn't have passed Captain's Inspection. In the Navy phrase, they were generally no better than "lash-ups." As to that, I plead *nolo contendere* and throw myself on the court's mercy. An officer, I was learning to do things again with my hands. My standards were humble. If anything, I was again a worshiping disciple of the

God of 2.5 of Naval Academy days, the god of the hairsbreadth passing grade, as personified by Tecumseh, at
whose bust we midshipmen used to chip penny offerings
as we marched to examinations. By Academy standards,
I should have "bilged out" of Advance Base on cooking
alone.

Breakfast didn't count. I rarely took more than tea and
a whole-wheat biscuit. Lunch was habitually an out-of-
the-can affair, consisting usually of tomato juice, Eskimo
biscuits, and frequently a cold meat or fish—either corned
beef, tongue, or sardines. These I prepared in masterly
fashion. But supper, by rights the high spot in an explorer's day, the hot meal toward which a cold and hungry
man looks with mounting anticipation—this meal for a
while was a daily fiasco.

I have only to close my eyes to witness again the succession of culinary disasters. Consider what my diary desig-
nated as The Corn Meal Incident. Into a boiler I dumped
what seemed a moderate quantity of meal, added a little
water, and stood it on the stove to boil. That simple formula gave birth to a Hydra-headed monster. The stuff
began to swell and dry up, swell and dry up, with fearful
blowing and sucking noises. All innocently I added water,
more water, and still more water. Whereupon the boiler
erupted like Vesuvius. All the pots and pans within reach
couldn't begin to contain the corn meal that overflowed.
It oozed over the stove. It spattered the ceiling. It covered
me from head to foot. If I hadn't acted resolutely, I might
have been drowned in corn meal. Seizing the container in
my mittened hands, I rushed it to the door and hurled it

far into the food tunnel. There it continued to give off deadly golden lava until the cold finally stilled the crater.

There were other disasters of the same order. There was the Dried Lima Beans Incident of April 10th. ("It's amazing," the diary reports soberly, "how much water lima beans can absorb, and how long it takes them to cook. At supper time I had enough half-cooked lima beans to feed a ship's company.") My first jelly dessert bounced like a rubber ball under my knife; the flapjacks had to be scraped from the pan with a chisel. ("And you, the man who sat at a thousand banquets," goes the accusing entry of April 12th.) I dreaded banquets before I went to Advance Base; and I have come to dread them since. But in April's dark hours I ransacked my memory, trying to remember what they were like. All that I could recall was filet mignon spiced and darkened to the color of an old cavalry boot; or lobster thermidor; or squabs perched on triangles of toast; or chicken salad heaped on billowing lettuce. All these were far beyond the simple foods in my larder. When I did experiment, the results filled the shack with pungent burning smells and coated the skillets with awful gummy residues. But, in spite of the missing cook book, the record was not one of unmitigated failure. Resolved to make a last stand, I took the surviving chicken, hung it for two days from a nail over the stove to thaw, boiled it all one day, seasoned it with salt and pepper, and served. The soup, which was an unexpected by-product, was delicious; that night I broached a bottle of cider and drank a toast to Escoffier.

* * *

Thus April moved along. Each night, as the last formal act of the day, I crossed off another date on the big calendar on the wall, and each morning consulted the calendar the first thing, to make sure that I hadn't forgotten. Above me the day was dying; the night was rising in its place. Ever since late in February, when the sun had rolled down from its lofty twenty-four-hour circuit around the sky, it had been setting a little earlier at night, rising a little later in the morning. Now, with less than a fortnight of daylight left in this latitude, it was just a monstrous ball which could barely hoist itself free from the horizon. It would wheel along for a few hours, obscured by mist, then sink out of sight in the north not long after noon. I found myself watching it as one might watch a departing lover.

April 9

... I have just seen (at 9 P.M.) a curious phenomenon. At first it appeared to be a ball of fire, which was smaller and redder than the sun. It bore about 205° true. I couldn't identify it. Going below, I got the field glasses and kept watching it. It changed from deep red to silver, and every now and then blanked out. It was astonishing how big it looked at first. But after long study I finally figured out that it consisted of four brilliant stars, very close together in a vertical line. However, they may not have been four stars but one having three images of itself refracted by ice crystals. ...

81

April 12

... It has been crystal clear, with a temperature of about 50° below zero, and a whispering southerly wind that set fire to the skin. Each day more light drains from the sky. The storm-blue bulge of darkness pushing out from the South Pole is now nearly overhead at noon. The sun rose this morning at about 9:30 o'clock, but never really left the horizon. Huge and red and solemn, it rolled like a wheel along the Barrier edge for about two and a half hours, when the sunrise met the sunset at noon. For another two and a half hours it rolled along the horizon, gradually sinking past it until nothing was left but a blood-red incandescence. The whole effect was something like that witnessed during an eclipse. An unearthly twilight spread over the Barrier, lit by flames thrown up as from a vast pit, and the snow flamed with liquid color.

At home I am used to seeing the sun leap straight out of the east, cross the sky overhead, and set in a line perpendicular to the western horizon. Here the sun swings to a different law. It lives by extremes. In the spring it rises for the first time at noon, and for the last time at midnight. As in the fall, it rises and sets daily for a month and a half. Then for four months and a half it never sets at all, never crosses directly overhead, but instead wheels around the horizon, nearly parallel to it and never rising higher than 33½°. In the fall it sets for the first time at midnight, and sets for good at noon. Then for four and a half months it does not rise at all, but instead sinks gradually below the horizon to a depth of 13½° before it begins to lift again. This is the period I am approaching now; a period when the day seems to be holding its breath.

Thus the coming of the polar night is not the spectacular rush that some imagine it to be. The day is not abruptly walled off; the night does not drop suddenly. Rather, the effect is a gradual accumulation, like that of an infinitely prolonged tide. Each day the darkness, which is the tide, washes in a little farther and stays a little longer; each time the day, which is a beach, contracts a little more, until at last it is covered. The onlooker is not conscious of haste. On the contrary, he is sensible of something of incalculable importance being accomplished with timeless patience. The going of the day is a gradual process, modulated by the intervention of twilight. You look up, and it is gone. But not completely. Long after the horizon has interposed itself, the sun continues to cast up a pale and dwindling imitation of the day. You can trace its progress by the glow thrown up as it makes its round just below the horizon.

These are the best times, the times when neglected senses expand to an exquisite sensitivity. You stand on the Barrier, and simply look and listen and feel. The morning may be compounded of an unfathomable, tantalizing fog in which you stumble over sastrugi you can't see, and detour past obstructions that don't exist, and take your bearings from tiny bamboo markers that loom as big as telephone poles and hang suspended in space. On such a day, I could swear that the instrument shelter was as big as an ocean liner. On one such day I saw the blank north-eastern sky become filled with the most magnificent Barrier coast I have ever seen, true in every line and faced with cliffs several thousand feet tall. A mirage, of course. Yet, a man who had never seen such things would have taken oath that it was real. The afternoon may be so clear that you dare not make a sound, lest it fall in pieces. And on such a day I have seen the sky shatter like a broken goblet, and dissolve into iridescent tipsy fragments—ice crystals falling across the face of the sun. And once in the golden downpour a slender column of platinum leaped up from the horizon, clean through the sun's core; a second luminous shadow formed horizontally through the sun, making a perfect cross. Presently two miniature suns, green and yellow in color, flipped simultaneously to the ends of each arm. These are parhelia, the most dramatic of all refraction phenomena; nothing is lovelier.

April 14

...Took my daily walk at 4 P.M. today, in 89° of frost. The sun had dropped below the horizon, and a blue—of a richness I've never seen anywhere else—flooded in, extinguishing all but the dying embers of the sunset.

Due west, halfway to the zenith, Venus was an un-blinking diamond; and opposite her, in the eastern sky, was a brilliant twinkling star set off exquisitely, as was Venus, in the sea of blue. In the northeast a silver-green serpentine aurora pulsed and quivered gently. In places the Barrier's whiteness had the appearance of dull platinum. It was all delicate and illusive. The colors were subdued and not numerous; the jewels few; the setting simple. But the way these things went together showed a master's touch.

I paused to listen to the silence. My breath, crystallized as it passed my cheeks, drifted on a breeze gentler than a whisper. The wind vane pointed toward the South Pole. Presently the wind cups ceased their gentle turning as the cold killed the breeze. My frozen breath hung like a cloud overhead.

The day was dying, the night being born—but with great peace. Here were the imponderable processes and forces of the cosmos, harmonious and soundless. Harmony, that was it! That was what came out of the silence—a gentle rhythm, the strain of a perfect chord, the music of the spheres, perhaps.

It was enough to catch that rhythm, momentarily to be myself a part of it. In that instant I could feel no doubt of man's oneness with the universe. The conviction came that that rhythm was too orderly, too harmonious, too perfect to be a product of blind chance—that, therefore, there must be purpose in the whole and that man was part of that whole and not an accidental offshoot. It was a feeling that transcended reason; that went to the heart of man's despair and found it groundless. The universe was a cosmos, not a chaos; man was as rightfully a part of that cosmos as were the day and night.

APRIL II: THE NIGHT

April 15

I have been cooking some dried lima beans for two hours in the hottest water I can manage. It is now 9 o'clock, and they are still granite-hard. By the great horn spoon, I am going to find out their softening point if it takes all night.

...This morning I had another radio contact with Little America. As were the two preceding affairs, it was a major operation; therefore, as with everything else important, I am trying to systematize the operation as best I can.... The fact that I haven't mastered the Morse code complicates the business infernally. Even though I have a conversion alphabet tacked to the table next to the key, I find it terribly difficult to think in terms of dots and dashes; and my thumb and forefinger are clumsy executing them with the key.

So this is what I'm doing: While the engine is heating on the stove, I sit down at the desk and write out on a sheet of paper whatever messages I have in mind. I spell them out vertically down the page—that is,

86

Chinese fashion, with the letters one under each other; then, opposite each letter, I write the equivalent dots and dashes. This is fine, as far as it goes. The trouble comes afterwards, when Charlie Murphy takes up some expedition matter or else is in a mood just to make conversation. Then I become as frantic as a tongue-tied Latin being interrogated in a strait jacket, who can't form the words in his mouth or use his hands to gesticulate. Yet, somehow, Dyer manages to follow me— he must have learned mind-reading along with his engineering. . . .

My first question today was, "How is Ken Rawson?" Charlie Murphy came on and said that Rawson's neck was still giving trouble. Aside from that, all's well at Little America.

Charlie gave me a digest of Little America weather; and, as we anticipated, it averages 15° to 20° warmer than here.

It's really comforting to talk this way with Little America, and yet in my heart I wish very much that I didn't have to have the radio. It connects me with places where speeches are made and with the importunities of the outer world. But at least I myself can't broadcast over this set, thank heaven. It won't carry voice; and, moreover, I haven't enough generator fuel to be sending long messages in code. Charlie Murphy will see to it that my friends understand the situation. But I know that some day, out of pure curiosity, I shall be tempted to ask how the stock market is going or what's happening in Washington. And, in view of my pre-carious finances, any news will probably bring restless-ness and discontent.

After the schedule I found that the ventilator pipe in the generator alcove was half filled with ice from the condensation of the hot gases, and sickening fumes filled the tunnel. Although I don't like this at all, I can't seem to find a remedy. The temperature today held between 50° and 60° below.

April 17

A momentous day. I found the cook book! Going through a homemade canvas bag full of navigational gear and various odds and ends, I came upon the pre-cious volume early this morning. The whoop of joy I uttered sounded so loud that I was actually embarrassed; it was the first sound to pass my lips, I realized, in twenty days.

No book washed ashore to a castaway could have been more avidly studied. I regret to say, though, that it doesn't solve all the mysteries of cooking. It doesn't tell me how to keep flapjacks from sticking to the pan. So I took advantage of the radio schedule today to ask Charlie Murphy if anyone in camp knew the answer. Greasing the pan, I explained, did no good. Charlie's reply came floating back. "You've got me there," he said. "I've never cooked a thing in my life. Maybe you'd better change your diet."

"Ask cook," I spelled out laboriously.

"Dick, if you were starving to death," my friend replied, "I still wouldn't trust that cleaver-wielding Marine."

"Ask somebody," I persisted.

"I'll tell you what," said Charlie. "I'll send a message to Oscar of the Waldorf. In a serious matter like this, we don't want to take any chances." *

Another important event occurred today. The sun departed for good. It peeped above the horizon at noon, and with that hasty gesture set for the last time. I am feeling no particular reaction over the loss of the sun— not even envy for the men at Little America, who have an appreciably shorter winter night. Wondering why, I concluded that the long period of preparation—the lingering twilight, the lengthening nights—had put me in the mood for the change. If you hadn't lost the sun, I told myself, you would have had something serious to think about, since that would mean that the earth's axis was pointing the wrong way, and the entire solar system was running amok.

April 18

Worked topside several hours today, leveling snow and getting rid of snow blocks from the Escape Tunnel. Slipped once and fell heavily on the bad shoulder; it hurt like the deuce. I was puffing a bit while I worked and apparently got a touch of frost in the lungs, because tonight, when I breathe, I notice a burning sensation.

* Fourteen days later, as he had promised, Charlie joyfully read a treatise by Oscar himself, the gist of which was buttering the pan. I gave up then, and resigned myself to continuing with the chisel.

The temperature was 60° below. My lantern froze and went out when I went topside on the last inspection trip. . . . This morning I found more ice in the stovepipe. I'll have to do something about that. The ice was incredibly hard. I was a long time breaking it out.

A day or two later, having meanwhile given serious thought to the whole problem of ventilation, I decided to change the position of the ventilator pipe in the center of the room. This, it will be recalled, was a U-shaped duct, one arm of which passed from a point three feet or so above the surface, down the outside of the hut, swung under the floor, and discharged the gravity-borne fresh air into the shack through a riser housed in a tall wooden pillar extending nearly to the ceiling. Although the arrangement had promised well, a month's trial had convinced me that it ought to be changed. For one thing, the pillar was always in the way. It stood right in the middle of the shack. If I collided with it once, I collided with it a hundred times. That, however, was only an inconvenience. My real objection was that the apparatus was failing to do its job. Mornings, the cold in the room lay like a congealed liquid. By midafternoon, when the stove was running hot, the air around my head would turn warm, though the floor and the corners stayed icy. A step or two carried me from equatorial warmth to polar cold. I wanted a more equable distribution of temperature, if I could get it; but more than anything else I wanted plenty of air in the place.

My theory was that I could get much better circulation

if I brought the outlet arm of the duct close to the stove; the vacuum effect caused by the heating of the air in the pipe would pull more air into the shack. Lacking pipe joints, and having no other tools than a hammer, saw, and wrench, I was puzzled for a while as to just how this might be done. I solved the problem, finally, in a simple way. After taking down the wooden pillar and pipe, I sawed off seven inches of the wooden housing, and nailed it over the vent in the middle of the floor. Over this I nailed a piece of heavy canvas, thus making a box. Then I let into the side of it a piece of pipe, which ran across the floor to the foot of the bunk. Here an empty five-gallon gasoline tin, pierced through one side and the top, was made to serve as a second joint. Into the top of the can I fitted a stand of pipe and leaned the top part of it against the horizontal section of the stovepipe near the ceiling.

I didn't finish until 3 o'clock in the morning; and, while the result was hardly a new advance in the technics of air conditioning, an improvement in my ventilation was noticeable. A piece of tissue paper held over the outlet fluttered convincingly. And now that that awkward pillar had been eliminated from the middle of the room, the shack seemed twice as large. However, the dispensation was limited; for, instead of bumping against the pipe, I was now tripping over it; but the increased elbow room was adequate compensation. Next morning, when I got up, the inside temperature was 30° below zero. The new arrangement was working quite nicely indeed.

* * *

Although the day was gone, the twilight lingered in the sun's wake. At noon the northern horizon continued to erupt with explosive reds and yellows and greens. There were still several hours on either side of noon when I could work and travel on the Barrier without a light. But the mornings and afternoons were dark as night; and I found that my routine was being regulated imperceptibly by the darkness, even as the daylight had regulated it before. In addition to the weather observations I now had to make five auroral observations every day. They came at 10 o'clock in the morning, then at 1 o'clock, 4 o'clock, 7 o'clock, and the last one at 10 o'clock. The aurora occurs in complicated patterns, called rays, arcs, curtains, bands, and coronas. Standing at the hatch, I would identify the structure, and note other relevant information, such as the bearing and estimated altitude of the center and the termini. These data were entered in a special book; and the auroral observations, like the meteorological observations, were timed to coincide with simultaneous observations at Little America to make for true correlations later on. A day broken up in this wise could never be a spacious day. Until I became used to it, my life seemed to be made up of busy, unrelated little fragments which I seldom succeeded in piecing together.

Now, I had always been a somewhat casual person, governed by moods as often as by necessities, and given to working at odd hours. My footless habits were practically ruinous to those who had to live with me. An explorer's home is his office, recruiting station, headquarters, and main cache. Mine was the mobilization and demobilization point of all my expeditions. The telephone used to ring at all hours. People tramped in and out as if it were a public place. Mukluks and sleeping bags and pemmican samples and sun compasses cluttered up the living room, the bedrooms, the closets—every nook, in fact, where I could find room to dump them. And meals were never on time because Daddy was (1) on the long-distance telephone; or (2) spinning yarns with an old shipmate; or (3) preparing a talk; or (4) getting ready to go off somewhere. Remembering the way it all was, I still wonder how my wife ever succeeded in bringing up four such splendid children as ours, wise each in his or her way, and each one as orderly as Father almost never was. Certainly it has been done in spite of the example set by that haphazard man who came and went at 9 Brimmer Street. However, I have often explained to the children how lucky they were to have in their mother one parent who offered a perfect example of what to do, and in their father another who was an example of what not to do.

Out at Advance Base I made a heroic effort to mend my ways. Not from conscience but from necessity. From the beginning I had recognized that an orderly, harmonious routine was the only lasting defense against my special circumstances. The brain-cracking loneliness of solitary confinement is the loneliness of a futile routine. I tried to keep my days crowded; and yet, at the same time, I, the most unsystematic of mortals, endeavored to be systematic. At night, before blowing out the lantern, I formed the habit of blocking out the morrow's work. Once the tunnels were cleared up and the shack was made shipshape,

I could afford to be more leisurely. In drafting the day's agenda, I seldom set up any special objectives. It was a case of assigning myself an hour, say, to the Escape Tunnel, half an hour to leveling drift, an hour to straightening up the fuel drums, an hour to cutting bookshelves in the walls of the food tunnel, and two hours to renewing a broken bridge in the man-hauling sledge.

If the time was not sufficient, well and good; let the job be resumed another day. It was wonderful to be able to dole out time in this way. It brought me an extraordinary sense of command over myself and simultaneously freighted my simplest doings with significance. Without that or an equivalent, the days would have been without purpose; and without purpose they would have ended, as such days always end, in disintegration.

April 21

The morning is the hardest time. It is hard enough anywhere for a man to begin the day's work in darkness; where I am it is doubly difficult. One may be a long time realizing it, but cold and darkness deplete the body gradually; the mind turns sluggish; and the nervous system slows up in its responses. This morning I had to admit to myself that I was lonely. Try as I may, I find I can't take my loneliness casually; it is too big. But I must not dwell on it. Otherwise I am undone.

At home I usually awaken instantly, in full possession of my faculties. But that's not the case here. It takes me some minutes to collect my wits; I seem to be groping in cold reaches of interstellar space, lost and bewildered.

The room is a non-dimensional darkness, without shadow or substance; even after all these days I sometimes ask myself: Where am I? What am I doing here? I discover myself straining, as if trying to hear something in a place where no sound could possibly exist. Ah, yes. Tick-tick, tick-tick-tick, tick. The busy, friendly voices of the register and thermograph on the shelves, each distinct and dramatic—sounds I can understand and follow, even as a mariner emerging from the darkness of the boundless ocean can recognize and follow a coast by the bell buoys offshore.

As I dread getting up, I just lie and listen to these sharp, clean beats, letting them form little conversations, little rhymes, even short stories in my mind. They have a pleasant, narcotizing effect. The slightest move, disturbing the nice temperature balance in the sleeping bag, sends a blast of frosty air down my back or stomach. My skin crawls at the thought of touching foot to the deck. But up I must for the 8 A.M. observation; and so I lie there, mustering resolve for a wrenching heave into the dark. Clear of the bag, I feel around on the shelf at the head of the bunk until I locate the silk gloves which I wear to protect my fingers while handling cold metal. After putting these on, I light the lantern, which hangs from a nail over the bunk. The wick, hard with frost, seldom takes fire easily. The flame catches and goes out, catches and goes out. Then, as it steadies on the wick, the light gradually pushes a liquid arc into the room, bringing my possessions one by one into its wavering yellow orbit. I suppose it is really a gloomy light. Things on the opposite wall are scarcely touched by it. But to me that feeble burning is a daily miracle. With light the day begins, the mind escapes from darkness, and numbness leaves the body. I sleep in my underclothes, with my pants and shirt and socks heaped upon the table. Needless to say, I dress faster than a fireman. . . .

Thus the Advance Base day began. The next day, exactly a month after I flew from Little America, I sat down and wrote—at odd moments during the day—exactly what I did from waking to sleeping. The whole entry ran close to 3,500 words. The day happened to be a Sunday, but the flow of the hours at Advance Base was no different from that of any other day. Since the entry describes a typical day, at least for this period, I have decided to include it, except for slight editing against repetition:

April 22
  . . . After dressing, the first thing I do, of course, and that right lively, is to start the stove. The fuel is usually somewhat congealed, and it takes ten minutes or so for enough to run from the tank to fill the burner. I crave hot tea in the morning; for, rather than wait for the stove to warm up, I heat a quart of water (ice, of course) with meta tablets, which are inch-long wafers of solidified alcohol. I dump half a dozen of these in a can, and set the pan of ice in a metal rack over the hot blue flame.
  The silence during these first minutes of the day is always depressing. It seems real, as if a gloomy critic

were brooding in the shadows, on the verge of saying something unpleasant. Sharing his mood, I merely grunt a good morning. My exercises help to snap me out of this. Stretched out flat on the bunk, I go through fifteen minutes of various kinds of muscle stretchings. By the time I've finished, the water is hot. I brew about a pint of tea in a big porcelain cup, and dump in lots of sugar and powdered milk. After a sip or two, I put the cup over the flame, and hold it there until it gets piping hot; so hot, in fact, that it burns the mouth and throat. Thus fortified, I am ready for the observation.

A few minutes before 8 o'clock, I noted the barometric pressure (28.79 inches). A quick glance at the inside thermograph, just before I buttoned on my canvas windbreaker, showed a topside temperature in the minus forties. I heated the flashlight a minute or two over the stove; that would keep the batteries from freezing. Without bothering to turn the switch, I went into the pitch-black veranda, and up the ladder. That little route I knew by heart: a step past the door, two to the left, six rungs up.

The trapdoor stuck a little. The violence of my second heave sent a shower of crystals down my neck, making me shiver. It was still very dark, but an impalpable fog lay close to the surface, giving the day a gray look; and a relentless flutter of snow was in my face. I still use the words "day" and "night," having no equivalents for the divisions whose differences are only in time; "day" seems a meaningless description of the soggy pall which this morning lay over the Barrier. As I looked about, I was conscious only of solitude and my own forlornness.

The thermograph in the shelter showed a minimum temperature of 48.5° below zero and a maximum of 46° since the last observation. I reset the pin in the minimum thermometer and brushed out the rime and snow with a whisk broom which I carried in my pocket. Altogether I was not on the surface more than five minutes, counting the time spent taking notes on cloudiness, mist, drift, precipitation, and the rest of it; but it was long enough for me to decide that a blow was in the making.

Although the fire had not yet driven the cold out of the room, the place seemed snug and pleasant when I returned. The first thing I did was to light a candle, which I put on the table to brighten the middle of the room. While still standing up with my coat on, I jotted down on a piece of scratch paper the data I had gathered topside—I felt too cold to sit down. Meanwhile I polished off another pint of tea. Except for a biscuit, which was hard as rock, this was my breakfast.

8:30 o'clock. Some of the ice in the water bucket had melted; before I fetched in another snow block from the veranda, I poured enough water into a basin to wash my hands. Now was the time to decide what to have for supper and to begin thawing it. My choice was pea soup, seal meat, and stewed corn. From the meat box I took a five-inch slab of seal, black and unappetizing, which I hung from a nail over the stove to thaw. The can of corn I lifted from the cold deck to the shelf close behind the stove. The four-gallon gravity tank on the stove needs filling every three days; today is a filling day. I shut off the flame, unshipped the tank, and carried it into the fuel tunnel, a matter of thirty-five feet or so to the farthest drum. A stick driven into the wall served as a peg for the lantern. By its dim light I found the rubber siphon coiled over one of the drums. I had to suck on this for dear life to start the flow; and, while waiting for the tank to fill, I examined the roof to make sure that it wasn't caving again. Everything was holding nicely.

Just about 9 o'clock, I commenced the usual rigamarole of preparations for the radio schedule. I finished barely in time to pop topside for the 10 A.M. auroral "ob." Nothing doing—heavy clouds still. As I tuned in the receiver, Dyer was calling KFY. Today's was an interesting conversation. The general objectives of the big exploration campaign in the spring had been set up before I left Little America, but certain revisions in the plan seemed desirable after closer scrutiny; and these Charlie Murphy took up, after discussions with Poulter, June, Innes-Taylor, Rawson, Siple, and the scientific staff. With the suggested revisions I was in accord.

Just before we shut down, Dyer gave me a time tick, which he had picked up from either the U. S. Naval Observatory or Greenwich, I've forgotten which. "When I say 'now,'" Dyer warned, "it will be 10:53 o'clock. You have thirty-five seconds to go . . . Twenty seconds . . . Ten seconds . . . Now." One chronometer, I found, was running 2 minutes, 10 seconds fast, the other 31 seconds fast, the third was 1 minute 20 seconds slow. I noted the facts in my records. I must know the exact time in order to synchronize my observations with those at Little America. After that I carefully wound all three chronometers.

After the schedule I had an hour to devote to the Escape Tunnel. It's just about a third done—thirteen feet, to be exact. I'm far behind my schedule of a foot a day, but my lame shoulder has been something of a handicap. This morning I finished cutting shelves in the sides for superfluous books. Later on I expect to build alcoves in the tunnel for other gear. There isn't an inch of blank space anywhere in the shack. That's because I've been bringing in so much stuff from the boxes in the tunnel. Looking around, I was almost horrified at the amount of clothing, food, tools, gear, and other things it takes to support even one man and a scientific station here. Much of the stuff could just as well remain outside; but I suppose I get bored trotting in and out every time I want something. . . .

*   *   *

The hour between 12 and 1 o'clock was, as always, the busiest. Exactly at noon I inked the register pens, changed the sheet, and wound the clock (the tracing had turned irregular, which meant that the contact points were foul).

So, topside, armed with a flashlight looped around my neck, a whisk broom, and an open knife in the chest pocket of my parka. Reaching the top of the pole, I whipped off the reindeer-skin mittens, which were also on a cord around my neck, and fell to work on the wind vane. I lifted it off its seat, brushed the snow out of the cups, and scraped the contact points clean, all the while cursing the cold torturing my fingers and face.

My wrist watch showed 1 o'clock. No necessity for an auroral observation—still overcast. But time to wind the inside thermograph and change the recording sheet. After that, lunch. I am half through Somerset Maugham's *Of Human Bondage,* and I read a chapter as I ate. A meal eaten alone and in silence is no pleasure. So I fell into the habit of reading while I ate. In that way I can lose myself completely for a time. The days I don't read I feel like a barbarian brooding over a chunk of meat.

A moment ago there came a tremendous boom, as if tons of dynamite had exploded in the Barrier.* The sound was muffled by distance; yet, it was inherently ominous breaking through the silence. But I confess that any sound which interrupts the evenness of this place is welcome. I had the feeling that the Barrier was moving slightly. The handle of the lantern rattled against the tin base. The flashlight, hanging from a nail on a shelf in front of me, seemed to sway a little. This is what is known as a Barrier quake—a subsidence of great areas of snow contracting from cold.

* From seismic soundings taken the following summer we learned that Advance Base was underlaid by a stratum of ice and snow about seven hundred feet thick. The presence of this perpetual carapace of ice throughout most of Antarctica is one of the principal features which differentiate it from the Arctic, where, with few exceptions, the ground is uncovered during the summer.

Half an hour of shoveling drift was on the afternoon program. Before I went topside, I picked up the slop pail, already half frozen from standing on the floor. I was careful to dump it to leeward so that a mound wouldn't be formed to catch drift. Put in my half hour leveling off the snow around the shack. Not so difficult today. The snow lies a couple of feet deep on the roof, but for the time being does not seem to be deepening. After finishing that I pulled the ventilator up through the roof, and carried it below to thaw on the stove. For once it was fairly free of ice. After a few minutes on the stove, the ice loosened; and I was able to jar it out with a hammer. The chunk of seal over the stove was steadily dripping blackish drops of blood and water.

Then I had an hour to myself. I spent part of it entering my rough meteorological notes on U. S. Weather Bureau form Number 1083. Then I tinkered with the handle of the victrola, which had come unscrewed the night before. Just before 4 o'clock I put on my windproofs and went topside for the auroral "ob." The overcast had thinned a little, and the snow had stopped; but, beyond a pale, trembling glow in the dark edging of cloud, there was no sign of the aurora. A quiet day for the auroral department, I said to myself, and went walking.

Because of the fog and the threat of blizzard in the air, I decided not to go very far. It is my practice to walk between an hour and two hours a day—when I have time. The walk gives me change and it also provides another means of exercise. Starting out, I usually stop every few steps and do a knee bend or stoop or any one of a dozen exercises I enjoy. Today, however, I favored myself. My lungs hurt a little when I breathe, and I may have frosted them on the 18th a little more than I realized.

The last half of the walk is the best part of the day, the time when I am most nearly at peace with myself and circumstances. Thoughts of life and the nature of things flow smoothly, so smoothly and so naturally as to create an illusion that one is swimming harmoniously in the broad current of the cosmos. During this hour I undergo a sort of intellectual levitation, although my thinking is usually on earthy, practical matters. Last night, before turning in, I read, in Santayana's *Soliloquies in England,* an essay on friendship. I thought of that and the structure of social relationships and the mechanics of friendship as they have operated in my life. The negative aspects—the betrayals, the disappointments, and the bitternesses—I shut out entirely. Only by ruthlessly exorcising the disillusioning and unpleasant thoughts can I maintain any feeling of real detachment, any sense of being wholly apart from selfish concerns.

I made many turns back and forth before I decided to go below. It was very dark then, too dark to see the upperworks of the hut or even the anemometer pole until I was hard by; so I finished the walk by flashlight. On the way down the ladder, I noticed that one of the rungs had sprung, and made a mental note to fix that tomorrow. After getting rid of my heavy clothes, I set about the afternoon ritual of lighting the gasoline pressure lamp. Anyhow, I have made it a ritual. Its light is twice as strong as that of the storm lantern; it reaches every corner of the room. But I have forced myself to use it sparingly because it consumes a lot of gasoline, and, also, because it gives off certain disagreeable fumes. But I find that I crave light as a thirsting man craves water; and just the fact of having this lantern alive in the night hours makes an immense difference. I feel like a rich man.

The water in the bucket was hot when I dipped my finger—just right for the soup. Making a great clatter of pans and whistling out of tune anything that came to my lips, I got the supper ready: hot pea soup (made from a stick of dried peas, called erbswurst) ; fried young seal, which was very tender; plus corn, tea, powdered milk, and canned peaches for dessert. Excellent, all of it. Just before dessert I went topside for the 7 P.M. auroral "ob." Sky had cleared quite a bit. A vague, luminous belt lay sprawled through the northeast and southwest quarters of the sky, but it had little color or life. The data were dutifully entered in the records; structure H.A. (made up of homogeneous quiet arcs) ; intensity 2; altitude, about 35° above the horizon. Slight glow about 10° to the right, in the direction of Little America.

When I had finished the peaches, I pushed my book and the dishes to one side, got out the deck of cards, and played two or three hands of Canfield. No luck. At a dollar a point, I lost $15 to my imaginary banker. And then my only real luxury—music. I wound up the battered green victrola, slipped on a Strauss waltz, "Wine, Women

and Song," released the brake, and jumped simultaneously for the dishes. The idea is to finish the dishes
before the phonograph runs down. The machine has a
double-length spring, and I've rigged a rude sort of
repeater which plays a small record four or five times
on one winding. Tonight, though, no sound came out.
Cause: frozen oil in the works. I stood the machine on
a corner of the stove. In a little while the record began
to turn, very slowly at first, making lugubrious notes,
then faster and faster. I transferred it to the table and
fell to on the dishes, going like mad. Tonight they out-
lasted the record by fifteen seconds: a very poor showing indeed, although I credit the defeat to the head
start the phonograph got while it was warming up on
the stove.

While adding to this diary, I suddenly realized that
I had almost forgotten the 8 P.M. "ob." Hurriedly threw
on a coat, cap, and mittens, and scrambled topside. Still
cloudy; the pin in the minimum thermometer stood at
50° below zero; the wind was still in the northwest and
very light. But I could still smell a blizzard. I was glad
to return to the snugness of the shack.

Except for the 10 P.M. auroral "ob," my day's work
was finished. I spent the few remaining hours playing
the phonograph and completing this entry. . . . The day
is about to end. I have just finished my nightly bath,
or, rather, third of a bath; for each night I wash a different third of my body. I don't know how I came to
decide upon that arbitrary division, unless it was that
I discovered my conscience could be placated by per-

forming the ritual in installments. Anyhow, I started bathing this way during my first stay at Little America, and have found it satisfactory. I really don't get dirty. The Barrier is as clean as the top of Mount Everest, but habits must be satisfied, and the truth is that I find the bath a diversion. And my body always feels refreshed afterwards.

It is now close to midnight. In a moment I shall go to bed. I know exactly what I shall do. With a pencil stroke, I shall cross this day off the calendar; then fetch snow and alcohol tablets for the morning tea, and, finally, make sure that the instruments are functioning properly. This inspection over, I shall take a quick glance from the hatch to see whether anything unusual is happening in the auroral department. After battening down the trapdoor, I shall undress, turn down the pressure lantern, put out the fire, open the door, and jump for the sleeping bag, leaving the storm lantern burning over my head. That part of the routine is automatic. As long as heat remains in the shack, I shall read; tonight it will be the second volume of the *Life of Alexander,* which I've nearly finished. That part is by choice. When my hands turn numb, I'll reach up and blow out the lantern, but not until I have first made sure that the flashlight is somewhere in the sleeping bag, where my body will keep the battery warm.

I don't try to force myself to sleep, as I sometimes do at home. My whole life here in a sense is an experiment in harmony, and I let the bodily processes achieve a natural equilibrium. As a rule, it doesn't take me long to go to sleep. But a man can live a lifetime in a few half-dreaming moments of introspection between going to bed and falling asleep: a lifetime reordered and edited to satisfy the ever-changing demands of the mind.

* * *

As predicted, Monday the 23rd brought a blizzard. I was aroused in the morning by the rattling of the anemometer cups. When I pushed back the trapdoor, the wind swooped down, and the drift came in a white smother. The wind sucked the heat out of the shack so that I couldn't keep warm; the stove flickered from the draft. The open outlet ventilator alone wasn't enough to make the difference; the perviousness of the snow, I decided, had a lot to do with it. Although the hatch was battened down and two feet of closely packed snow insulated me from the surface, a strong draft moved steadily in the tunnels.

April ran out its time like a ship on a close reach. From the 23rd to the 29th the wind blew fairly steadily, though on no occasion did it rise over 27 miles per hour; but, since the wind begins to pick up drift at 15 miles per hour, and at 20 miles an hour is thick with it, the conditions topside were not very pleasant. The raking winds furrowed the Barrier with sastrugi as symmetrical as waves, hard at the crest and soft in the trough, so that walking was difficult. On the days the air was fairly quiet, a cottony gray fog deadened the twilight hours, and a somber red tinge smeared the northern horizon at noon. I continued working on the Escape Tunnel. My right arm was nearly well again. At Little America, I learned on the radio, they were being whaled by continuous blizzards, which had put a stop to outside work. But all was well.

April 30

Today came in fine and clear. So bright was the moonlight at the beginning of my walk that I could read the second hand on the wrist watch. The whole sky was bathed with light, and the Barrier seemed to exhale a soft, internal luminescence of its own. At first there was not a cloud anywhere, and the stars glittered with an unnatural brightness. Overhead, in the shape of a great ellipse, was a brilliant aurora. It ran across the sky from north to south. The short diameter of the ellipse ran east and west from where I stood, and the eastern segment of the curve was at my zenith. Waves of light pulsed rapidly through the structure. Beyond the south end of the ellipse, scintillating in the sky, was what appeared to be a drapery hanging over the South Pole. It hung in folds, like a gigantic curtain, and was composed of brilliant light rays.

The snow was different shades of silver gray (not white as one would suppose) with the brightest gray making a pathway to the moon. And to the eastward was another faint patch of aurora.

The wind blew gently from the pole, and the temperature was between 40° and 50° below. When Antarctica displays her beauty, she seems to give pause to the winds, which at such times are always still.

Overhead the aurora began to change its shape and

became a great, lustrous serpent moving slowly across the zenith. The small patch in the eastern sky now expanded and grew brighter; and almost at the same instant the folds in the curtain over the pole began to undulate, as if stirred by a celestial presence.

Star after star disappeared as the serpentine folds covered them. It was like witnessing a tragedy on a cosmic scale; the serpent, representing the forces of evil, was annihilating beauty.

Suddenly the serpent disappeared. Where it had been only a moment before, the sky was once more clear; the stars showed as if they had never been dimmed. When I looked for the luminous patch in the eastern sky, it, too, was gone; and the curtain was lifting over the pole, as if parted by the wind which at that instant came throbbing over the Barrier. I was left with the tingling feeling that I had witnessed a scene denied to all other mortal men.

* * *

Yet, this harmony was mostly of the mind: a temporary peace won by a physically occupied body. But the glory of the celestial is one, and the glory of the terrestrial is another. Even in my most exalted moods I never quite lost the feeling of being poised over an undermined footing, like a man negotiating a precipice who pauses to admire the sunset, but takes care where he places his feet. There were few days, even in April, that did not produce a reminder of the varied hazards of isolation. Rime was forever choking the stovepipe, ventilators, even the exhaust duct from the radio generator alcove, hindering the ventilation and making for fumes in the hut. And, though walking had always been my principal relaxation, I almost never dared to get out of sight of the anemometer pole, or the ten-foot snow beacon marking the Southern Party's depot, about seventy-five yards west of the hut. These were the only identifiable landmarks between the Queen Mauds and Little America. If a wind came up suddenly, or fog shut down, I could—and, on occasion, did—lose them in an instant.

The tolerable quality of a dangerous existence is the fact that the human mind cannot remain continuously sensitive to anything. Repetition's dulling impact sees to that. The threat of sudden death can scare a man for only so long; then he dismisses it as he might a mealymouthed beggar. When Bennett and I were on our way to the North Pole, and not quite halfway there, something let go in one of the engines, and ropy streaks of oil, whipped by the wind, coated the cowling. Bennett went white, and into my throat came a choking like that of suffocation. Then the feeling vanished. "Hold your course," I scratched on the pad which we used for communication. Bennett jerked his thumb down at the broken pack, 2,000 feet below, and made a wry grimace. Although the panic was gone, the leak fascinated us both. My eyes kept straying from the cowling to the oil pressure gauge and back again to see whether the leak was increasing. "Suppose it gets worse," Bennett yelled into my ear. Knowing that his pilot's instincts had already measured the possibilities, I didn't bother to answer. Either all the oil would trickle away before we managed to regain King's Bay, or it wouldn't; and, whichever happened, the outcome was out of our hands. Presently an angling wind fetched Bennett's attention back to the problem of holding his course, and mine to the drift indicator. And throughout the rest of the flight we paid little more attention to the leak.

Fright and pain are the most transitory of emotions. And, since they are so easily forgotten, I never ceased drilling into the men who served under me the absolute authority of safety rules. "Not just for today or tomorrow; but so long as you are on this expedition," is the way I'd put it to a new man. Relax once in the polar regions, and the artificial wall of security which you have so painstakingly erected about yourself may give way without warning. That appreciation of discipline I carried with me to Advance Base; and, though at times I had to drive myself to respect it, the necessity was always there.

As I saw it, three risks stood out before all the others. One was fire. Another was getting lost on the Barrier. And the third was being incapacitated, either by injury or illness. Of the three, the last was the most difficult to anticipate and prepare for. Yet, the possibilities were authentic enough, and I had carefully taken them into account. My health was sound. A thoroughgoing medical examination, before I left New Zealand, had confirmed that fact. From disease I had little to fear. Antarctica is a paradise in that respect. It is the germless continent. Vast oceans, frozen most of the time, seal it from the germ-laden civilization to the north; and the refrigerating temperatures of an active Ice Age, which even in the summer—

and then only for a few hours—rarely rise from freezing, have reduced the surviving micro-organisms to a largely encysted existence. The only germs are those you bring. In the bitter cold I've seen men shake to the periodic gusts of malarial fever contracted in the tropics; and once, in the winter night, flu laid half of Little America low—the result, according to the doctor, of opening a box of old clothing. I believe that, if any germs did survive at Advance Base, the temperature even in the hut never became warm enough for them to become active.

With the help of a doctor friend, I had equipped the Base with a medical library, containing, among other books, a medical dictionary, Gray's *Anatomy,* and Strumpell's *Practice of Medicine.* With these, if I thumbed far enough, I could recognize the symptoms of anything from AAA (a form of hookworm) to caries. A small supply of narcotics and anesthetics (such as novocaine), plus hypodermic needles, was available. These were stored on a shelf in the food tunnel, next to the surgical instruments, of which I had a fairly complete set—complete enough, in all events, for any operation up to a leg amputation. God knows, I had no desire to use these instruments, and only the vaguest idea what each one was for; but there they were, shiny and sharp.

But I did not expect anything serious to happen. A man never does. My preparations were of a piece with the methodical, impersonal preparations which I had learned in flying. For example, in taking fuel for the stove, I made a practice of drawing upon the drums at the distant end of the tunnel. Thus, in the event of my ever being crippled to such an extent that I might not be able to move very far or do much carrying, I should be able to struggle along with the nearby drums at the tunnel entrance.

Fire was a serious hazard, and one very much on my mind. I had plenty of liquid fire bombs; but the cold had cracked most of them; and I was afraid that, if the hut ever caught fire, nothing could save it. Stowed at the far end of the fuel tunnel, I had in reserve a complete trail outfit, including tent, sleeping bag, cooker, and primus stove, also a flare and even a kite for signaling. If I ever lost the shack, I could gouge the tunnel a little wider, pitch the tent inside, and get by. But I was careful that this necessity should never arise. Going for a walk, I always shut down the stove before leaving the shack; and at night I put it out before getting into the sleeping bag, knowing the drowsiness that came with books and the temptation to let the fire run until morning.

This filling of cracks and chinks, this constant watchfulness, used to remind me of how my brothers Harry and Tom and I used to play war as children. Although Harry was just old enough to be somewhat contemptuous of games, Tom and I were always building forts. Not just "pretend" forts: flimsy box structures to be brushed away as soon as the game palled, but elaborate earthworks and bastions which transformed the Byrd grounds into an armed city and kept Mother wavering between indignation and terror, since her gardens were ruined, and an innocent step might at any instant bring a blood-chilling imitation of musketry from an unseen ambuscade. No beleaguered city was ever more faithfully defended. Besides the other boys, who liked to shy rocks every now and then to test the garrison, our defenses were menaced by enemies whose numbers, in Tom's phrase, were never less than "annihilatin'." And, fearing that they might strike when we were supposedly asleep, we'd steal out of the house and man the watch towers, until one of us would softly call that Pop, whom we could see in the library, was putting away his law books, a signal to retreat while the way was still open.

Except that I was now alone, Advance Base was something like this. It, too, was a fort, whose enemies were likewise invisible and often, I suppose, no less imaginary. The daily business of inspecting the defenses, and prying the ice out of the ventilators with a long stick armed with a sharp nail, and storing the scientific records in a safe place in the tunnels, sometimes seemed a ridiculous game. Yet, it was a game I played with deadly seriousness, even in the simple matter of my daily walks. North and south of the shack I marked a path about one hundred yards long, which I called the hurricane deck. Every three paces a two-foot bamboo stick was driven into the crust, and along these poles I ultimately strung a life line. By running my hand over this, blindman fashion, I could feel my way back and forth in the worst weather; and many were the times I did it when the air was so thick with drift that I could not see past the cowling of my windproof, and the line was a thin cord through chaos.

On clear days I could extend my path in any direction. Then I'd tuck a bundle of split bamboo sticks under my arms; and every thirty yards or so, as I went along, I'd prick one of these sticks into the surface. When the bundle was used up, I'd retrace my steps, picking up the sticks on the way, the last stick fetching me hard by my path. The sticks weighed very little, and I could easily carry enough to mark a path a quarter of a mile long. Although I varied the route often, the change really made no difference. No matter which quarter I faced, an identical sameness met the view. I could have walked 175 miles northeast to the Rockefeller Mountains, or 300 miles south to the Queen Mauds, or 400 miles west to the mountains of South Victoria Land, and not seen anything different.

Yet, I could, with a little imagination, make every walk *seem* different. One day I would imagine that my path was the Esplanade, on the water side of Beacon Hill in Boston, where, in my mind's eye, I often walked with my wife. I would meet people I knew along the bank, and drink in the perfection of a Boston spring. There was no need for the path's ever becoming a rut. Like a rubber band, it could be stretched to suit my mood; and I could move it forward and backward in time and space, as when, in the midst of reading Yule's *Travels of Marco Polo*, I divided the path into stages of that miraculous journey, and in six days and eighteen miles wandered from Venice to China, seeing everything that Marco Polo saw. And on occasion the path led back down the eons, while I watched the slow pulsations of the Ice Age, which today grips the once semi-tropical Antarctic Continent even as it once gripped North America.

By speeding up the centuries I could visualize a tidal wave of ice flooding down from the Arctic and crushing everything before it. I could see it surging forward until the advancing edge made a zigzag line from what is now New York to what is now California, blotting out everything but the peaks of the mountains, and forming towering barriers on the margins of the sea. I could see bottomless chasms and enormous ridges thrown up by pressure, and blocks of ice strewn about in endless confusion. And for centuries I could see nothing but the obliterating ice, hear nothing but the wind, and feel nothing but the rigidity of death. But, finally, I could see the ice imperceptibly sinking; and the ocean rising as the ice melted; and the land resurrecting under the sun, with the mountains scoured and planed, and the rivers pushed into new courses. And along the edges of the land in Europe and Asia I could see men with primitive tools laying the foundations of history.

Thus it was in the Northern Hemisphere, and so it will some day be in the Antarctic, where the ice still holds mastery over the land. Except, I used to tell myself, that long before the ice rolls back, excursion boats will be steaming down from Sandy Hook and every moraine will have its tourist hotel.

All this was fun. But, if I wasn't careful, it could also be dangerous, as an experience which I went through just about this time will testify. Being in a particularly fine mood, I had decided to take a longer walk than usual. It was drifting a bit, and the Barrier was pretty dark, but that didn't bother me. After parading up and down for

half an hour, I turned around to go back. The line of
bamboo sticks was nowhere in sight! In my abstraction,
I had walked completely past and beyond it; and now,
wondering which way to turn, I was overwhelmed by the
realization that I had no idea of how far I had walked,
nor the direction in which I was heading. On the chance
that my footsteps would show, I scanned the Barrier with
a flashlight; but my boots had left no marks on the hard
sastrugi. It was scary. The first impulse was to run. I
quelled that, and soberly took stock of my predicament.

Since it was the one fact I had to work with, I again
pulled the flashlight up out of my pants, where I carried
it to keep it from freezing, and scratched into the
snow with the butt end an arrow in the direction whence
I had come. I remembered also, from having glanced
at the wind vane as I started, that the wind was
in the south. It was then on my left cheek and was still
on the same cheek, but that meant little. For the wind
might have changed, and subconsciously I might have
veered with it. I was lost, and I was sick inside.

In order to keep from wandering still farther from the
shack, I made a reference point. I broke off pieces of
sastrugi with my heel and heaped them into a little beacon
about eighteen inches high at the butt of the arrow. This
took quite a little while. Straightening up and consulting
the sky, I discovered two stars which were in line with
the direction in which I had been walking when I stopped.
This was a lucky break, as the sky had been overcast until
now and had only cleared in a couple of places. In the
navigator's phrase, the stars gave me a range and the

beacon a departure. So, taking careful steps and with my eyes on the stars, I started forward; after 100 paces I stopped. I swung the flashlight all around and could see nothing but blank Barrier.

Not daring to go farther for fear of losing the snow beacon, I started back, glancing over my shoulder at the two stars to hold my line. At the end of a hundred steps I failed to fetch the beacon. For an instant I was on the edge of panic. Then the flashlight beam picked it up about twenty feet or so on my left hand. That miserable pile of snow was nothing to rejoice over, but at least it kept me from feeling that I was stabbing blindfolded. On the next sortie, I swung the course 30° to the left. And as before, after a hundred steps, I saw nothing.

You're lost now, I told myself. I was appalled. I realized that I should have to lengthen my radius from the beacon; and in lengthening it I might never be able to find the way back to the one certainty. However, there was no alternative unless I preferred to freeze to death, and I could do that just as thoroughly 1,000 yards from the hut as 500. So now I decided to take 30 steps more in the same direction, after scraping a little heap of snow together to mark the 100-pace point. On the 29th step, I picked up the first of the bamboo sticks, not more than 30 feet away. No shipwrecked mariner, sighting a distant sail, could have been more overjoyed.

MAY I: THE INTIMATION

MAY I: THE INTIMATION

THE FIRST DAYS OF MAY CARRIED NO HINT OF THE CALAMI-
ties that would overtake me at the month's end. On the
contrary, they were among the most wonderful days
I had ever known. The blizzards departed, the cold moved
down from the South Pole, and opposite the moon in a
coal-black sky the cast-up light from the departed sun
burned like a bonfire. During the first six days the temperature averaged $-47.03°$; much of the time it was deep
in the minus forties and fifties. The winds scarcely blew.
And a soundlessness fell over the Barrier. I have never
known such utter quiet. Sometimes it lulled and hypno-
tized, like a waterfall or any other steady, familiar sound.
At other times it struck into the consciousness as per-
emptorily as a sudden noise. It made me think of the fatal
emptiness that comes when an airplane engine cuts out
abruptly in flight. Up on the Barrier it was taut and immense; and, in spite of myself, I would be straining to
listen—for nothing, really, nothing but the sheer excitement of silence. Underground, it became intense and concentrated. In the middle of a task or while reading a book,

119

I was sometimes brought up hard with all my senses alert and suspicious, like a householder who imagines he hears a burglar in the house. Then, the small sounds of the hut —the hiss of the stove, the chatter of the instruments, the overlapping beats of the chronometers—would suddenly leap out against the soundlessness, all seeming self-conscious and hurried. And after a big wind I have been startled out of a sound sleep, without understanding why, until I realized that my subconscious self, which had become attuned to the rattling of the stovepipe and the surf-like pounding of the blizzard overhead, had been unsettled by the abrupt calm.

It was a queer business. I felt as though I had been plumped upon another planet or into another geologic horizon of which man had no knowelge or memory. And yet, I thought at the time it was very good for me; I was learning what the philosophers have long been harping on —that a man can live profoundly without masses of things. For all my realism and skepticism there came over me, too powerfully to be denied, that exalted sense of iden-tification—of oneness—with the outer world which is partly mystical but also certainty. I came to understand what Thoreau meant when he said, "My body is all sentient." There were moments when I felt more *alive* than at any other time in my life. Freed from materialistic distrac-tions, my senses sharpened in new directions, and the ran-dom or commonplace affairs of the sky and the earth and the spirit, which ordinarily I would have ignored if I had noticed them at all, became exciting and portentous. Thus:

May 1

This afternoon, in the lee of the sastrugi formed by the last blow, I discovered some extraordinarily fluffy snow. It was so light that my breath alone was enough to send the crystals scurrying like tumbleweed; so fragile that, when I blew hard, they fell to pieces. I have named it "snow down." Although most of the crystals were not much bigger around than a quarter, some were as small as marbles and others as big as goose eggs. Apparently they were blown in on this morning's light westerly wind. I scooped up enough to fill a box—no easy task, for even so slight a disturbance as that created by my hands caused the crystals to fly away. The box was half again as big as a shoe box (approximately 600 cubic inches), but the contents, melted in the bucket, yielded barely half a cup of water....

Later, during my walk, I saw a moon halo, the first since I've been here. I had remarked inwardly that the moon seemed almost unnaturally bright, but thought no more about it until something—perhaps a subtle change in the quality of moonlight—fetched my attention back to the sky. When I glanced up, a haze was spreading over the moon's face; and, as I watched, a system of luminous circles formed themselves gracefully around it. Almost instantly the moon was wholly surrounded by concentric bands of color, and the effect was as if a rainbow had been looped around a huge silver coin. Apple-green was the color of the wide outer band, whose diameter, I estimated, was nineteen times that of the moon itself. The effect lasted only five minutes or so. Then the colors drained from the moon, as they do from a rainbow; and almost simultaneously a dozen massive streamers of crimson-stained aurora, laced together with blackish stripes, seemed to leap straight out from the moon's brow. Then they, too, vanished.

May 3

...I again saw in the southeast, touching the horizon, a star so bright as to be startling. The first time I saw it several weeks ago I yielded for an instant to the fantastic notion that somebody was trying to signal me; that thought came to me again this afternoon. It's a queer sort of star, which appears and disappears irregularly, like the winking of a light.

The wind vane has been giving quite a bit of trouble lately. I've had to climb the pole once or twice every day to scrape the contact points. The temperature is holding pretty steadily between 50° and 60° below zero; and I must admit that the job is chillier than I bargained for. Freezing my hands, nose, and cheeks, separately or all together every time I mount the pole is an old story by now; today, for a change, I froze my chin. But all this is not as bad as it sounds....

May 5

This has been a beautiful day. Although the sky was almost cloudless, an impalpable haze hung in the air, doubtless from falling crystals. In midafternoon it disappeared, and the Barrier to the north flooded with a rare pink light, pastel in its delicacy. The horizon line was a long slash of crimson, brighter than blood; and over this welled a straw-yellow ocean whose shores were the boundless blue of the night. I watched the sky a long time, concluding that such beauty was reserved for distant, dangerous places, and that nature has good reason for exacting her own special sacrifices from those determined to witness them. An intimation of my isolation seeped into my mood; this cold but lively afterglow was my compensation for the loss of the sun whose warmth and light were enriching the world beyond the horizon.

That afternoon, for variety's sake, I decided to direct my walk out along the radio antenna, which extended on a line about due east from the shack. The cold was not excessive—somewhere between 50° and 60° below zero—but I was astonished to find how much rime had collected on the wire. It was swollen to many times its natural size; so much so, in fact, that I could just encircle it with my fingers; and the weight of the ice had caused it to sag in great loops between the poles.

A day or so before the sun had departed I had planted a bamboo stick about twenty yards beyond the last antenna pole. This was to serve as a beacon in case I ever happened to miss the pole in fog or storm. On this day I found the marker without difficulty.

I was standing there, thinking about something, when I suddenly remembered that I had left the stove going. So I turned back, making for the last antenna pole, whose shadowy pencil form I could just see. Head screwed down inside the windproof hood out of the wind, I paid no attention to where I was stepping. Then I had a horrible feeling of falling, and at the same time of being hurled sideways. Afterwards I could not remember hearing any sound. When my wits returned, I was sprawled out full length on the snow with one leg dangling over the side of an open crevasse.

I lay still, not daring to make a move lest I shake down the ledge supporting me. Then, an inch at a time, I crawled away. When I had gone about two yards, I came slowly to my feet, shivering from the closeness of the escape.

I had broken through the snow bridging of a blind crevasse—a roofed-over one which you cannot tell from solid surface. I edged back with my flashlight and took a look. The hole I had made was barely two feet across, and I could see that the roof was twelve inches or so thick. Stretched out on my belly, I pounded the roof in with the marker stick for a distance of several feet; then I turned the flashlight into the crevasse. I could see no bottom. My guess was that the crevasse was at least several hundred feet deep. At the surface it was not more than three feet across; but a little way down it bellied out, making a vast cave. The walls changed from blue to an emerald green, the color of sea ice. The usual crystals, created by the condensed exhalations from the warmer depths, did not festoon the walls; their absence indicated that the crevasse was of fairly recent origin.

I was glad to leave that place. Good luck had carried me across the crevasse at right angles to its length. Had

I been walking in any other direction, I might well have gone to the bottom. Odd, I thought, that it hadn't let me through when I passed over it on the way out. Possibly I had hit the one weak spot. So as not to make a similar mistake, I fetched back two bamboo poles and planted them in front of the hole.

May 6

Today I broke the thermometer I keep in the hut. It is not important, really, as inside temperatures are not a part of my meteorological records; but I have been interested in finding out how cold it gets in the hut during the night when the fire is out.

Curiosity tempted me to ask Little America how the stock market was going. It was a ghastly mistake. I can in no earthly way alter the situation. Worry, therefore, is needless. Before leaving [home] I had invested my own funds—carefully, I thought—in the hope of making a little money and thus reducing the expedition's debt. This additional loss, on top of ever-mounting operating expenses, may be disastrous. Well, I don't need money here. The wisest course is to close off my mind to the bothersome details of the world.

* * *

It was one thing to instruct the mind; it was another to make the mind obey. The nature of the distinction was to be a fundamental part of my self-instruction at Advance Base, as is evidenced by a diary entry about this time: "Something—I don't know what—is getting me down," the entry goes. "I've been strangely irritable all day, and since supper have been depressed.... [This] would not seem important if I could only put my finger on the trouble, but I can't find any single thing to account for the mood. Yet, it has been there; and tonight, for the first time, I must admit that the problem of keeping my mind on an even keel is a serious one...."

The entire entry, a longish one, is before me now. I have a clear recollection of how it came to be written. Supper was over, the dishes had been washed, the 8 P.M. "ob" was out of the way, and I had settled down to read. I picked up Veblen's *Theory of the Leisure Class,* which I was halfway through, but its concerns seemed fantastically remote to the monocracy of Advance Base. I went from that to *Heloïse and Abélard,* a story I have always loved; after a little while the words began to run together. Queerly, my eyes hurt, my head ached a little, though not enough to bother.

So I turned up the lamp a little, thinking that more light might help, and tried a few hands of solitaire. But this did no good. Nor did bathing my eyes in boric acid. I couldn't concentrate. My whole being was restive and unaccountably troubled. I got up and paced the room. My movements were almost automatic. Two strides—duck the light, sidestep the stove—another step—full turn at the bunk—back again—three strides from the door to the radio set—three back—and so on, tracing an endlessly repeated L. Months after I had left Advance Base, when the pain was ebbing into forgetfulness, I used to pace my room that way, my steps unconsciously regulated to the dimensions of the shack, and my head jerking away from an imaginary lantern.

That night the peace did not come that should have come. I was like a clock wound up to strike in an empty house. Everything I was doing seemed unfinished and crude, without relationship to the unfathomable desires in my mind. The futility and emptiness of my existence were symbolized by the simple act of jumping up from the chair. Nothing in the everyday habits of a man is ordinarily freighted with more purposefulness than the business of quitting a chair. The swift leverage may impel him on any one of a thousand different errands and opportunities. But with me it led only to blank walls.

I tried to be rational about it. The diary testifies to that. I took my mood apart and studied it as I might have studied the register. Had anything gone wrong during the day? No, it had been a very pleasant day. Though the temperature was in the minus fifties, I had worked hard on the Escape Tunnel; I had supped well on chicken soup, beans, dehydrated potatoes, spinach, and canned peaches. Had I reason to be worried about matters in the world to the north? On the contrary, the news over the last radio schedule had been reassuring. My family was well, and nothing was wrong at Little America. The debt was a problem, but I was used to debts; I could pay off this one as I had paid off the others. My physical condition? Except for the dull ache in my eyes and head, I felt fine; the ache came only at night, anyway, and was gone before I fell asleep. Maybe the fumes from the stove accounted for it. If this was the case, I had better crack the door when the stove was going during the day, and spend more time outside. The diet might also be a contributing cause, but I doubted it. I had been careful about vitamins.

"The most likely explanation," I concluded that night in the diary, "is that the trouble lies with myself. Manifestly, if I can harmonize the various things within me that may be in conflict and also fit myself more smoothly into this environment, I shall be at peace. It may be that the evenness and the darkness and the absence of life are too much for me to absorb in one chunk. I cannot accept that as a fact, if only because I have been here but forty-three days and many months must be lived out which will be no different from the first.... If I am to survive—or at least keep my mental balance—I must control and direct my thoughts. This should not be difficult. Any intelligent man should be able to find means of existence within himself...."

Even from this distance I maintain that the attitude was a sensible one. The only fault was its glibness. The reasoning was too pat. I can see that now, but I lacked the prescience to see it then. It was true, as I reasoned that night in May, that the concerns and practices of the outer world had not intruded into my existence. That was proved by the weeks of utter tranquillity. It was also true, as I had concluded, that the way to keep them from intruding was through the censorship and control of the mind. But beyond these was a truth which that night I did not recognize; and this truth was that the whole complex nervous-muscular mechanism which is the body was waiting, as if with bated breath, for the intrusion of familiar stimuli from the outside world, and could not comprehend why they were denied.

A man can isolate himself from habits and conveniences —deliberately, as I have done; or accidentally, as a ship-wrecked sailor might—and force his mind to forget. But the body is not so easily sidetracked. It keeps on remembering. Habit has set up in the core of the being a system of automatic physio-chemical actions and reactions which insist upon replenishment. That is where the conflict arises. I don't think that a man can do without sounds and smells and voices and touch, any more than he can do without phosphorus and calcium. This is, in general, what I meant by the vague term "evenness."

So I learned at Latitude 80° 08′ South. It was exhilarating to stand on the Barrier and contemplate the sky and luxuriate in a beauty I did not aspire to possess. In the presence of such beauty we are lifted above natural crassness. And it was a fine thing, too, to surrender to the illusion of intellectual disembodiment, to feel the mind go voyaging through space as smoothly and felicitously as it passes through the objects of its reflections. The body stood still, but the mind was free. It could travel the universe with the audacious mobility of a Wellsian time-space machine.

The senses were isolated in soundless dark; so, for that matter, was the mind; but one was stayed, while the other possessed the flight of a falcon; and the free choice and opportunity of the one everlastingly emphasized the poverty of the other. From the depth of my being would sometimes surge a fierce desire to be projected spectacu-

ALONE

larly into the living warmths and movements the mind revisited. Usually the desire had no special focus. It sought no single thing. Rather it darted and wavered over a panorama of human aspects—my family at dinner time, the sound of voices in a downstairs room, the cool feeling of rain.

Small matters, all of them; not realities but only the manifestations of reality. Yet, they and a thousand other remembrances of like substance assailed me at night. Not with the calm, revivifying strength of treasured memories; but bitterly and provokingly, as if they were fragments of something vast and not wholly recognizable which I had lost forever. This was the basis of my mood that night in May. Like fingers plucking at a counterpane, my thoughts moved through the days and nights of an existence that seemed to be irrevocably gone. In that mood I had walked before; I would walk like that again; and the glowing tranquillity built up in the afternoon would go out like a spent rocket.

*   *   *

Nevertheless, I practiced my preachments of a disciplined mind. Or perhaps discipline isn't exactly the right word; for what I did, or tried to do, was to focus my thinking on healthy, constructive images and concepts and thus crowd out the unhealthy ones. I built a wall between myself and the past in an effort to extract every ounce of diversion and creativeness inherent in my immediate surroundings. Every day I experimented with new schemes for increasing the content of the hours. "A grateful en-

130

vironment," according to Santayana, "is a substitute for happiness," for it can stimulate us from without just as good works can stimulate us from within. My environment was intrinsically treacherous and difficult, but I saw ways to make it agreeable. I tried to cook more rapidly, take weather and auroral observations more expertly, and do routine things systematically. Full mastery of the imping-ing moment was my goal. I lengthened my walks and did more reading, and kept my thoughts upon an impersonal plane. In other words, I tried resolutely to attend to my business.

All the while I experimented steadily with cold weather clothing. Inside the shack my usual outfit consisted of a thick woolen shirt, breeches, and underwear (medium weight); plus two pairs of woolen socks (one pair heavy, the other medium); plus a pair of homemade canvas boots, which were soled with thin strips of hairless sealskin, lined with a half-inch thickness of felt, and secured to the ankles by means of leather thongs fastened to the soles. The feet are most vulnerable to cold. They feel chilly sooner and stay that way longer than any other part of the body. This is partly because the circulation in the feet is not so good as in the rest of the body and because the cold from the snow gets to them from conduction and causes condensa-tion. The permeability of canvas was a partial solution to the second difficulty. By making the boots two inches longer and half again as wide as ordinary shoes, I assisted the circulation. The boots were about as handsome as potato sacks, but they worked very well indeed. Whenever I had been a considerable time in the cold, I always changed my socks and inner liners and let the wet ones dry on the stove. The inner soles of my boots were coated with a layer of ice that never thawed. Cold was nothing new to me; and experience had taught me that the secret of protection is not so much the quantity or weight of the clothes as it is the size and quality and, above all, the way they are worn and cared for.

After I'd been at Advance Base a little while I could tell, from a glance at the thermograph, exactly what clothing I would need topside. If it were a matter of taking a quick observation, I'd just slip on a canvas windbreaker, mittens, and a woolen cap that pulled down over the ears. If I had shoveling to do, I'd substitute a helmet for the cap, and add windproof socks, pants, and parka. Walking, I'd wear a woolen parka under the windproofs, which are nothing more mysterious than fine-spun unbleached cotton blouses and pants, made of material no heavier than ordinary sheeting. I've felt wind cut through half an inch of wool as if it were nothing at all; whereas, paper-thin windproofs, closed at the ankles, chin, and waist with draw strings or elastics, were scarcely penetrated. The ideal material is not completely windproof, but lets enough air through to prevent moisture from collecting. At 65° below zero, I usually wore a mask. A simple thing, it consisted of a wire framework overlaid with windproof cloth. Two funnels led to the nose and mouth, and oval slits allowed me to see. I'd breathe in through the nose funnel, and out through the mouth funnel; and, when the latter clogged with ice from the breath's freezing, as it would in short order, I brushed it out with a mitten. On the very cold days, if I had to be out two hours or more, I usually wore my fur outfit (pants, parka, mittens, and mukluks), which was made of reindeer skin, the lightest and most flexible of the warm furs. Thus protected, I could walk through my own inhospitable medium as well insulated as a diver moving through his.

Thus in May, as in April, I never really lacked for something to do. For all the hush and evenness and the slow pulse of the night, my existence was anything but static. I was the inspector of snowstorms and the aurora, the night watchman, and father confessor to myself. Something was always happening, for better or worse. For example, the Tuesday radio schedule with Little America was eliminated, to save gasoline; while this left a blank spot in the hours, the remaining two schedules in turn became more animated. There was always a message from the family in our own private code, which Dyer read with a gracious and unflagging courtesy: "A as in Arthur, L as in laughter, C as in ceiling ..." I can still hear him going on. Sometimes there were messages from friends. One message came from my old friend Franklin D. Roosevelt in the White House, saying that he hoped that "the night was not too cold or the wind too strong for an occasional promenade in the dark." And almost always Poulter, or Rawson (now fully recovered), or Siple, or Noville, or Haines, or Innes-Taylor entered into the conversation to discuss an expedition problem or merely pass the time of day.

When I gained in one direction, I seemed to lose in another. Just when I was congratulating myself on having mastered the job of weather observer, the outside thermo-

133

graph began to act up. A devilish contrivance, it occupied the instrument shelter topside, where hoarfrost settled on the trace, the pen, the drum, and even the workings. On the one occasion I brought the instrument into the shack to change the sheet and make an adjustment, the difference in temperature coated the metal with rime and stopped it dead. Thereafter I had no choice but to make the adjustments in the chill of the tunnel, with no protection for my hands except thin silk gloves; even these seemed infernally clumsy when I had to deal with the speed regulator, which must have been invented for the specific purpose of plaguing weather men.

Thus, even in the heart of the Ross Ice Barrier a solitary man had plenty to occupy him. Thus in the diary: ". . . I got Canfield twice tonight—extraordinary! The only games I played, too." And again: ". . . One of my favorite records is 'Home on the Range.' It's the second song I've ever learned to sing. (The other was 'Carry Me Back to Old Virginny,' and even that I never dared to sing except in the cockpit of an airplane, where nobody could hear me.) And tonight I sang while washing the dishes. Solitude hasn't mellowed my voice any, but I had great fun. A gala evening, in fact." The diary became more than a record; it became a means to think out loud. This was a pleasant way of filling the last hour; also, it helped to stabilize my philosophy. For example:

May 9

. . . I have been persistent in my effort to eliminate the after-supper periods of depression. Until tonight my

mood has been progressively better; now I am despond-
ent again. Reason tells me that I have no right to be
depressed. My progress in eliminating the indefinable
irritants has been better than I expected. I seem to be
learning how to keep my thoughts and feelings on an
even keel, for I have not been sensible of undue anxiety.
Therefore, I suspect that my dark moods come from
something affecting my physical being—possibly fumes
from the stove, the lantern, or the gasoline generator.
If that be the case, then my state of mind may possibly
have helped to offset the depressing consequences of the
poisoning—if that is what is affecting me.

It is really essential that I take careful stock of my
situation because my enemy is subtle. This doesn't mean
that I have become too introspective or that I am taking
myself too seriously. My thoughts have been objective
enough. But, if something is poisoning or otherwise
afflicting my body, what effect will this have on my peace
of mind? Certain types of physical ailments have a definitely depressing effect. The question is, how much can
this effect be overcome by disregarding or even denying
its existence? Suppose the disorder is organic and lies in
a deep-seated complaint. Suppose it comes from bad
food, from germs, or from the gases given off by the
stove. How much resistance, then, can my mind impart
to the body if the mind is properly directed?

Possibly something is harming me physically, and I am
making things worse by some negative subconscious emotion. Then my mind and body are both sick, and I have
a vicious circle to break. Do the mind and the body

135

exist separately, along parallel lines? Is the physical part mostly mental, or the mind mostly physical? How much does the mental control the physical? Indeed, how much division is there between mind and body? The body can take charge of the mind, but isn't it natural and best for the mind to take charge of the body? The brain is part of the body, but I am not conscious of my brain. The mind seems to be the real "I"....

Which is it, then? My mind or my body or both? It is of vital importance that I find the truth. Aside from the slight trouble with my eyes and the fact that my lungs are still sensitive to cold, I am not conscious of any physical deterioration. Diet, I am sure, has nothing to do with my moodiness. The fumes are the one question mark. The pain in my eyes and the headachy feeling come in the early evening, after the stove has been on a long time. And sometimes the air in the tunnel is thick after the gasoline engine has been running during a radio schedule. But it is hard to believe that the exhaust gases from either the stove or the engine are really damaging. The ventilation seems to be adequate, so long as I keep the vents clear of ice....

I remember that after finishing the foregoing entry I got up and inspected the stove. I walked all around, covertly scrutinizing the simple structure as I might a friend whose motives I had come to suspect. But my expression must have been anything but grave. The stove was more ludicrous than sinister. At that moment it was performing the humble duty of warming the water bucket in which my underwear was soaking. Even the gentle hiss of the burner seemed ineffectual; and the contrast between the tiny stove, which came just above my knees, and the grotesquely attenuated length of pipe was as ridiculous as anything of the sort could be. The only faults I could find with it were two. One was the burner's tendency to splutter and smoke from the water dripping down from the bucket when I melted snow. The other was the tendency of the pipe to fill with ice, and then, as it thawed, to let the water pour down into the stove. I had already made a hole in a right-angle joint to catch the water before it reached the burner; if that didn't work I could bend the joint into a V, making an easily drained trap.

Beyond this I could not think of anything important to do; for that matter, nothing more seemed necessary. The ventilating pipes were drawing well, considering the conditions under which they were operating. Certainly I had plenty of air. Every now and then during the day I'd crack the door an inch or two; when the room turned so cold that my nose hurt, I'd shut it again. To make the relatively distant reaches more attractive, I named one corner Palm Beach and the other Malibu; but with the door open I seldom felt very comfortable in either place without fur pants on. This is the honest truth. Indeed, on more than one occasion the glass of water which I put down beside the key at the start of a radio schedule was skimmed over with ice before I had time to drink it.

As the diary testifies, my mind was satisfied that the diet was providing the proper amount of vitamins. True, I had already pulled in my belt two notches, and would take in a third notch before the month was out. But that was to be expected. Although I had made an exhaustive study of dietetics, especially vitamins, in connection with provisioning my expeditions, just to be on the safe side, I decided to consult an excellent authority, called *New Dietetics,* a present from my friend John H. Kellogg. At first, though I hunted high and low, I couldn't find the book; finally I asked Dyer, on a radio schedule, please to send somebody after Siple and find out from him where it had been stowed. Ten minutes later Siple sent word back that he had last seen the book in a box on the veranda. And there I found it.

A quick reading of the book confirmed what I knew already: namely, that so far as choice of foods went, my diet was thoroughly balanced. But, as a double check, I asked Little America to consult a nationally known food laboratory in Rochester, New York. The experts there promptly reported back that my diet was adequate in every respect.

May 11

12:15 A.M. It is late, but I've just had an experience which I wish to record. At midnight I went topside to have a last look at the aurora, but found only a spotty glow on the horizon extending from north to northeast. I had been playing the victrola while I waited for the midnight hour. I was using my homemade repeater and was playing one of the records of Beethoven's Fifth Symphony. The night was calm and clear. I left the door to my shack open and also my trapdoor. I stood there in the darkness to look around at some of my favorite constellations, which were as bright as I had ever seen them.

Presently I began to have the illusion that what I was seeing was also what I was hearing, so perfectly did the music seem to blend with what was happening in the sky. As the notes swelled, the dull aurora on the horizon pulsed and quickened and draped itself into arches and fanning beams which reached across the sky until at my zenith the display attained its crescendo. The music and the night became one; and I told myself that all beauty was akin and sprang from the same substance. I recalled a gallant, unselfish act that was of the same essence as the music and the aurora.

10 P.M. Solitude is an excellent laboratory in which to observe the extent to which manners and habits are conditioned by others. My table manners are atrocious —in this respect I've slipped back hundreds of years; in fact, I have no manners whatsoever. If I feel like it, I eat with my fingers, or out of a can, or standing up—in other words, whichever is easiest. What's left over, I just heave into the slop pail, close to my feet. Come to think of it, no reason why I shouldn't. It's rather a convenient way to eat; I seem to remember reading in Epicurus that a man living alone lives the life of a wolf.

A life alone makes the need for external demonstration almost disappear. Now I seldom cuss, although at first I was quick to open fire at everything that tried my patience. Attending to the electrical circuit on the ane-

mometer pole is no less cold than it was in the beginning; but I work in soundless torment, knowing that
the night is vast and profanity can shock no one but
myself.

My sense of humor remains, but the only sources of
it are my books and myself, and, after all, my time to
read is limited. Earlier today, when I came into the hut
with my water bucket in one hand and the lantern in
the other, I put the lantern on the stove and hung up
the bucket. I laughed at this; but, now when I laugh, I
laugh inside; for I seem to have forgotten how to do it
out loud. This leads me to think that audible laughter
is principally a mechanism for sharing pleasure.

I find, too, that absence of conversation makes it
harder for me to think in words. Sometimes, while walking, I talk to myself and listen to the words, but they
sound hollow and unfamiliar. Today, for instance, I
was thinking of the extraordinary effect of the lack of
diversions upon my existence; but describing it is beyond my power. I could feel the difference between this
life and a normal life; I could see the difference in my
mind's eye, but I couldn't satisfactorily express the
subtleties in words. That may be because I have already
come to live more deeply within myself; what I feel
needs no further definition, since the senses are intuitive
and exact. . . .

My hair hasn't been cut in months. I've let it grow
because it comes down around my neck and keeps it
warm. I still shave once a week—and that only because
I have found that a beard is an infernal nuisance out-

side on account of its tendency to ice up from the breath and freeze the face. Looking in the mirror this morning, I decided that a man without women around him is a man without vanity; my cheeks are blistered and my nose is red and bulbous from a hundred frostbites. How I look is no longer of the least importance; all that matters is how I feel. However, I have kept clean, as clean as I would keep myself at home. But cleanliness has nothing to do with etiquette or coquetry. It is comfort. My senses enjoy the evening bath and are uncomfortable at the touch of underwear that is too dirty.

I've been trying to analyze the effect of isolation on a man. As I said, it is difficult for me to put this into words. I can only feel the absence of certain things, the exaggeration of others. In civilization my necessarily gregarious life with its countless distractions and diversions had blinded me to how vitally important a role they really did play. I find that their sudden removal has been much more of a wrench than I had anticipated. As much as anything, I miss being insulted every now and then, which is probably the Virginian in me.

May 12

... The silence of this place is as real and solid as sound. More real, in fact, than the occasional creaks of the Barrier and the heavier concussions of snow quakes. ... It seems to merge in and become part of the indescribable *evenness,* as do the cold and the dark and the relentless ticking of the clocks. This evenness fills the air with its mood of unchangeableness; it sits across from me at the table, and gets into the bunk with me at night. And no thought will wander so far as not eventually to be brought up hard by it. This is timelessness in its ultimate meaning. Very often my mood soars above it; but, when this mood goes, I find myself craving change —a look at trees, a rock, a handful of earth, the sound of foghorns, anything belonging to the world of movement and living things.

But I refuse to be disconcerted. This is a great experience. The despondency which used to come after supper—probably because that is the hour when we expect companionship—seems to have disappeared. Incidentally, I have mastered the business of waking myself in the morning; it has returned as mysteriously as it disappeared. Every morning for the last fortnight I've awakened within five minutes of the time I set in my mind.

I'm getting absent-minded. Last night I put sugar in the soup, and tonight I plunked a spoonful of corn-meal mush on the table where the plate should have been. I've been reading stories from several old English magazines. I got started on a murder serial, but I'll be damned if I can find two crucial installments. So I've had no choice but to try the love stories, and it is queer to reflect that beyond the horizon the joyful aspects of life go on. Well, this is the one continent where no woman has ever set foot; I can't say that it is any better on that account. In fact, the stampede to the altar that took place after the return of my previous expedition would seem to offer strong corroboration of that. Of the forty-one men with me at Little America, thirty were bachelors. Several married the first girls they met in New Zealand; most of the rest got married immediately upon their return to the United States. Two of the bachelors were around fifty years old, and both were married shortly after reaching home. There are only a few left, and I suspect their lonesome state is not entirely their fault.

May 16

It's just a week since the last after-supper depression. I don't want to be overconfident, but I believe I have it licked....

May 17

... I have more leisure than I shall probably ever have again. Thanks to the routine way I do things, my opportunities for intellectual exercise are virtually unlimited. I can, if I choose, spend hours over a single page in a book. I thought tonight what a very full and simple life it is—indeed, all I really lack is temptation.

Partly as an amusement I have been speculating on thought harmony. If man is, as I believe, an integral part of the universe and since grace and smoothness mark the movements of most things in it—such as the electrons and protons within the atom and the planets within the solar system and the stars within the galaxies—

then a normal mind should function with something of the same harmoniousness.

Anyhow, my thoughts seem to come together more smoothly than ever before....

*   *   *

This was a grand period; I was conscious only of a mind utterly at peace, a mind adrift upon the smooth, romantic tides of imagination, like a ship responding to the strength and purpose in the enveloping medium. A man's moments of serenity are few, but a few will sustain him a lifetime. I found my measure of inward peace then; the stately echoes lasted a long time. For the world then was like poetry—that poetry which is "emotion remembered in tranquillity."

Perhaps this period was just the repeated pattern of my youth. I sometimes think so. When I was growing up, I used to steal out of the house at night, and go walking in Glass's woods, which were a little way up the road from our place. In the heavy shadows of the Shenandoah Valley hills, the darkness was a little terrifying, as it always is to small boys; but, when I would pause and look up into the sky, a feeling that was midway between peace and exhilaration would seize me. I never quite succeeded, as a boy, in analyzing that feeling, any more than I did when it used to come to me as a naval officer, in the night watches at sea, and later when, as an explorer, I first looked upon mountains and lands which no one before me had ever seen. No doubt it was partly animal: the sheer expanding discovery of being alive, of growing, of no longer being afraid. But there was more to it than just that. There was the sense of identification with vast movements: the premonition of destiny that is implicit in every man; and the sense of waiting for the momentary revelation.

MAY II: THE BLOW

MAY WAS A ROUND BOULDER SINKING BEFORE A TIDE. Time sloughed off the last implication of urgency, and the days moved imperceptibly one into the other. The few world news items which Dyer read to me from time to time seemed almost as meaningless and blurred as they might to a Martian. My world was insulated against the shocks running through distant economies. Advance Base was geared to different laws. On getting up in the morning, it was enough for me to say to myself: Today is the day to change the barograph sheet, or, Today is the day to fill the stove tank. The night was settling down in earnest. By May 17th, one month after the sun had sunk below the horizon, the noon twilight was dwindling to a mere chink in the darkness, lit by a cold reddish glow. Days when the wind brooded in the north or east, the Barrier became a vast stagnant shadow surmounted by swollen masses of clouds, one layer of darkness piled on top of the other. This was the polar night, the morbid countenance of the Ice Age. Nothing moved; nothing was visible. This was the soul of inertness. One could almost

146

hear a distant creaking as if a great weight were settling.

Out of the deepening darkness came the cold. On May 19th, when I took the usual walk, the temperature was 65° below zero. For the first time the canvas boots failed to protect my feet. One heel was nipped, and I was forced to return to the hut and change to reindeer mukluks. That day I felt miserable; my body was racked by shooting pains —exactly as if I had been gassed. Very likely I was; in inspecting the ventilator pipes next morning I discovered that the intake pipe was completely clogged with rime and that the outlet pipe was two-thirds full. Next day— Sunday the 20th—was the coldest yet. The minimum thermometer dropped to 72° below zero; the inside thermograph, which always read a bit lower than the instruments in the shelter, stood at −74°; and the thermograph in the shelter was stopped dead—the ink, though well laced with glycerine, and the lubricant were both frozen. So violently did the air in the fuel tank expand after the stove was lit that oil went shooting all over the place; to insulate the tank against similar temperature spreads I wrapped around it the rubber air cushion which by some lucky error had been included among my gear. In the glow of a flashlight the vapor rising from the stovepipe and the outlet ventilator looked like the discharge from two steam engines. My fingers agonized over the thermograph, and I was hours putting it to rights. The fuel wouldn't flow from the drums; I had to take one inside and heat it near the stove. All day long I kept two primus stoves burning in the tunnel.

Sunday the 20th also brought a radio schedule; I had

the devil's own time trying to meet it. The engine balked for an hour; my fingers were so brittle and frostbitten from tinkering with the carburetor that, when I actually made contact with Little America, I could scarcely work the key. "Ask Haines come on," was my first request. While Hutcheson searched the tunnels of Little America for the Senior Meteorologist, I chatted briefly with Charlie Murphy. Little America claimed only — 60°. But we're moving the brass monkeys below," Charlie advised. "Seventy-one below here now," I said. "You can have it," was the closing comment from the north.

Then Bill Haines's merry voice sounded in the earphones. I explained the difficulty with the thermograph. "Same trouble we've had," Bill said. "It's probably due to frozen oil. I'd suggest you bring the instrument inside, and try soaking it in gasoline, to cut whatever oil traces remain. Then rinse it in ether. As for the ink's freezing, you might try adding more glycerine." Bill was in a jovial mood. "Look at me, Admiral," he boomed. "I never have any trouble with the instruments. The trick is in having an ambitious and docile assistant." I really chuckled over that because I knew, from the first expedition, what Grimminger, the Junior Meteorologist, was going through: Bill, with his back to the fire and blandishment on his tongue, persuading the recruit that duty and the opportunity for self-improvement required him to go up into the blizzard to fix a balky trace; Bill humming to himself in the warmth of a shack while the assistant in an open pit kept a theodolite trained on the sounding balloon soaring into the night, and stuttered into a telephone the different vernier readings from which Bill was calculating the velocities and directions of the upper air currents. That day I rather wished that I, too, had an assistant. He would have taken his turn on the anemometer pole, no mistake. The frost in the iron cleats went through the fur soles of the mukluks, and froze the balls of my feet. My breath made little explosive sounds on the wind; my lungs, already sore, seemed to shrivel when I breathed.

Seldom had the aurora flamed more brilliantly. For hours the night danced to its frenetic excitement. And at times the sound of Barrier quakes was like that of heavy guns. My tongue was swollen and sore from drinking scalding hot tea, and the tip of my nose ached from frostbite. A big wind, I guessed, would come out of this still cold; it behooved me to look to my roof. I carried gallons of water topside, and poured it around the edges of the shack. It froze almost as soon as it hit. The ice was an armor plating over the packed drift.

At midnight, when I clambered topside for an auroral "ob," a wild sense of suffocation came over me the instant I pushed my shoulders through the trapdoor. My lungs gasped, but no air reached them. Bewildered and perhaps a little frightened, I slid down the ladder and lunged into the shack. In the warm air the feeling passed as quickly as it had come. Curious but cautious, I again made my way up the ladder. And again the same thing happened; I lost my breath, but I perceived why. A light air was moving down from eastward; and its bitter touch, when I faced into it, was constricting the breathing passages. So I turned my face away from it, breathing into my glove;

and in that attitude finished the "ob." Before going below, I made an interesting experiment. I put a thermometer on the snow, let it lie there awhile, and discovered that the temperature at the surface was actually 5° colder than at the level of the instrument shelter, four feet higher. Reading in the sleeping bag afterwards, I froze one finger, although I shifted the book steadily from one hand to the other, slipping the unoccupied hand into the warmth of the bag.

* * *

Out of the cold and out of the east came the wind. It came on gradually, as if the sheer weight of the cold were almost too much to be moved. On the night of the 21st the barometer started down. The night was black as a thunderhead when I made my first trip topside; and a tension in the wind, a bulking of shadows in the night indicated that a new storm center was forming. Next morning, glad of an excuse to stay underground, I worked a long time on the Escape Tunnel by the light of a red candle standing in a snow recess. That day I pushed the emergency exit to a distance of twenty-two feet, the farthest it was ever to go. My stint done, I sat down on a box, thinking how beautiful was the red of the candle, how white the rough-hewn snow. Soon I became aware of an increasing clatter of the anemometer cups. Realizing that the wind was picking up, I went topside to make sure that everything was secured. It is a queer experience to watch a blizzard rise. First there is the wind, rising out of nowhere. Then the Barrier unwrenches itself from quietude; and the surface, which just before had seemed as hard and polished as metal, begins to run like a making sea. Sometimes, if the wind strikes hard, the drift comes across the Barrier like a hurrying white cloud, tossed hundreds of feet in the air. Other times the growth is gradual. You become conscious of a general slithering movement on all sides. The air fills with tiny scraping and sliding and rustling sounds as the first loose crystals stir. In a little while they are moving as solidly as an incoming tide, which creams over the ankles, then surges to the waist, and finally is at the throat. I have walked in drift so thick as not to be able to see a foot ahead of me; yet, when I glanced up, I could see the stars shining through the thin layer just overhead.

Smoking tendrils were creeping up the anemometer pole when I finished my inspection. I hurriedly made the trap-door fast, as a sailor might batten down a hatch; and knowing that my ship was well secured, I retired to the cabin to ride out the storm. It could not reach me, hidden deep in the Barrier crust; nevertheless the sounds came down. The gale sobbed in the ventilators, shook the stove-pipe until I thought it would be jerked out by the roots, pounded the roof with sledge-hammer blows. I could actually feel the suction effect through the pervious snow. A breeze flickered in the room and the tunnels. The candles wavered and went out. My only light was the feeble storm lantern.

Even so, I didn't have any idea how really bad it was until I went aloft for an observation. As I pushed back the trap-door, the drift met me like a moving wall. It was only a few steps from the ladder to the instrument shelter, but it seemed more like a mile. The air came at me in snowy rushes; I breasted it as I might a heavy surf. No night had ever seemed so dark. The beam from the flashlight was choked in its throat; I could not see my hand before my face.

My windproofs were caked with drift by the time I got below. I had a vague feeling that something had changed while I was gone, but what, I couldn't tell. Presently I noticed that the shack was appreciably colder. Raising the stove lid, I was surprised to find that the fire was out, though the tank was half full. I decided that I must have turned off the valve unconsciously before going aloft; but, when I put a match to the burner, the draught down the pipe blew out the flame. The wind, then, must have killed the fire. I got it going again, and watched it carefully.

The blizzard vaulted to gale force. Above the roar the deep, taut thrumming note of the radio antenna and the anemometer guy wires reminded me of wind in a ship's rigging. The wind direction trace turned scratchy on the sheet; no doubt drift had short-circuited the electric contacts, I decided. Realizing that it was hopeless to attempt to try to keep them clear, I let the instrument be. There were other ways of getting the wind direction. I tied a handkerchief to a bamboo pole and ran it through the outlet ventilator; with a flashlight I could tell which way the cloth was whipped. I did this at hourly intervals, noting any change of direction on the sheet. But by 2 o'clock in the morning I had had enough of this periscope sighting. If I expected to sleep and at the same time maintain the continuity of the records, I had no choice but to clean the contact points.

The wind was blowing hard then. The Barrier shook from the concussions overhead; and the noise was as if the entire physical world were tearing itself to pieces. I could scarcely heave the trapdoor open. The instant it came clear I was plunged into a blinding smother. I came out crawling, clinging to the handle of the door until I made sure of my bearings. Then I let the door fall shut, not wanting the tunnel filled with drift. To see was impossible. Millions of tiny pellets exploded in my eyes, stinging like BB shot. It was even hard to breathe, because snow instantly clogged the mouth and nostrils. I made my way toward the anemometer pole on hands and knees, scared that I might be bowled off my feet if I stood erect; one false step and I should be lost forever.

I found the pole all right; but not until my head collided with a cleat. I managed to climb it, too, though ten million ghosts were tearing at me, ramming their thumbs into my eyes. But the errand was useless. Drift as thick as this would mess up the contact points as quickly as they were cleared; besides, the wind cups were spinning so fast that I stood a good chance of losing a couple of fingers in the process. Coming down the pole, I had a sense of being whirled violently through the air, with no control over my movements. The trapdoor was completely buried when I found it again, after scraping around for some time with my mittens. I pulled at the handle, first with one hand, then with both. It did not give. It's a tight fit, anyway, I mumbled to myself. The drift has probably wedged the corners. Standing astride the hatch, I braced myself and heaved with all my strength. I might just as well have tried hoisting the Barrier.

Panic took me then, I must confess. Reason fled. I clawed at the three-foot square of timber like a madman. I beat on it with my fists, trying to shake the snow loose; and, when that did no good, I lay flat on my belly and pulled until my hands went weak from cold and weariness. Then I crooked my elbow, put my face down, and said over and over again, You damn fool, you damn fool. Here for weeks I had been defending myself against the danger of being penned inside the shack; instead, I was now locked out; and nothing could be worse, especially since I had only a wool parka and pants under my windproofs. Just two feet below was sanctuary—warmth, food, tools, all the means of survival. All these things were an arm's length away, but I was powerless to reach them.

There is something extravagantly insensate about an Antarctic blizzard at night. Its vindictiveness cannot be measured on an anemometer sheet. It is more than just wind: it is a solid wall of snow moving at gale force, pounding like surf.* The whole malevolent rush is concentrated upon you as upon a personal enemy. In the senseless explosion of sound you are reduced to a crawling thing on the margin of a disintegrating world; you can't see, you can't hear, you can hardly move. The lungs gasp after

* Because of this blinding, suffocating drift, in the Antarctic winds of only moderate velocity have the punishing force of full-fledged hurricanes elsewhere.

the air sucked out of them, and the brain is shaken. Nothing in the world will so quickly isolate a man.

Half-frozen, I stabbed toward one of the ventilators, a few feet away. My mittens touched something round and cold. Cupping it in my hands, I pulled myself up. This was the outlet ventilator. Just why, I don't know—but instinct made me kneel and press my face against the opening. Nothing in the room was visible, but a dim patch of light illuminated the floor, and warmth rose up to my face. That steadied me.

Still kneeling, I turned my back to the blizzard and considered what might be done. I thought of breaking in the windows in the roof, but they lay two feet down in hard crust, and were reinforced with wire besides. If I only had something to dig with, I could break the crust and stamp the windows in with my feet. The pipe cupped between my hands supplied the first inspiration; maybe I could use that to dig with. It, too, was wedged tight; I pulled until my arms ached, without budging it; I had lost all track of time, and the despairing thought came to me that I was lost in a task without an end. Then I remembered the shovel. A week before, after leveling drift from the last light blow, I had stabbed a shovel handle up in the crust somewhere to leeward. That shovel would save me. But how to find it in the avalanche of the blizzard?

I lay down and stretched out full length. Still holding the pipe, I thrashed around with my feet, but pummeled only empty air. Then I worked back to the hatch. The hard edges at the opening provided another grip, and

155

ALONE

again I stretched out and kicked. Again no luck. I dared
not let go until I had something else familiar to cling to.
My foot came up against the other ventilator pipe. I edged
back to that, and from the new anchorage repeated the
maneuver. This time my ankle struck something hard.
When I felt it and recognized the handle, I wanted to
caress it.

Embracing this thrice-blessed tool, I inched back to the
trapdoor. The handle of the shovel was just small enough
to pass under the little wooden bridge which served as
a grip. I got both hands on the shovel and tried to wrench
the door up; my strength was not enough, however. So I
lay down flat on my belly and worked my shoulders under
the shovel. Then I heaved, the door sprang open, and I
rolled down the shaft. When I tumbled into the light
and warmth of the room, I kept thinking, How wonderful, how perfectly wonderful.

* * *

My wrist watch had stopped; the chronometers showed
that I had been gone just under an hour. The stove had
blown out again, but I did not bother to light it. Enough
warmth remained for me to undress. I was exhausted; it
was all I could do to hoist myself into the bunk. But I
did not sleep at first. The blizzard scuffled and pounded
gigantically overhead; and my mind refused to drop the
thought of what I might still be doing if the shovel hadn't
been there. Still struggling, probably. Or maybe not. There
are harder ways to die than freezing to death. The lush
numbness and the peace that lulls the mind when the ears

cease listening to the blizzard's ridiculous noise, could make death seem easy.

The wind was still blowing, but not so violently, when I awakened at 7 o'clock the next morning. Dressing in the yellow light of the storm lantern, I shivered in every bone. My clothes, rigid with frost, lay in a grotesque heap on the floor, exactly as they had fallen a few hours before; they crackled like paper when I put them on. Starting up the ladder, I thought glumly, It will be stuck again for sure. Therefore, I had no misgivings at finding the door jammed. Armed with a saw, a shovel, alpine rope, and a lantern, I walked to the far end of the Escape Tunnel. It didn't take long to breach a hole in the roof, which was less than two feet thick at this point.

Before leaving the tunnel, I drove a stout stick into the roof, to which I made fast one end of the line. With the other end secured to my belt, I clambered to the surface over a ladder made of boxes. The drift was still heavy, but with a flashlight it was possible to see a yard or two. After a couple of false stabs I finally fetched the anemometer pole. The drift packed in the cups was almost as compact as cement; I cleaned them out and scraped the contact points. It was an abominable task; but it had to be done, because the fouling slowed down the cups and hence the wind-speed reading. Yet, after what I had been through the night before, there was little reason to complain.

For once "daily promenade" was missed. Every moment that could be spared from the instruments and my own personal needs was devoted to leveling drift around the shack. Luckily the new snow wasn't packed hard. I just shoveled it into the air and let the wind dissipate it to leeward. That done, I sealed off the breach in the Escape Tunnel with the sides of a couple of food boxes and re-opened the hatch. The faint lightening in the gloom that came with midday was draining away; heavy shadows were pressing down through the ghostly billowing of drift. But the wind was spent; and so was the cold, temporarily. The temperature kited to 10° below. Safe in the bunk, I slept the sleep of a man who had been working a hundred years.

Thursday the 24th was unbelievably warm. At the 8 A.M. "ob" the maximum thermometer read 2° above zero. The wind still haunted the east; and puffs of drift came erratically from that quarter, thickening the steady fall of snow from the sky. I was nearly an hour late meeting the radio schedule, because the antenna had been blown down and I didn't find it out until after I had checked the transmitter and receiver. I made a hurried splice at a break and re-rigged the antenna temporarily on two poles. Dyer was still calling patiently when I made contact. My signals, he said, were weak but intelligible. Beyond dis-cussing arrangements for me to participate in a special broadcast, we had little to talk about. At Little America the temperature was 25° above zero, and Bill Haines offi-cially announced a "heat wave."

I was informed that on Saturday Little America was broadcasting a special program to the Chicago World Fair; would I mind adding my greetings? Certainly not. It was agreed that I should spell out in code, "Greetings from the bottom of the world," which message was to be picked up and relayed by Little America's more powerful transmitter. I reduced the message to dots and dashes and practiced religiously. When Saturday came, Charlie Murphy broke the news, just before the broadcast, that New York now wanted me to spell, "Antarctic greetings," instead. "I'm given to understand," he said sententiously, "they intend to translate the damn thing into fireworks."

"Let it be on their own heads, then,"I said.

Charlie chuckled. "If the fireworks are supposed to spell out what you send, then Chicago is in for the wildest display since the Fire."

As excited as an actor making his debut, I sat at Advance Base listening to the broadcast from Little America; and, when somebody said, "We shall now attempt to make contact with Admiral Byrd," I reached for the key and worked it furiously. But it went for naught. Dyer reported a few minutes after that he had heard it clearly, but Chicago hadn't heard anything. "No doubt the fireworks went off anyway," he observed dryly.

Bill Haines's forecast of a "heat wave" was no jest. That afternoon the thermometer rose to 18° above zero—the second highest point it ever reached. The wind, dallying in the east, flooded the Barrier with warm air from the distant ocean. From then until the end of the month the coldest temperature recorded was 23° below zero; and most of the time it was above zero or close to it.* Snow fell in a relentless flutter; the Barrier became a concentrated gloom, except when the moon, fetched back on its

* Studied as a whole, the records show that May was not exactly a hot month. The cold passed 40° below zero 20 days out of the 31, crossed 50° below, 12 days; crossed 60° below, 3 days; and 70° below, 2 days.

fortnightly errand, was able to break through the cloud rack and bathe it briefly in an astringent light.

May 25

This is my sixty-fourth day at Advance Base, and it just so happened that I had some leisure time. I have been taking advantage of this to think back over my stay here and take stock of my situation.

There are three things for which I am particularly thankful. The first is that my records so far are complete (though blotted and splotched a bit). The second is that my defenses are perfected, and the third is that I have become well adjusted to conditions—especially psychologically. I feel able now to withstand any assaults the beleaguering night may launch. Indeed, I look forward to the rest of my sojourn with pleasure.

Though I am not quite as heavy as when I came out here, I feel all right. I was probably a bit overweight, anyway. Perhaps the fumes have had something to do with the lost pounds, though because of my precautions I think I am getting less fumes than at first.

I am finding that life here has become largely a life of the mind. Unhurried reflection is a sort of companion. Yes, solitude is greater than I anticipated. My sense of values is changing, and many things which before were in solution in my mind now seem to be crystallizing. I am better able to tell what in the world is wheat for me and what is chaff. In fact, my definition of success itself is changing. Just lately my views about man and his place in the cosmic scheme have begun to run something like this:

If I had never seen a watch and should see one for the first time, I should be sure its hands were moving according to some plan and not at random. Nor does it seem any more reasonable for me to conceive that the precision and order of the universe is the product of blind chance. This whole concept is summed up in the word harmony. For those who seek it, there is inexhaustible evidence of an all-pervading intelligence.

The human race, my intuition tells me, is not outside the cosmic process and is not an accident. It is as much a part of the universe as the trees, the mountains, the aurora, and the stars. My reason approves this; and the findings of science, as I see them, point in the same direction. And, since man is a part of the cosmos and subject to its laws, I see no reason to doubt that these same natural laws operate in the psychological as well as in the physical sphere and that their operation is manifest in the workings of the consciousness.

Therefore, it seems to me that convictions of right and wrong, being, as they are, products of the consciousness, must also be formed in accordance with these laws. I look upon the conscience as the mechanism which makes us directly aware of them and their significance and serves as a link with the universal intelligence which gives them form and harmoniousness.

I believe further that the age-tested convictions of

ALONE

right and wrong, in which individual aberrations must
have been largely canceled out, are as much a mani-
festation of cosmic law and intelligence as are all other
phenomena.

Therefore, the things that mankind has tested and
found right make for harmony and progress—or peace;
and the things it has found wrong hinder progress and
make for discord. The right things lead to rational be-
havior—such as the substitution of reason for force—
and so to freedom. The wrong things lead to brute
force and slavery.

But the peace I describe is not passive. It must be
won. Real peace comes from struggle that involves
such things as effort, discipline, enthusiasm. This is
also the way to strength. An inactive peace may lead
to sensuality and flabbiness, which are discordant. It
is often necessary to fight to lessen discord. This is the
paradox.

When a man achieves a fair measure of harmony
within himself and his family circle, he achieves
peace; and a nation made up of such individuals and
groups is a happy nation. As the harmony of a star
in its course is expressed by rhythm and grace, so the
harmony of a man's life-course is expressed by happiness; this, I believe, is the prime desire of mankind.

"The universe is an almost untouched reservoir of
significance and value," and man need not be discouraged because he cannot fathom it. His view of
life is no more than a flash in time. The details and
distractions are infinite. It is only natural, therefore,

that we should never see the picture whole. But the universal goal—the attainment of harmony—is apparent. The very act of perceiving this goal and striving constantly toward it does much in itself to bring us closer and, therefore, becomes an end in itself.

* * *

Snow was still falling on Thursday the 31st. The morning was dreary and stagnant; the temperature about 5° above. The calendar warned: "Radio schedule." I went about the preparations methodically. Before me now are the messages which I dispatched to Little America that day. One was to Chief Pilot June and Navigator Rawson, reminding them to swing the planes for compass deviations. Another was to my wife, suggesting that she take up with my secretary, Miss McKercher, and my representatives in the United States ways and means of reducing the expedition's expenses.

Dyer took these messages down, then read them back. Poulter, he said, had already arrived in the radio shack in response to my summons. I had a long talk with him and Charlie Murphy over the proposed operations, and was particularly emphatic about the dangers from crevasses confronting the tractors. Poulter finished his business with me; and Charlie Murphy stayed to finish a few matters, one having to do with the engagement of an ice pilot for the *Jacob Ruppert* on her return voyage to Little America in December. We talked back and forth nearly an hour and a half. From my desk in the shack I could hear the engine in the tunnel; for some reason it started

163

skipping. "Wait," I spelled out to Dyer. Unhooking the lantern, I went into the tunnel. The air was thick with exhaust gases. Thinking the mixture was at fault, I bent over the carburetor and tinkered with the needle valve. This had little effect. I remember straightening up. And that was the last conscious act of mine that I do remember. The next thing I recall, I was down on my hands and knees; and through the drowsiness, like an echo from far away, came an insistent notion that something terribly important ought to be done. What it was exactly my mind couldn't tell; and I felt helpless to do anything about it. I don't know how long I remained in that position. It may be that the cold aroused me. Anyhow, after a little while I crawled into the shack. The radio desk emerged from the blur, and then I remembered what I was supposed to do. I fumbled for the key and signed off, thinking how hard it was to spell out what I had to say. If any acknowledgment came, I did not hear it; for I couldn't get the earphones on.*

My actions thereafter are uncertain; I don't really know which were nightmare and which were fact. I remember lying on the bunk, fully dressed, and hearing, as if with surprise, the irregular beat of the engine in the tunnel and realizing that I must shut it off to escape asphyxiation. I rolled off the bunk and staggered to the door. Dizziness seized me, and my heart turned fantastic somersaults; but,

* The radio log at Little America shows that twenty minutes or so elapsed between the time I said, "Wait" and the time I signed off, saying, "See you Sunday." This fixes approximately the interval I was in the tunnel.

as from a great distance, I could see the gray fumes of the exhaust smoke curling under the top sill; and the upper half of the tunnel, when I entered, was so foggy that I could not see as far as the alcove where the engine lay.

Very probably I dropped to my hands and knees, as I must have appreciated the necessity for keeping my head under the fumes and in the uncontaminated air near the floor. Anyhow, I was on my knees when I reached into the recess and threw the ignition switch. When I turned around, the light was gone in the doorway; this was puzzling until I recalled that the only light in the shack was the electric bulb over the radio desk, which burned only while the engine supplied current. Luckily the lantern was still burning on a box, where I had set it down before adjusting the engine. Pushing the lantern ahead of me, I crawled back to the shack and to the bunk.

Whatever did, in fact, occur during the rest of this last day in May, this I do know: that much of it was probably fantasy—a slow and wearying fantasy. Perhaps I did in truth roll off the bunk and try to replace the sheets on the register drum; else how to account for the vague recollection of seeing the glass frame on the floor some time in the afternoon. But the rest of it—the skyrocketing pain in my forehead and eyes, the nausea, the violent beating of my heart, the illusion of being a thin flame drawn between two voids—they could not have been real. Only the cold was real: the numbness in the hands and feet, creeping like a slow paralysis through my body. At least, I could cope with cold. I grasped for the throat of the sleeping bag, and eased in.

Once the ticking of the clocks roused me out of the stupor. I have no sure memory of winding them; but, so strong was the compulsion of habit, I do remember thinking bitterly that they ought to be wound and that the register and thermograph sheets ought to be changed. Evidently I performed these tasks; for the instruments were still going next day; and the records, now in the possession of the U. S. Weather Bureau, show that the sheets were shifted at 2 P.M., two hours late. My only distinct memory from that period was arousing and thinking that I was blind. My eyes were open, but I could see nothing. Then I realized that I must be facing the wall. The lantern was out (from lack of fuel, I learned presently), but a dim glow showed in the side of the stove.

There is nothing more panicky than the loss of sight. I shall never forget the agony in Floyd Bennett's voice when we pulled him, terribly smashed up, from the debris of our crash landing. "I'm done for," he whispered; "I can't see anything." His face was a smear of oil; when I wiped it away and he could see again, the expression that .transfigured his face was beautiful.

* * *

It is painful for me to dwell on the details of my collapse, particularly as the affairs of Advance Base are now receding into the gentling haze of the past. The subject is one that does not easily bear discussion, if only because a man's hurt, like his love, is most seemly when concealed. From my youth I have believed that sickness was somehow humiliating, something to be kept hidden. But the consequences of this collapse were never to depart during the rest of my stay at Advance Base; and my struggle against the one universal certainty played too large a part in my experience there to be omitted from this account.

I have a pretty clear idea concerning much that happened, almost too clear, in fact. I shall not, however, depend upon memory alone. During the days that followed, I set forth in the diary—as far as I was able—what I knew and remembered. How natural is the instinct which drives a man alone to pencil and paper, as if his destiny required the right last word and period.

The afternoon ran out its time; though my eyes would not stop aching and the pain would not quit my temples, just lying in the sleeping bag quieted the hammering of my heart. Gradually my mind cleared, and I tried to reconstruct the events preceding the episode in the tunnel. The exhaust vent over the engine, I decided, must have filled with rime, causing the poisonous gases to back into the tunnel. I was pretty sure that it was carbon monoxide. The instantaneous way I was struck down, the absence of any consciousness of suffocation bespoke these things, plus the symptoms—the splitting headaches, the nausea, the stabbing pains in my body and eyes, the hot and cold rushes of dizziness. What had saved me in the tunnel was the fact of my being dropped as though poleaxed. Since monoxide rises, the air at the bottom of the tunnel must have been all right; and the oxygen entering my blood brought me around.

All this represented a mind groping for bearings. To know I had escaped disaster in one form was only a preliminary step in the process of preparing to avert it in another. The fact was manifest that I was helpless, at least for the time being. I barely had strength to light the candle standing on the tin ledge directly over my head. If so simple a movement could empty me of the little strength that had returned, what chance did I have of bringing in food and fuel from the tunnels, let alone attending to the instruments? I could live many days without food. I could suck snow to quench thirst. But, ill and weak as I was, I could not live long without heat; and the fuel tank had to be filled every three days. Pondering such difficult matters was too much for me; my mind went blank again. When I awakened and looked at my wrist watch, the time was 7 o'clock. I wasn't quite so weak, and my body craved water.

So I drew the flashlight from the sleeping bag and propped it on the edge of the bunk in order to direct the beam toward the stove. With this to guide me, I slipped from the bunk, clinging to the side for support. Waves of dizziness swept from head to foot, but after a little while I was able to reach the chair and push it toward the stove. A little water remained in the bucket on the stove; I dipped it out with a can. The first few swallows my stomach threw up; nevertheless, I persevered until I had at least a cupful down. Wondering why my teeth chattered so, I put my hand against the stove. It was out—no longer than a few minutes, evidently, else the water would have frozen. *Thursday . . . Thursday . . . the day to fill the tank.* So the tank was dry, as was the lantern; and if I wanted to have light and warmth, both must be filled at once.

The notes which I jotted down a few days afterwards insist this stranger reeling in the dark acted with the utmost deliberation. Perhaps so. Between the pain and the weakness it was hard for more than one thought to find a lodgment. I managed to pull on my parka and mittens. Then I lifted the empty tank from the stand. Holding it by the handle with one hand and the flashlight with the other, I started into the tunnel. The nearest fuel drum— by the grace of God equipped with a spigot—was only fourteen feet from the door; but to make the distance I had to stop and put around my neck the loop attached to the flashlight so as to free one hand with which to steady myself. I walked slowly and uncertainly; as, years ago, I had walked for the first time after being desperately ill of typhoid fever while on a midshipman cruise to England.

The funnel lay on top of a barrel. I fitted it into the tank; and, while the tank was filling, I rested on a box. But, though I had the strength to lift the tank (it weighed about twenty-one pounds filled to the brim), I could not carry it far. After a few steps my heart was pounding, and the dizziness returned. I let go and slumped on the tool box, near the head of the tunnel. For how long? I really don't know. Long enough, anyhow, to be shaken by the cold. If I couldn't carry the tank, perhaps I could pull it, which was what I did—a few feet at a time. At least, I remember doing that.

Inside the shack, I poured half a gallon or so of the precious stuff into a pitcher; this would do for the lantern. A lot spilled on the floor. Presently I succeeded in lifting the tank itself to the stand behind the stove. With that a feeling of relief possessed me for a moment. I could now hold off the cold for at least two days, and maybe three if I economized. Nevertheless, I didn't attempt to light the stove, dreading the effort and knowing that I ought to be in the bunk; but, craving light after the long darkness, I did light the lantern. The light was so cheery that I was encouraged to attempt an observation at 10 P.M. (Actually 8 P.M. my old time; for, a day or two previously, I had advanced my clock two hours, as an experiment in moonlight saving, so to speak.)

That was a mistake. I was able to climb the ladder all right, resting at every rung; I pushed the door back with my head, waited a moment, and then hobbled to the instrument shelter, feeling dizzy and utterly forlorn. I guessed the wind's velocity as being seventeen miles per hour (the register trace shows an actual wind speed of only seven miles), and noted the absence of aurora. But I was unspeakably weak and sick again when I reached the bottom of the ladder. I must sleep. I must sleep, something was saying inside me. In the Escape Tunnel I groped around until I found the box of phenobarbital pills. With the box in my hand I stumbled to the hut. I got my parka, pants, and shoes off; but the shirt was beyond me. Using the chair as a step, I hung the lantern from its peg above the bunk, then climbed in, weighed down by a sense of complete futility.

The instant the candle died, the darkness dropped like a blow. Sleep was the great hunger; but it would not come, so cruel was the pain in my head and back and legs. As I lay there, the intimation came that I would not recover. Carbon monoxide poisoning is an insidious thing. Once the haemoglobin in the blood stream and the lungs is broken down, it takes the liver and spleen a long time to restore the oxygen-carrying material. Even with the best of hospital care this is a matter of weeks and sometimes months. For me the worst of the cold and the darkest part of the night were yet to come. The sun was nearly three months away. I could not persuade myself that I had the strength to meet it. To some men sickness brings a desire to be left alone; animal-like, their one instinct is to crawl into a hole and lick the hurt. It used to be so with me. But that night, as never before, I discovered how alone I was; and the realization evoked an indescribable desire to have about me those who knew me best. Remembering the meticulous preparations, the safeguards which I had thrown about myself, my soul was bitter with reproaches. My fort had become an ambush. Nothing within the power of the night or cold had made it so. My stupidity was to blame, and this I should have feared before the others.

Even in my stupor I seem to have recognized that the gasoline engine was not solely responsible. The engine dealt the blow which knocked me down, but long before then I had partially perceived a developing weakness. I remembered the notches I had taken up in my belt; the headaches and hurt in my eyes earlier in the month. Maybe the frost in my lungs was at fault. Maybe something was organically wrong with me. But I doubted that these by themselves could have depleted me so much. What reason I could muster indicted the stinking stove as the principal villain. Monoxide poisoning is not necessarily an instantaneous matter. It may be a gradual and cumulative process, brought about by intermittent exposure to the chemistry of the fumes. And the more I thought about the leaky joints in the stove, the more I blamed it.

But all this was shadowy in my mind that last night in May. I wavered between self-recrimination and hopefulness, between pain and an emptiness devoid of feeling. I knew that I was in a frightful mess, one that would involve my family, the expedition, and God only knew whom else. But it was hard to see what could be done about that. I lighted the candle, intending to write certain messages; but no paper was within reach. After a little while I blew out the candle. In my hand was the box of sleeping pills. I was reluctant to take one, not from squeamishness but from the fear that the drug would weaken me further. So, telling myself I would wait until 4 o'clock before resorting to the sedative, I put the box down. Sometime after 3 o'clock I drifted off into a dream of horrors.

JUNE I: DESPAIR

JUNE 1ST WAS A FRIDAY. A BLACK FRIDAY FOR ME. THE nightmare left me, and about 9 o'clock in the morning I awakened with a violent start, as if I had been thrown down a well in my sleep. I found myself staring wildly into the darkness of the shack, not knowing where I was. The weakness that filled my body when I turned in the sleeping bag and tried to throw the flashlight on my wrist watch was an eloquent reminder. I was Richard E. Byrd, United States Navy. (Ret.), temporarily sojourning at Latitude 80° 08' South, and not worth a damn to myself or anybody else. My mouth was dry and tasted foul. God, I was thirsty. But I had hardly strength to move. I clung to the sleeping bag, which was the only source of comfort and warmth left to me, and mournfully debated the little that might be done.

Two facts stood clear. One was that my chances of recovering were slim. The other was that in my weakness I was incapable of taking care of myself. These were desperate conclusions, but my mood allowed no others. All that I could reasonably hope for was to prolong my

existence for a few days by hoarding my remaining resources; by doing the necessary things *very slowly* and
with *great deliberation*. So long as he did that and main-
tained the right frame of mind, even a very ill man
should be able to last a time. So I reasoned, anyway. There
was no alternative. My hopes of survival had to be staked
on the theory.

But you must have *faith*—you must have faith in the
outcome, I whispered to myself. It is like a flight, a flight
into another unknown. You start and you cannot turn
back. You must go on and on and on, trusting your instruments, the course you have plotted on the charts, and
the reasonableness of events. Whatever goes wrong will be
mostly of your own making; if it is to be tragedy, then it
will be the commonplace tragedy of human vulnerability.

My first need was warmth and food. The fire had been
out about twelve hours; I had not eaten in nearly thirty-
six. Toward providing those necessities I began to mobi-
lize my slender resources. If there had been a movie
camera to record my movements, the resulting picture
could have been passed off as slow motion. Every act was
performed with the utmost patience. I lifted the lantern
—and waited. I edged out of the sleeping bag—and rested
on the chair beside the stove. I pulled on my pants, hiking
them up a little bit at a time. Then the shirt. Then the
socks. And shoes. And finally the parka. All this took a
long time. I was shaking so from the cold that, when my
elbow struck the wall, the sound was like a peremptory
knock at the door. Too miserable to stick it out, I retreated to the sleeping bag; half an hour later the chill

in my body drove me into a fresh attempt to reach the stove.

Faintness seized me as I touched foot to the floor. I barely made the chair. There I sat for some minutes, not moving, just staring at the candle. Then I turned the valve, and with the stove lids off waited for the wick to become saturated with the cold, sluggish oil. Thirst continued to plague me. Several inches of ice were in the water bucket. I dropped it on the floor, bottom up. A sliver of ice fell out, which I sucked until my teeth rattled from the cold. A box of matches was on the table. I touched one to the burner. A red flame licked over the metal ring; it was a beautiful thing to see. I sat there ten or fifteen minutes at least, absorbing the column of warmth. The flame burned red and smoky, when it should have been blue and clear; and, studying it, I knew that this was from faulty combustion and was one source of my misfortunes. This fire was my enemy, but I could not live without it.

Thus this never-ending day began. To describe it all would be tedious. Nothing really happened; and yet, no day in my life was more momentous. I lived a thousand years, and all of them were agonizing. I won a little and lost a lot. At the day's end—if it can be said to have had an end—all that I could say was that I was still alive. Granting the conditions, I had no right to expect more. Life seldom ends gracefully or sensibly. The protesting body succumbs like a sinking ship going down with the certificate of seaworthiness nailed fast to the wheelhouse bulkhead; but the mind, like the man on the bridge, realizes at last the weakness of the hull and ponders the irony. If the business drags out long enough, as mine did, the essence of things in time becomes pitifully clear; except that by then it is wadded into a tight little scrap ready to be thrown away, as the knowledge is of no earthly use.

My thirst was the tallest tree in a forest of pain. The Escape Tunnel was a hundred miles away, but I started out, carrying the bucket and lantern. Somewhere along the way I slipped and fell. I licked the snow until my tongue burned. The Escape Tunnel was too far. But in the food tunnel my boots had worn a rut eighteen inches wide and six inches deep, which was full of loose snow. The snow was dirty, but I scraped the bucket along until it was nearly full, then pulled it into the shack, a foot or so at a time.

Snow took a long time to melt in the bucket, and I could not wait. I poured a little into a pan and heated it with alcohol tablets. It was still a soggy mass of snow when I raised it to my lips. My hands were shaking, and the water spilled down the front of my parka; then I vomited, and all that I had drunk came up. In a little while I tried again, taking sips too small to be thrown up. Then I crawled on top of the sleeping bag, drawing a heavy blanket over my shoulders, hoping I should somehow regain strength.

Nevertheless, I was able to do a number of small things, in a series of stealthy, deliberate sorties from the bunk. I attended to the inside thermograph and register, changing the sheets, winding the clocks, and inking the pens.

JUNE I: DESPAIR

The outlet ventilator was two-thirds filled with ice; I
could just reach it from the bunk with a stick which had
a big nail in the end. After every exertion I rested; the
pain in my arms and back and head was almost crucifying.
I filled a thermos jug with warm water, added powdered
milk and sugar, and carried the jug into the sleeping bag.
My stomach crawled with nauseous sensations; but, by
taking a teaspoonful at a time, I finally managed to get
a cupful down. After a while the weakness left me, and
I felt strong enough to start for the instrument shelter.
I reached the hatch and pushed it open, but could go
no farther. The night was a gray fog, full of shadows, like
my mood. In the shack I lost the milk I had drunk. On
the verge of fainting, I made for the bunk.

* * *

I won't even attempt to recall all the melancholy
thoughts that drifted through my mind that long afternoon. But I can say truthfully that at no time did I have
any feeling of resignation. My whole being rebelled
against my low estate. As the afternoon wore on, I felt
myself sinking. Now I became alarmed. This was not the
first time I had ever faced death. It had confronted me
many times in the air. But then it had seemed altogether
different. In flying things happen fast: you make a decision; the verdict crowds you instantly; and, when the
invisible and neglected passenger comes lunging into the
cockpit, he is but one of countless distractions. But now
death was a stranger sitting in a darkened room, secure in
the knowledge that he would be there when I was gone.

177

Great waves of fear, a fear I had never known before, swept through me and settled deep within. But it wasn't the fear of suffering or even of death itself. It was a terrible anxiety over the consequences to those at home if I failed to return. I had done a damnable thing in going to Advance Base, I told myself. Also, during those hours of bitterness, I saw my whole life pass in review. I realized how wrong my sense of values had been and how I had failed to see that the simple, homely, unpretentious things of life are the most important.

Much as I should have liked to, I couldn't consider myself a martyr to science; nor could I blame the circumstances that had prevented staffing the base with three men, according to the original plan. I had gone there looking for peace and enlightenment, thinking that they might in some way enrich my life and make me a more useful man. I had also gone armed with the justification of a scientific mission. Now I saw both for what they really were: the first as a delusion, the second as a dead-end street. My thoughts turned to gall and wormwood. I was bitter toward the whole world except my family and friends. The clocks ticked on in the gloom, and a subdued whir came from the register at my feet. The confidence implicit in these unhurried sounds emphasized my own debasement. What right had they to be confident and unhurried? Without me they could not last a day.

The one aspiration I still had was to be vindicated by the tiny heap of data collected on the shelf in the Escape Tunnel. But, even as I seized upon this, I recognized its flimsiness; a romanticized rationalization, as are most of

178

the things which men are anxious to be judged by. We men of action who serve science serve only a reflection in a mirror. The tasks are difficult, the objectives remote; but scholars sitting in bookish surroundings tell us where to go, what to look for, and even what we are apt to find. Likewise, they pass dispassionate judgment on whatever we bring back. We are nothing more than glamorous middlemen between theory and fact, materialists jobbing in the substance of universal truths.

Beyond the fact that I had suffered to secure them, what did I know about the theoretical significance of the records in the Escape Tunnel, of the implications which might differentiate them from a similar heap of records gathered at Keokuk? I really didn't know. I was a fool, lost on a fool's errand, and that was how I should be judged.

At the end only two things really matter to a man, regardless of who he is; and they are the affection and understanding of his family. Anything and everything else he creates are insubstantial; they are ships given over to the mercy of the winds and tides of prejudice. But the family is an everlasting anchorage, a quiet harbor where a man's ships can be left to swing to the moorings of pride and loyalty.

*   *   *

The chill went out of the shack; and the heat from the stove, accumulating in a layer under the ceiling, wrapped the bunk as in a blanket. A little after 6 o'clock, as nearly as I could remember afterwards, I sipped the last of the milk in the thermos jug. My body needed stronger nourishment, but I possessed nothing like the strength to cook a meal. I nibbled an Eskimo biscuit and a piece of chocolate, but my stomach was turning somersaults. So I got up and refilled the thermos jug with hot water and powdered milk, a really desperate task, as I had to cling to the table to keep from falling. The next several hours are a blank. Later, when I was able to make notes of what had happened to me, I could not remember anything at all. Perhaps I slept. When I looked at my watch again the time was about 9:30. I was dazed and exhausted. The idea came to me that I ought to put out the stove to give myself a needed rest from the fumes; besides, there was no telling when I should have strength to fill the tank again. As I twisted the valve, the room went black. The next thing I knew I was on the floor. I pulled myself up by the stove. It was still warm; so I could not have been out very long.

I dropped into the chair, convinced that the end was near. Up till now I had been sustained by a conviction that the only way I could nullify my mistake and make reparation to my family was by transcending myself and surviving. But I had lost. I flung my arms across the table, and put my head down, spilling a cup of water I had in my hand. My bitterness evaporated, and the only resentment I felt was concentrated on myself. I lay there a long time, sobbing, "What a pity, what an infinite pity!" So my pride was gone as well. A Virginian, I was brought up to believe that a gentleman never gives way to his feelings. I felt no shame then, although I do now. Fear was gone, also. When hope goes, uncertainty goes, too; and men don't fear certainties.

The only conscious resolve left was to write a message to my wife—a last groping touch of the hand. Beyond the very personal things, I wanted her to understand why I had not tried to inform Little America of my plight (forgetting that it needed no explanation) and my reasons for going to Advance Base. There had to be that. Pencil and paper were on a shelf nearby. When I went to reach out, my arm would not come free; my sleeve had frozen in the spilled water. I wrenched it loose. The frenzy to write supplied its own strength. After the first few paragraphs my mind calmed. But I was too weak to write sitting up. My head kept jerking forward; and, now that the fire was out, the shack was unbearably cold.

The bunk was a continent's breadth away, and I had to cross an interminable plateau to reach it. Safe at last in the sleeping bag, I lay still many minutes, shivering and gasping for breath. Then I finished the letter; and, as I did so, I thought of the last entry in Scott's diary: "For God's sake, look after our people." I had often pondered that simple phrase, but only intellectually. That night I understood what Scott meant. It seemed a pity that men must undergo a cataclysmic experience to perceive this simplest of truths.

The lantern flicked and grew dim. I managed to light two candles which stood on a ledge over the bunk. Just as the second one flamed, the lantern went out. Then, after a while, I wrote a letter to my mother, and another to my children, a few messages, very brief, of instruction to Dr. Poulter and Charlie Murphy concerning the welfare of the expedition, and a final letter to the men at Little America. On the shelf was the green metal box which held my personal papers. I have had it for years. In this I stowed the letters to my family. The ensuing periods are not very clear. I may have lapsed into a coma. A sensation of freezing came; my next recollection is of hoisting myself into a sitting position and composing a message to Murphy regarding the disposal of my papers. This, with the other messages, I secured with a string to the nail from which the lantern usually hung.

Something approaching gratitude flowed into me. Over my head the two candles still burned. Both were red. One stood in a cracked china holder. The other was planted in its own tallow. I looked up at them, thinking vaguely that, when they went out, I should never again see anything so friendly. After a little while I doused the wicks against the wall. Presently another reaction set in. My mind wandered off into a vision of the past, in which I seemed to be wrestling again for the welterweight championship of the Naval Academy. An agonizing pain was in my body; I had given up all hope of winning; there remained only an insane determination not to bring shame to my mother in the gallery. It was vivid, and the reason it was vivid was that I was again in almost the same situation, except that the stakes were infinitely greater and the chances of winning even less. Then the same determination that had kept me fighting on to the finish that day again came surging back. I saw that, although I seemed absolutely washed up, there was a

chance I was mistaken. Anyway, I would have another
try.

About 3 o'clock on the morning of June 2nd, I had
another lucid phase. I tried without success to force my
body into sleep. The sleeping pills were on the shelf.
The flashlight fingered the bottle. I took it down and
dumped the pellets into my cupped palm. There were
more than two dozen, white and round; they bespoke a
lovely promise. I reached for the bottle. But then I
stopped. It was impossible to go on like this. I should
become a madman, shrinking from every shadow and
touch of pain. I found a match and lighted a candle. An
unused sheet of paper lay on the bunk, on top of the
diary. I wrote:

The universe is not dead. Therefore, there is an
Intelligence there, and it is all pervading. At least one
purpose, possibly the major purpose, of that Intelligence is the achievement of universal harmony.

Striving in the right direction for Peace (Harmony),
therefore, as well as the achievement of it, is the result
of accord with that Intelligence.

It is desirable to effect that accord.

The human race, then, is not alone in the universe.
Though I am cut off from human beings, *I* am not
alone.

For untold ages man has felt an awareness of that
Intelligence. Belief in it is the one point where all re-
ligions agree. It has been called by many names. Many
call it God.

This was the gist of the philosophy which had come to me out of April's hush. Dousing the candle, I slipped into the bag, and repeated the sentiments, over and over again. Sleep came after a while. It was intruded upon by another nightmare in which I seemed to be struggling desperately to awaken and take charge of my faculties. The struggle went on interminably in a half-lighted borderland divided by a great white wall. Several times I was nearly across the wall into a field flooded with a golden light, but each time I slipped back into a spinning darkness. Instinct plucked at my sleeve: You must wake up. You must wake up. I pinched the flesh over my ribs. I pulled my long hair. Then the tension eased; I fell across the wall; and, instead of warm sunlight, I found myself in darkness, shivering from cold and thirsting for water.

* * *

June 2nd was a Saturday and a prolongation of the melancholy events of the day before. I was as weak as ever, and just as certain that I was at the end of my tether. The anemometer cups rattled most of the day; drift sifted down the ventilator in a fine haze, and dripped in hot, pinging pellets from the stovepipe to the deck. From the register I learned that the wind was in the northeast and blowing about twenty miles an hour. I prayed for it to stay in that quarter, since it would mean a continuation of the warm weather. Although the temperature did drop to − 19° in the evening, it was above zero part of the day. If the cold held off, I could do without the stove for long periods and give my system a chance to throw off the effects of the fumes. Altogether, I could not have been out of the bunk more than two or three hours during the day.

As before, I did what had to be done piecemeal, doling out my strength in miserly driblets, creeping rather than walking, and resting long intervals after each small effort. Toward the middle of the day I made several sorties into the tunnels, once after snow and three times after fuel. I relayed the fuel in a tin pitcher, which held about a gallon, since the stove tank was too heavy for me. Later, when the snow had melted, I mixed more milk in the thermos jug. My stomach would not hold anything more solid, although I did manage to down a cup of tea.

I have a vague memory of climbing the ladder to see what the day was like. This was the period of the moon; but, if it showed, I have no recollection of it; my mind remembered a depressing darkness and drift burning against the cheek. In the late afternoon, when the shack had warmed up, I shut down the stove. The thermograph trace shows a minimum temperature of − 22° for the day—a really moderate reading. But the water which I had spewed up was frozen on the floor; a film of ice was creeping up the shack walls; and the slop pail was a solid, messy chunk of ice.

That night, as well as I could estimate, I slept seven or eight hours. Sunday morning brought another anguished struggle to awaken. Sunday meant a radio schedule with Little America and a lie about my condition which every pain-ridden fiber entreated me not to make. God knows where the strength came from to slide the thirty-five-pound engine into the shack, get it up on the stove, and push it back into the tunnel again, a distance of some forty feet, all told. It was my good fortune to find the tank nearly half full of gasoline. The last thing I did was to pick the rime out of the surface ventilator pipe with a spiked stick. The pipe was almost solidly clogged. No wonder the tunnel had filled with fumes during the last schedule.

By the Little America radio log, I was about twenty minutes late reporting. Dyer's voice was saying, "KFZ calling KFY," in the same crisp, matter-of-fact way; but the sound was a surpassing miracle.

It took only the pressure of a finger to work the key; I knew that code would not betray me. Some days before, Charlie Murphy had asked me to give him certain weather information. The data had been lying on my desk for nearly a week. I sent that. Then some of the camp officers took up certain aspects of the proposed spring operations. I am not sure that I wholly understood everything that was said, for the sickness was coming on again. My answers were a simple yes or no or, "Will think over." Finally Dyer's stately "Thank you, sir. We shall meet you again Thursday," came through the confusion. I shut off the engine, utterly spent.

I have often been asked why I did not tell Little America what had happened. My answer is that it was too dangerous for the men to come to me. This conviction was so strong that I took it for granted. But I was no automaton. When contact was made and Dyer remarked at the outset, as he always did, "We hope that everything is well with you," it was hard to say "OK." But it would have been harder to say anything else. The intervening darkness, the cold, the rolling vacancies of the Barrier, and the crevasses were all immutable facts. Advance Base was my responsibility. It was unthinkable that willing men at Little America should be made to suffer.

That afternoon I may have been close to going out of my mind; the strain of preparing for the schedule had raised Cain with me. I know that I was in torment, and the notion that I was dying would not leave me. Some time during the evening I came out of the delirium, thirsty and hungry. Along with some milk, I managed to down half a dozen salt crackers, the first solid food since Thursday morning. That night I slept a little longer, though my slumber was lighted by unspeakable nightmares. Monday I scarcely left the sleeping bag. The rest did me good; as did, perhaps, my keeping the fire out most of the afternoon. At night I got up and supped on malted milk, salted crackers, almonds, and dried apples soaked in warm water. A queer mixture, which I myself cannot explain otherwise than by a dim notion that of all the edibles in the shack, these were the only ones that my stomach would tolerate.

I still had no endurance. The pain came and went in my eyes and head and back. And I was always cold.

That night, as before, I ranged the whole broad reaches of hell before finding sleep. Next morning I had much less difficulty waking up, which heartened me. Indeed,

matters went somewhat easier. I even managed to empty
the slop pail in the food tunnel. In the afternoon I had
strength enough to crank the phonograph. The song "In
the Gypsy's Life" from *Bohemian Girl* was on the disk.
I played that, then the drinking song in *Heidelberg*. And
"Adeste Fidelis." It was magnificent to hear the sound
of many voices throbbing in every corner of the shack.
You are on the mend, an inner voice said; *you really have
a chance. One in a hundred, perhaps, but still a chance.*

* * *

Afterwards, lying in the sleeping bag, I tried to analyze the possibilities. By then I had been through five
days of it—five everlasting, interminable days. I had been
lost on a great plateau of pain where all the passes were
barred. I had suffered and struggled; I had hoped and
stopped hoping. Still, it is not in a man to stop, anyhow;
something animal and automatic keeps him propped on
his feet long after the light has gone from his heart. And
as I lay there thinking, I finally asked myself: What are
your assets? What might be done that has not already been
done?

To begin with, there were two certainties. One was
that no help was to be had from the outside—the Barrier
was a wall between. The other was that little could be
done about improving the ventilation in the shack. Even
if materials had been available to make a drastic change,
I was palpably too weak to undertake anything of that
order. Here the warmish weather had been an unexpected
ally. I had been able to do without the stove for long

intervals during the day; and the relief from the fumes
had given my body respite. This was sheer luck, however.
The greatest cold was yet to come, and might come any
day.

These were facts. To the degree that a man is superior
to his destiny, I should be able to rise above them. Few
men during their lifetime come anywhere near exhausting
the resources dwelling within them. There are deep wells
of strength that are never used. Could I find a way to tap
those physical potentialities locked up within myself?
Well, suppose I were able to. It still wouldn't mean a great
deal. Clearly, my remaining material resources couldn't
be very much. Therefore I must find other sources of replenishment. In such times, when the tricks and expedi-
encies of cornered men fall to pieces in their hands, they
turn to God—as I did, after my fashion.

The articles of my faith were in part set forth in the
paragraphs I wrote after Friday's despair. They represented no new convictions. I had always had them in a
dim way. The difference was that the peacefulness of
April and May had crystallized my old beliefs as it was
adding new ones; and the time had come to test them.

And yet, being a practical man, I recognized a big difference between the mere affirmation of faith and its
effective implementation. To desire harmony, or peace,
or whatever word you care to give to the sense of identification with the orderly processes of life, would be a step
in the right direction; but this by itself was not enough.
I had to work for it. Above everything else, what I sought
must be logical; it must be brought about by following

189

ALONE

the laws of nature. It didn't occur to me to formulate a prayer. I would express whatever urge to pray I had in action—besides, the sheer hunger to live was prayer enough.

As I saw the situation, the necessities were these: To survive I must continue to husband my strength, doing whatever had to be done in the simplest manner possible and without strain. I must sleep and eat and build up strength. To avoid further poisoning from the fumes, I must use the stove sparingly and the gasoline pressure lantern not at all. Giving up the lantern meant surrendering its bright light, which was one of my few luxuries; but I could do without luxuries for a while. As to the stove, the choice there lay between freezing and inevitable poisoning. Cold I could feel, but carbon monoxide was invisible and tasteless. So I chose the cold, knowing that the sleeping bag provided a retreat. From now on, I decided, I would make a strict rule of doing without the fire for two or three hours every afternoon.

So much for the practical procedure. If I depended on this alone, I should go mad from the hourly reminders of my own futility. Something more—the will and desire to endure these hardships—was necessary. They must come from deep inside me. But how? By taking control of my thought. By extirpating all lugubrious ideas the instant they appeared and dwelling only on those conceptions which would make for peace. A discordant mind, black with confusion and despair, would finish me off as thoroughly as the cold. Discipline of this sort is not easy. Even

190

in April's and May's serenity I had failed to master it entirely.

That evening I made a desperate effort to make these conclusions work for me. Although my stomach was rebellious, I forced down a big bowl of thin soup, plus some vegetables and milk. Then I put the fire out; afterwards, propped up in the sleeping bag, I tried to play Canfield. But the games, I remember, went against me; and this made me profoundly irritable. I tried to read Ben Ames Williams' *All the Brothers Were Valiant;* but, after a page or two, the letters became indistinct; and my eyes ached—in fact, they had never stopped aching. I cursed inwardly, telling myself that the way the cards fell and the state of my eyes were typical of my wretched luck. The truth is that the dim light from the lantern was beginning to get on my nerves. In spite of my earlier resolve to dispense with it, I would have lighted the pressure lantern, except that I wasn't able to pump up the pressure. Only when you've been through something like that do you begin to appreciate how utterly precious light is.

Something persuaded me to take down the shaving mirror from its nail near the shelf. The face that looked back at me was that of an old and feeble man. The cheeks were sunken and scabrous from frostbite, and the bloodshot eyes were those of a man who has been on a prolonged debauch. Something broke inside me then. What was to be gained by struggling? No matter what happened, if I survived at all, I should always be a physical wreck, a burden upon my family. It was a dreadful business. All the fine conceptions of the afternoon dissolved in black despair.

The dark side of a man's mind seems to be a sort of antenna tuned to catch gloomy thoughts from all directions. I found it so with mine. That was an evil night. It was as if all the world's vindictiveness were concentrated upon me as upon a personal enemy. I sank to depths of disillusionment which I had not believed possible. It would be tedious to discuss them. Misery, after all, is the tritest of emotions. All that need be said is that eventually my faith began to make itself felt; and by concentrating on it and reaffirming the truth about the universe as I saw it, I was able again to fill my mind with the fine and comforting things of the world that had seemed irretrievably lost. I surrounded myself with my family and my friends; I projected myself into the sunlight, into the midst of green, growing things. I thought of all the things I would do when I got home; and a thousand matters which had never been more than casual now became surpassingly attractive and important. But time after time I slipped back into despond. Concentration was difficult, and only by the utmost persistence could I bring myself out of it. But ultimately the disorder left my mind; and, when I blew out the candles and the lantern, I was living in the world of the imagination—a simple, uncomplicated world made up of people who wished each other well, who were peaceful and easy-going and kindly.

The aches and pains had not subsided; and it took me several hours to fall asleep; but that night I slept better

than on any night since May 31st; and in the morning was
better in mind and body both.

* * *

The melancholy began to lift, and I was able to do a
little more for myself. Wednesday the 6th I succeeded in
getting topside for the 8 A.M. weather "ob." Although the
morning was clear, drift still blurred the horizon and
peppered my face. I sank to my knees in soft snow at
every step. It was good to possess the spaciousness of the
Barrier after the narrowness of the shack. I threw the
beam of my flashlight at the wind vane, and saw that the
wind was in the southeast. That means cold, I muttered.
Rime covered everything. The breathing slats in the sides
of the instrument shelter were thick with drift, but I did
not feel up to brushing it off. I was satisfied to read the
thermometer, reset the pin, and retreat below.

Later, I crept to the far end of the fuel tunnel and
secured a small piece of asbestos, which I cut to fit over
the top of the stove. My idea was that it would help to
shut off the initial fumes that poured through the chinks
while the burner was still cold and smoky. I cut the piece
to fit snugly around the stovepipe and fold over the edges
of the stove.

In the afternoon I eavesdropped on Little America's
weekly broadcast to the United States.* One reason was
that prudence suggested testing my handiness with the
battery-powered emergency set. But the moving reason

* 2 o'clock Little America time; 9 o'clock Eastern Standard time.

was a hunger for familiar voices. I missed much of what was said, but I did catch the solemn to-do over the three cows at Little America; how one stood up all the time and refused to lie down; and how another, which was accustomed to lying down every night, lay down with the coming of the winter night and refused to stand up; and how the third, poor thing, couldn't make up her mind just what to do, except roll her eyes at Cox, the carpenter, who haunted the cowbarn. I really chuckled over that and over "Ike" Schlossbach's baritone solo called "Love, You Funny Thing." Other people in Antarctica, I realized, had their problems too.

JUNE II: THE STRUGGLE

MY SCHEDULED CONTACT WITH LITTLE AMERICA WHICH fell on the next day—Thursday the 7th—confirmed what I knew in my heart: that the improvement in my condition was more mental than physical. Though I was less weak, I was at least three hours getting fuel, heating the engine, sweating it into the shack and out, and completing the other preparations. I moved feebly like a very old man. Once I leaned against the tunnel wall, too far gone to push the engine another inch. You're mad, I whispered to myself. It would be better to stay in the bunk and cut out paper dolls than keep up this damnable nonsense.

That day the cold was worse. The thermograph showed a minimum of 48° below zero. From all indications the "heat wave" was broken. The slick white film of ice on the walls had climbed from the floor halfway to the ceiling. All my resistance to cold seemed to have vanished. My flesh crawled, and my fingers beat an uncontrollable tattoo against everything they touched. It was disheartening to be so much at the mercy of something from which there was no lasting escape. Resting betweenwhiles, I huddled over the stove. The warmth was only superficial. My blood ran cold as ice.

In spite of all my efforts, I was late making contact. Dyer was playing a record, as he sometimes did when he grew tired of repeating the call. I finally recognized what it was—"The Pilgrim's Song" from *Tannhäuser;* I waited much stirred, until the record was played out. When I broke in, Charlie Murphy chided me: "Oversleep, Dick?"

"No, busy."

Charlie had little to say. Siple, however, was waiting to read a paper. As well as I can remember, it dealt with the theoretical configuration of the undiscovered coastal reaches of the Pacific Quadrant, where I was supposed to make a flight of exploration in the spring. Interesting, yes; there was no denying the thought that Siple had put into it. And, desperate as I was to close the conversation, I could not help but reflect that this was the most exquisite of ironies: that I should sit there, gripping the table for support, and listen to a theory about a coast I had never seen and now might never see.

If I remember rightly, I said: "Very interesting. Submit to scientific staff." Dyer broke in to ask if I had any further messages before signing off. I asked him if it would be possible to shift the schedules from the morning to the afternoon. He replied: "Wait a minute, please." Although the words were unintelligible, I could hear voices talking in the background. Dyer said that they were perfectly willing to make the change if I wished it, but that to do so would involve shifting their own schedules with the United States, which had been fixed after long testing. "Never mind," I said. And, for the time being, let the subject drop, not wishing to excite suspicion. Directly after the schedule I took to my bunk, and scarcely moved the rest of the day. The pain was back, and with it the bitterness and the discouragement.

Why bother? they argued mockingly. Why not let things drift? That would be the simple way. Your philosophy tells you to immerse yourself in the universal processes. Well, the processes here are in the direction of uninterrupted disintegration. That is the direction of everlasting peace. So why resist?

From that day on I came to dread the radio schedules with Little America. The task of getting the engine ready, together with the ever-present fumes, emptied me of whatever strength and resistance I had accumulated meanwhile. It seemed almost better to let the radio go by the board. I tried to think up excuses for stopping the contacts altogether which I could present to Little America over the next schedule, but none made sense. I couldn't very well say that the conversations were beginning to bore me or that the transmitter was on the verge of breakdown and not to be worried if Advance Base went off the air. For one thing, many expedition problems remained to be discussed with Poulter and Murphy; and, in spite of the explicit orders I had left with the officers at Little America and reiterated to the tractor crew just before they departed for Advance Base, I couldn't help but feel that any lasting silence on my part might tempt the camp into some rash move.

Thus, I was caught up in a vicious circle. If I kept up the

197

schedules, the drain upon my strength plus the fumes would almost certainly finish me off; if I failed to keep them up, I had better be finished off anyway. This was the way I looked at the situation—the way I believe that any member of the expedition in my position would have viewed it. Just as any normal man would be, I was doggedly determined to keep them from attempting a possibly disastrous relief excursion.

So I came to dread the schedules for a second reason: the fear that I would betray the condition which I was trying to hide by maintaining them. I knew that Murphy was always studying me in his cynical, penetrating fashion. As time went on, I sent amusing messages to throw him off. (I must say, though, that most of these looked pretty silly afterwards.) But, when a course of action is obvious, you take it for granted that you could not deliberately do otherwise; and, when your conscience is too weak to hold you to that course, you continue along it from momentum. By an ironical twist of circumstances the radio, which should have been the greatest safety factor, had instead become my greatest enemy.

That Thursday night I really grasped how far I had fallen. In the diary I wrote: ". . . These early morning schedules are killing. They leave me without strength to go through the day. Tremendously difficult to get even a little sleep. There are strange nagging pains in my arms, legs, shoulders, and lungs. . . . I'm doing everything possible to hold out. Could I but read, the hours would not seem half so long, the darkness half so oppressive, and my minor misfortunes half so formidable. . . ."

JUNE II: THE STRUGGLE

Across the room, in the shadows beyond the reach of the storm lantern, were rows of books, many of them great books, preserving the distillates of profound lives. But I could not read them. The pain in my eyes would not let me. The phonograph was there, but the energy to crank it had to be saved for the business of living. Every small aspect of the shack bespoke my weakness: the wavering, smoking flame in the lantern and the limp outlines of the clothing on the walls; the frozen cans of food on the table, the slick patches of ice on the deck, the darker stains of spilt kerosene, and the yellowed places where I had vomited; the overturned chair beside the stove which I hadn't bothered to pick up, and the book—John Marquand's *Lord Timothy Dexter of Newburyport*—which lay face down on the table.

* * *

June 8

I am endeavoring to set forth, day by day, the way I live. I am steadfastly holding to a routine designed to give me the best chance of pulling through. Though the mere thought of food is revolting, I force myself to eat— a mouthful at a time. It takes me two or three minutes just to get down a single mouthful. Mostly I eat dehydrated vegetables—dried lima beans, rice, turnip tops, corn, and canned tomatoes—which contain the necessary vitamins—occasionally cold cereals slaked with powdered milk. When I feel up to it, I cook fresh seal meat.

The uncertainty of my existence rises from the realization, when I blow out the candles at night, that I may lack the strength to get up on the morrow. In my

199

stronger moments I fill the oil tank supplying the stove. I use kerosene exclusively now. Its fumes seem less injurious than those from the solvent. I no longer carry the tank into the tunnel as at first. My only container holds just one gallon, and I must make four trips into the tunnel to fill the tank and supply fuel for my lantern. I creep a bit, then rest a bit—over an hour at the job this morning. I froze my hand rather badly. Little by little I've added to the food stores on the shelves within reach of my bunk. They are my emergency cache. The last thing I do when I turn in is to make sure that the lantern is full of oil. If some morning I cannot get out of my bunk, I shall have enough food and light at hand to carry on for a while.

What baffles me is that I have no reserve strength whatever. Climbing the ladder to go topside, I must rest at every other rung. The temperature today was only 40° below zero; but, though I was clad in furs, the cold seemed to shrivel my bones. It's been blowing pretty steadily from the southeast, and I can't seem to keep any heat in the shack. At night the pains in my body nag incessantly. Sleep is what I need most, but it seldom comes. I drift into a torpor, lighted up by fearful nightmares. Mornings it's a tough job to drive myself out of the sleeping bag. I feel as if I had been drugged. But I tell myself, over and over again, that if I give in—if I let this stupor claim me—I may never awaken.

Little by little I came to my feet and regained a measure of control over my affairs. But the improvement came so gradually and was interrupted by so many attacks that it was perceptible only over a long period; it was most apparent in my somewhat improved ability to control my moods of depression. Although I tried to resume the auroral observations, I was in truth too weak to stay for more than a few minutes topside. What I did was to brace the trapdoor with a stick, and peer from underneath while clinging to the ladder. Sunday came in gloomy and on the warm side. On the register trace a wind no stronger than a whisper slewed out of the north, through east and into the southeast; the temperature rose to 4°. I was grateful for that. Most of the afternoon the fire was out; and I persuaded myself that the letup from the fumes was helping me to throw off the exhaustion that followed the radio schedule.

Now that the agony in my eyes and head was diminishing, the hardest thing to put up with was the gloom in the shack. I had craved light before, but in June I lusted for it. The storm lantern and the candles were at best only yellow puddles in a cave. I was afraid to light the gasoline pressure lamp. For one thing, I had to pump air into it with a small piston, which took more strength than I was willing to expend. Another thing, the burner had first to be heated with meta tablets, and the fumes at first were always noticeable. No man could have been more careful than I was. During the brief conversation with Little America, I asked them to have Dr. Poulter consult with the Bureau of Standards in Washington and find out: (1) whether the wick lantern gave off less fumes than the pressure lantern; and (2) whether moisture in the kerosene or Stoddard solvent (in consequence of thawing rime in the stovepipe) would be apt to cause carbon monoxide. I presented the questions in an offhand way; and Guy Hutcheson, the other radio engineer, who occasionally relieved Dyer, said he would deliver the message to Poulter and in all probability I would have a reply from Washington by the next schedule, which was Thursday. My life at this time is summed up in the diary entry for this day:

June 10

... During my rare "up" moments I compel myself to draw all my fuel from the farther drum in the tunnel. The roof is caving in again at that end, and I haven't the strength to shore it properly. These few extra steps I may presently be unable to take, and I want a full drum nearby. Even now I sometimes can hardly reach the nearer drum.

I dare say that every ounce of egotism has been knocked out of me; and yet, today, when I looked at the small heap of data in the tunnel, I felt some stirrings of pride. But I wish that the instruments did not always make their inevitable demands, even though they require little actual strength. How pitilessly resolute and faithful they are. In the cold and darkness of this polar silence they steadfastly do their appointed jobs, clicking day and night, demanding a replenishment I cannot give myself. Sometimes, when my body is aching and fingers won't obey, they appear utterly remorseless. Over and over they seem to say, "If we stop, you stop; if you stop, we stop."

June 11

I'm trying to reduce fumes by lagging the stovepipe with surgical tape. The stove burns low most of the day, and to be sure of good ventilation I keep the shack door open into the tunnel much of the time. So it's always cold. A piece of meat left lying on the table hasn't thawed out in five days.

In the afternoon I put the fire out to cut fumes and got in my sleeping bag until 6:30. The pain in my shoulders is so intense that at times I cannot lie on my back. I crave sedatives, but dare not risk them. Too near the ragged edge to let down even for an hour.

Still can't eat properly—have to force food down by chewing it to the point of dissolution. To take my mind off the distress of my stomach, I sometimes play solitaire while I eat. I use three decks of cards. They are marked A, B, C. I keep score and bet against myself. My arms grow weary just dealing the cards. Finished a whole game tonight before I downed three mouthfuls of food.

By then it was time for the 8 P.M. "ob." Rested afterwards, and went above again to note the 10 P.M. aurora. You see, my existence, like the most commonplace life, is regulated by routine—a pattern endlessly and inexorably repeating itself. Nevertheless, since the 31st it is almost always precarious.

Snow fell during the night. When I crept up the ladder this morning, I found I couldn't budge the hatch by my usual method. I rested and tried to lift it with my shoulders. Not a stir. I came below and got a hammer. Pounding finally broke it loose. It left me exhausted for quite a while.

June 13

For an Antarctic June the weather has been surprisingly mild. I have the thermograph sheets and the Weather Bureau forms beside me as I write this (I'm stretched out in the sleeping bag), and from them I find that the lowest reading since the first was $-46°$, on the 7th. Yesterday's minimum was $-38°$; today's $-34°$. Also, the air has been almost dead still, which helped, too.

Nevertheless, I've had the fire out so much of the time that the ice on the walls never melts. I've been watching it creep slowly toward the ceiling. It seems to rise at the rate of an inch or so every day. But in spite of everything I seem to be improving. Incidentally, I have given up the morning tea. It was a wrench to do that, having been a tea-drinker all my life; but it seemed best to give up all stimulants, however mild.

Thursday the 14th brought a radio schedule. Murphy was in high good humor. He said everything was fine at Little America, and passed on a couple of jokes which he had picked up while chatting with somebody in New York during a broadcast test. "I can't vouch for their authenticity," he said dryly, "because they come secondhand." Then Dr. Poulter came on, with the answers to the questions I had asked about the fumes from the stove and the lanterns. From the elegance of the language, I judged he was reading from a prepared statement; I even fancied that I could hear the rustle of the paper in the microphone. If he had been lecturing a class in physics at Iowa Wesleyan, he could not have been more earnest, more impersonal.

As between two kinds of lamps, Dr. Poulter thought that the storm lantern was the safer. He warned me that, if moisture was consistently present in the fuel, it could cause the stove or lamp to burn with a dirty yellowish flame which would give off some CO. He also advised me to mend all leaks around the burners in the stove where drip or the hot metal would vaporize the kerosene and give rise to nauseating fumes.

That settled the matter temporarily, so far as Dr. Poulter was concerned. As it also did for me, since I had done everything that was humanly possible along the lines suggested. Moreover, I was reluctant to press the matter further, lest I arouse suspicion. Whereupon my Senior Scientist launched into a subject very close to his scientist's heart: meteor observations. Ever since darkness had fallen, he and his crew, in co-operation with observatories scattered throughout the world, had been keeping a continuous watch on the sky for meteors. As I was interested in this and frequently found meteoric fragments in the snow I melted for water, I was informed from time to time about the progress of these observations, either by Dr. Poulter directly or by Charlie Murphy. Into the roof of his own shack at Little America, Dr. Poulter had built a transparent turret, almost flush with the surface, which faced the four quadrants of the sky and was manned continuously by observers when the sky was clear. The results had been phenomenal. On account of the extraordinary clarity of the Antarctic atmosphere, vast numbers of meteors were observed which would not ordinarily be visible through the layer of dust and water particles which obscures the sky over more temperate regions. This was an important astronomical discovery which changed upwards the prevailing estimates of how much material was constantly being received by the earth from this source.

"We're delighted with this piece of research," Dr. Poulter said. "I had no idea that it would turn out so well. Now, we're planning to go a step farther. Demas, as you know, is overhauling the tractors. The canvas tops are being replaced with stout wooden bodies, equipped with bunks, stoves, radio—complete trail units, in other words. What we'd like to do is to take one of the cars out and set up a second meteor station on the Barrier about thirty miles out on the Southern Trail."

"How long expect occupy base?" I keyed back.

"A couple of days, during a clear spell," was the answer in the earphones. "That way, we can get a base line from which to calculate the radients, the altitude at which the meteors enter the atmosphere, and so forth."

"When will tractors be ready?" was my next question.

Poulter wasn't sure. That would depend upon Demas and the mechanics. "But Number One should be ready within a few days."

"Test run?" I guessed.

"To Amundsen Arm and back," * the scientist said. "That's far enough to give us a line on the extent to which the flags are snowed under, and whether we'll be able to follow the trail."

"When?"

"Oh, in about a month. We'll see how things turn out, then we'll discuss the whole project with you."

"OK." I keyed a closing message to Dyer: "Sked Sunday?"

Dyer broke in. "Yes, we shall look for you at the usual time Sunday. Good night, sir. This is KFZ signing off." That was Dyer, as brilliant a young man as ever served under me, never ruffled, never at a loss, and as courteous as the winter night was long.

Curiously, the implications of the proposition at first passed over my head, so casually was it presented. Perhaps in my weariness I could not see them. Only once before had anyone seriously undertaken a major journey during the Antarctic winter night.* The cold was too great for dogs, and for airplanes the risks—particularly those surrounding a forced landing—were almost overwhelming. A month is a long time in the Antarctic; the best-laid plans have a way of vanishing into thin air. We shall see, I muttered to myself as I stumbled into the tunnel to shut off the engine. It did not occur to me for an instant that this

---

* A heavily crevassed arm of the Bay of Whales, lying about 10 miles south of Little America.

* The celebrated winter journey made on foot from Cape Evans to Cape Crozier by Dr. Wilson, Cherry-Gerrard, Evans, and Bowers of the Scott expedition.

development could have any connection with my dwindling fortunes. Nor was it so intended at Little America.

As had the others, this schedule left me worn out; the difference was the speed with which I recuperated. Toward late afternoon, after several hours in the bunk, I felt strong enough to attempt a stroll—the first in a fortnight. Or perhaps "stroll" isn't quite the word, because I leaned on a bamboo staff and rested every other step to catch my breath and calm the rapid beating of my heart. Altogether I did not walk more than twenty yards, but I was grateful for that little. You are getting well, I told myself; and the words sounded convincing.

I do not recall ever seeing the aurora more active. Even through the ventilator I could see flashes of it. In addition to the regular "obs," I made several other excursions topside to watch the show. The sky had been obscured all day, but in the evening the clouds seemed to roll back especially for the aurora. At first it was a sheaf of tremulous rays; then it became a great river of silver shot through with flaming gold. About 10:30 o'clock, when I pushed open the trapdoor for a last look, it was a swollen mass of gauzy vapor which lay sprawled uneasily through the zenith, between the northern and southern horizons. It began to pulsate, gently at first, then faster and faster. The whole structure dissolved into a system of virescent arches, all sharply defiant. Above these revolved battery upon battery of searchlights, which fanned the heavens with a heightening lustrousness. Pale greens and reds and yellows touched the stately structures; the whole dark sky came to life.

The graceful, trembling movements were somehow suggestively feminine. I sat and watched, my weakness momentarily forgotten. Swinging faster and faster, the crisscrossing rays suddenly became curling spirals which heaved into a system of immense convolutions, all profoundly agitated and touched with a fragile coloration. In an instant the immense arrangement was gone, as if drained through a spigot. All that remained were a few rays whose stenthic excitement was a signal saying: "It's not over yet, not yet."

Gazing up from under the trapdoor, I divined that a climax was coming. And then from all around the horizon—north, east, south, and west—there leaped up countless numbers of towering rays, as though a great city were springing from sleep to finger the sky for air raiders. The columns of light would rush two-thirds of the way up to the zenith, slide back with a draining of color, then surge up again. Finally, with a mighty push, they freed themselves from the horizon, gliding with infinite grace into the zenith. There, in the height of the sky, they flowered in the surpassing geometry of a corona, laced with gorgeous streams of radial light. And red Mars and the Southern Cross and Orion's belted brightness were contrastingly as pale as the candles in the shack.

* * *

On Friday the 15th the temperature rose to 7° in the early morning, then turned and nose-dived through the minus 20's. Rime sheathed everything in a swollen insulation. The wind vane was stuck, and in the forenoon I

209

climbed the anemometer pole to free it and clean the copper contact points at the same time. ("I haven't yet sufficient strength to do this sort of thing—it took a tremendous lot out of me," the diary says.) Saturday was pitch-black. The barometer dropped to 28.04 inches, after a long, slow fall; and the days of quietude were broken by the wind, which made up afresh in the northeast. Snow fell, and drift surged over the Barrier in wind-flattened rushes. All day long there was a steady spiraling of drift through the ventilator and part of the stovepipe. After the windless silence, the sound of the storm was singularly exciting; its distant thumping reminded me of my returning strength and security. I found that I could read again, without hurting my eyes, and spent a wonderful hour or so finishing Marquand's tale about that eccentric eighteenth-century gentleman, Lord Timothy Dexter. Later, I played the phonograph, for the first time in nearly a week. It seems incredible that a person should lack strength to wind such a small spring, but this was the case. I remember the records well, having noted them in the diary. One was "The Parade of the Wooden Soldiers"; the other, "Holy Night," sung by Lucy Marsh. The last was one of my favorites, especially the melody in the beginning, which goes:

Oh, Holy Night, the stars are brightly shining
'Tis the night of our dear Saviour's birth.

After this came an unintelligible sentence, followed by a phrase about a thrill of hope. In the past I had played the record over and over again, trying to make out the words so that I could sing them. I have never succeeded; and that day I vowed that, if I came out of this affair alive, I would lead a national reform movement insisting upon clearer diction by sopranos for the peace of mind of explorers who might be tempted to take up singing late in life.

JUNE III: THE PROPOSAL

JUNE WAS A PERIOD OF MARCHES AND COUNTER-MARCHES, of victories and retreats. Now I was overtaken by the first serious reverse since May's disastrous ending. The 17th was a Sunday—a radio schedule day. My diary has no entry covering the date for the reason that I could not summon up the will to write. All the ground that had been so painfully recovered meanwhile was whipped from under my feet in a single morning.

June 18

... Yesterday my invisible enemy struck again. The engine had been running badly toward the end of my previous schedule, so for this one I started the engine about half an hour before schedule time in order to make whatever adjustments were necessary. As usual, since May 31st, I took the precaution of clearing the ice out of the ventilator over the engine. Tinkered with the mixture valve for about twenty minutes or so; the engine was just running nicely when I felt very dizzy and dropped to my knees. Dropping to my knees was

212

instinctive. I crawled back to my shack, shut the door, and lay on the bunk waiting for schedule time. I believe that I was late coming on and had a very tough time holding out during the conversation. Hope my answers to Charlie's questions satisfied him.

I kept my head low when I turned off the engine, but it was running smoother and there were less fumes. I'm back, I'm afraid, where I was the first four days of this month. I'd like to say more, but for some reason writing is taking too much out of me tonight. The worst of it is that Murphy, Poulter, and Innes-Taylor were standing by to discuss a plan for advancing the date set for the start of the spring operations. Indeed, they are already talking at Little America about the possibilities of laying bases with the tractors as early as August, in order to lengthen the field season and with it the scope of the scientific program. Apparently they have been inspired to attempt this as a result of reconstructing the tractor. But it was all pretty vague.

This entry is significant, at least to me, for what it fails to say. Grim as it is, it does not begin to describe what I went through. All this time I was deliberately understating the facts, since the diary was written primarily for my family, and in case I did not survive they would be spared the unpleasant details of my last days. For example, that evening I was too far gone to go topside for the 8 P.M. observation, or even to transfer data from the automatic instruments to the Weather Bureau form. That night I scarcely slept at all, but tossed instead in my sleeping bag,

racked by pain and literally shaken by the thumping in
my heart. At times I thought that if this kept up I must
go out of my head. I vomited up the little milk I was able
to swallow, and my arms were too weak to mop up the
mess. Curled up in the bunk, I mumbled like a monk
fingering his beads. When my voice stopped, the silence
crowded in. In the calm between the rushes of pain I
had the sense of waiting, of waiting and listening for something to happen; waiting with a pent-up expectancy that
was neither fear nor hope, but rather midway between.

Starting the day had always been hard; now it became
a task for Hercules. I had to push the night back and the
day ahead; the weight of the solar system cut into my
shoulders. It was all I could do to force myself out of the
sleeping bag in the morning. By then the stove would have
been out at least twelve hours; my lips bled from where
my teeth bit into them. You asked for it, the small voice
within me said; and here it is. For all my resolve, I doubt
whether I'd have been able to survive this second relapse
if it had not been for half a dozen heat pads which I found
in a box in the food tunnel.

These little flat pads, shaped like envelopes and weighing about a pound, contained a sandlike chemical which
gives off heat when water is added. At night I took two
of these pads to bed with me, together with a full thermos
jug. On awakening, I'd pour a little water into the pads
and knead them gently until the warmth came; then, with
a string around my waist, I'd wear them, one fore and
one aft, between the pants and underwear. Without re-
filling, the pads stayed warm for about an hour, by which

time the stove would have heated up the shack. I used the pads sparingly, not knowing how long the supply would last; but I blessed the supply officer for the illogical impulse which had prompted him to throw those things into the Advance Base gear.

The days that followed were hardening knots in the strands of the hours. I managed to keep up the observations; I wound the clocks and changed the sheets; and when I couldn't get topside I faithfully copied the data on form 1083. But none of these things seemed to have any connection with reality. While one part of me groped about these tasks, another part seemed to be watching from the bunk. At night it was just as bad. Propped up in the sleeping bag, with the top of a box resting on my knees, I tried to play Canfield. The baffling weakness in my arms as I dealt out the cards continued to vex me unreasonably; when the game went against me I threw the cards on the deck. I picked up Ludwig's *Napoleon*, but after a page or two the letters became blurred and my eyes ached. You can't go on, the querulous small voice insisted. This is habit carrying on, not you. You are through.

Wednesday noon, June 20th, with two heat pads belted around my waist and wearing furs, I climbed topside to escape the unmitigated gloom of the shack. A heap of drift lay in the lee of the stovepipe; on this I sat, too exhausted to walk. It was snowing gently. In the east and south the horizon was as dark as the Barrier itself; but in the north a watery smear of crimson rouged the horizon line, the farthest light that the vanished sun could throw past the earth's round. The winter night was approaching its climax. In two days would come the winter solstice, when the sun, at its maximum declination of 23½ degrees below the horizon, would stand still on its northward journey, and then head back into the Southern Hemisphere.

Beyond the Barrier, beyond Little America, and beyond the frozen wastes of the Ross Sea, the sun was still performing its daily, inevitable miracle. It was queer to think that at a calculable instant warmth and light were washing into one part of the world as they ebbed from another. That in some longitudes millions of people were going to bed, and in other longitudes other millions, speaking different languages, were responding to different compulsions, were awakening to the full light of day. All that seemed unbearably remote. Where I was, it would take the sun as long to return as it had taken it to go. Here it was June. It would be August 27th—by the nautical almanac and a little arithmetic—before the sun returned to Latitude 80° 08′ South. And by that time I should be past caring.

But you have been through the worst of it, the inner voice said; now is the time for stocktaking. Every day after the solstice the sun would climb a little higher, and the light in the north would wax a little stronger at noon; and every day, as the dawn-light washed in over the Barrier, the flag-marked trail between Advance Base and Little America would be lifted a little out of darkness and toward the light. But you won't see it accomplished, the inner voice said; yet something desperate within me denied the prophecy. For, if I had one incorruptible hope now, it was to see the sun and the daylight marching over the Barrier. That much at least I must have; the will to live would concede nothing short of it.

As I sat there, this thought suddenly brought to mind the idle conversation that Little America had had with me over starting base-laying operations with the return of the sun in August. For the first time I perceived a possible relevance to my own desperate affairs. They must come this way—*they must come here.* Now at last I had an overwhelming incentive for wanting to see the sun.

Until then I had paid little attention to the base-laying talk, leaving it for the officers at Little America to decide for themselves the details of these preliminary operations. There were two directions these operations would take. One was to the east, toward Marie Byrd Land. The other was to the south toward the Queen Mauds. The second would carry them past my door; and, since this was so, the conviction took root in my mind that I owed it to my family and myself to bring them here first, and at the earliest possible date consistent with safety. This was the only sensible attitude to take. The next day was schedule day. When I talked to Little America tomorrow, I would give Poulter a carefully-phrased directive, urging him to hasten preparations for the early journey, and yet phrased so carefully that he would have no reason to read any personal urgency into it. It had to be handled that way, or not at all.

Having made this resolve, I went below feeling more hopeful than I had felt in nearly four months. In the diary that evening I wrote, "... For the first time since the 16th I feel strong enough not to find writing a chore. The sun

217

is a long way off, but October is a whole light year farther. If they will only change the radio schedule to the afternoon, my cup will be running over."

* * *

In the morning I met Little America on the dot. "Congratulations on the punctuality," Charlie Murphy said. "How come you were so curt with us last Sunday?"

The directness of the question took me aback for an instant. Well, the truth would do no harm. I keyed a short message saying that fumes from the engine had made me feel "rocky," and I had therefore decided to shut down until I could find out what was wrong.

"Is everything all right now?" Charlie wanted to know.

"OK."

"Good."

"Thanks," I replied. Then, to disarm any possible suspicion, I gave him a brief report on how I averted monotony—a grim and for me humorless digest of the tricks I had used in May, by then an eternity once removed.

"Myself, I just count sheep by the millions," Charlie agreeably said. "And before I forget it, Tractor Number One is having its coming-out party tomorrow, if weather holds good. Poulter and Demas are taking it for a short trial spin. That is, if we can muster enough hands to dig away about fifty tons of snow from the garage ramp so as to get the damn thing on the surface."

My heart went up at that. "Have message for Poulter," I said.

"All right. John is ready."

JUNE III: THE PROPOSAL

Although I didn't know it then, Poulter was working in the radio shack, virtually at Dyer's elbow.

The message was brief and matter of fact. Giving as my reasons the depleted state of the expedition treasury and the consequent necessity of winding up our affairs as rapidly as possible after the arrival of the ships from New Zealand, I said that I favored a very early start of field operations and that, if it were practicable, I should probably take advantage of the base-laying trip south to return to Little America somewhat earlier than I had expected to. I ended up with the usual admonition to prepare carefully and wait for ample daylight on the Barrier.

Dyer read back the message without comment.

"OK," I said. The last thing Dyer did before signing off was to advance the schedules to 2 o'clock in the afternoon, in response to my previous request.

"I hope this will be satisfactory," he said.

"Fine."

Then we shut down.

*　　*　　*

Friday the 22nd was wine in a glass. This was the day the sun stood still on the turntable of the solstice. A mackerel sky and a gliding half-moon. The temperature was 50° below, the coldest registration thus far in June. Next day was just as cold, just as clear; but the moon was rounding out and looked like an ancient silver coin, a little squashed out on one side. I was learning new things about myself. Whereas, seventy-two hours before I was reconciled to the hopeless business of waiting for help until October, now my hopes were clasping the end of August. I couldn't think of anything else. And yet, there was no peace in it. My good sense would not let me be. With the best of fortunes it would still be a struggle for men to make good the distance between Little America and Advance Base. The Col on Mount Everest is no more punishing than the Barrier at the end of the winter night. There must be no mistakes, no rash plans. The whole idea might fall dead at my feet.

June 23

For the last few days I've had a rough time. In an effort to rid my body of the poison and so get my strength back, I have lain in the sleeping bag hour after hour, with the fire out and even the lantern dark. I have no appetite, but I force myself to eat.

June 24

Still feeling miserable. Today on the schedule Bailey asked me to move my schedule back to the morning, explaining that the new time interrupted Little America's midday schedules with the U. S. When I asked Dyer how important he thought this was, he said it was up to me, and that he was agreeable to continuing our afternoon schedule. "Then let it stand," I said. And yet, Bailey's request, which at first struck me as being selfish and harsh, was on second thought a good sign. Proof to me that the men at Little America, always independent and touchy about their rights, construed my own request as nothing worse than an arbitrary whim on the part of the C. O. to coddle himself.

June 25

Nothing . . . nothing. . . .

June 26

I've been counting calories, and find that I average about 1,200 daily. Not enough. I should average about 2,500. This morning, for the sake of the extra calories, I melted a big chunk of butter into the hot, sweet milk. Supper menu tonight: dried lima beans, rice, and tomatoes, plus canned turnip tops, plus Virginia ham. I'm eating more nowadays, but my appetite is zero.

June 27

Nothing—and yet, there must be countless things to write about, if I had the will to look. . . .

Next day brought news in plenty. I met the radio schedule on time. Dyer said briskly and with characteristic Yankee understatement: "Doc and Charlie are both waiting. I think you will be interested in what they have to say."

Tractor Number One, with Poulter himself aboard, two days before had made the trial run through Amundsen Arm and to the crest of high Barrier just beyond, approximately eleven miles south of Little America. "Everything went very nicely," Poulter said. "We side-stepped the crevasses and had no special difficulty following the trail. The flags are standing all right, and don't seem to have been frayed much by the wind. Just about the time we'd have one flag abeam, the next flag would be showing up in the headlights. However, I may be able to throw together a makeshift searchlight, which ought to help a lot."

Then, without preliminaries, the Senior Scientist launched into a proposal of his own. It was that the meteor trip proposed earlier be extended to Advance Base in order to observe a meteor shower which was due early in August. Two errands might therefore be disposed of in a single stroke. By continuing on to Advance Base, he said, the observations would benefit from the extended base line and the observers would have the protection of my shack; on my side, I could return with the tractor, if I wished to come, instead of waiting for the base-laying expedition later on. The size of the party was still indefinite, but his first estimate was five men. Of these, two would remain a month at Advance Base and continue the meteor and weather observations.

The present plan, Dr. Poulter continued, was to shove off from Little America at the first clear spell between July 23rd and the 29th. At that time the moon at midnight would be full in the south dead ahead, and the light of the sun would be strongest at their backs at noon. Poulter did not wish to leave much later than that because the oncoming dawn would ruin the opportunities for continuous observations; but, on the other hand, neither he nor the other officers at Little America thought it would be wise to leave earlier. Besides, Demas estimated that it would require at least three weeks to complete the overhauling of the other two machines; it did not seem prudent to start out before they were available as a reserve.

That was the story, presented as matter-of-factly as a

meteorological summary. I couldn't believe the words striking like pebbles on the earphones. It was more like one of the hallucinations which had bedeviled me after the first collapse. But no: that calm, hesitant voice went on and on, discussing the various aspects of the journey with a logic and reasonableness that couldn't spring from a fevered imagination. No such great good news was ever broken so unexpectedly. It flashed through my mind that if Poulter and Murphy, both men of rare judgment, wanted to make the trip, it could not be considered too hazardous at Little America. This is their show, not yours, the inner voice said; they want to come here on their own account, and you need have no shame.

Then I heard Poulter ask, "Well, what do you think of it?"

Though my hand was on the key, my mind was irresolute. "Wait a minute," I tapped out. No matter what happened, it would still be my show; the consequences of failure would still be on my head. And, not knowing what to answer, I finally told him to make more trial runs and let me know the results. Yet, even as I said this, I knew deep in my heart that I should never have the will to refuse him. I had been through too much to cast aside any straw. Moreover, the consequences of this affair would involve more than my family and myself. I had a huge debt, and an expedition poised for a great task in the spring. If I went down, a frightful mess would almost certainly result. Not just because I, Richard Byrd, had died, as all men must die; but because with me would vanish the ephemeral tensions that held a hundred men to a single cause—the leadership, the plan, and the name which had been able to command credit to pay for the outfitting of ships, tractors, airplanes, and men, because that name was able to draw profitable numbers of people into lecture halls, movie theaters, and before radio loud-speakers. The name was the asset, not the pain-ridden, bankrupt body which bore it. But what has this to do with me?

All that afternoon and well into the night, I sat cross-legged in the sleeping bag, weighing the pros and cons. In my lap were the nautical almanac, logarithm tables, pencil and a pad, and a chart of the Southern Trail. As Poulter had said, the moon would be back during the second fortnight in July, and full commencing the third week; and the sun, mounting to the horizon at accelerating speed, would be near enough to make for some light at noon. I covered sheets of paper with figures. I tried to estimate the fuel consumption and capacity of the tractors, and to envisage the safety precautions which should be outlined for the tractor crews. In the end everything must turn upon the men. If they were resolute, prudent, and trail-wise, the risks ought not to be too great nor the hardships too severe.

The big question was whether the trail could be followed with the amount of light there would be in July. On account of the danger of crevasses, particularly those lying in the valley just beyond 50-Mile Depot, this journey would be no straight compass run from Little America. The tractor must hold to the trail flagged by the Southern Party, if it expected to negotiate safely the detour beyond 50-Mile Depot. On the way back to Little America from

Advance Base in March, the tractor party had doubled the flags, spacing them at intervals of one-sixth of a mile. The danger was that the blizzards might have blown down or obliterated scores of them, leaving big gaps in the 123-mile line.

There was no sure way to judge this, short of attempting the journey. True, the results of Poulter's trial run had been encouraging; and in the vicinity of Advance Base the flags, when I had last seen them by moonlight, had appeared to be standing all right. Drift hadn't mounted more than five or six inches around the staffs, although in one or two cases the edges of the flags had been caught and pinned down, making them hard to see.* Hereabouts, however, the Barrier was flat, and the drift didn't pile up so much. In the hollows and troughs the flags might be entirely buried. Well, if the flags were buried and the trail couldn't be followed, that would end the matter, at least until after the sun returned.

I really tried hard to be impersonal in my calculations, and so the difficulties confronting the journey began to loom larger. The great hope unloosed in the afternoon slowly died, and a reaction set in. I blew out the candle, depressed and infinitely weary.

* * *

June went out on a shrinking moon with rising cold. On Thursday the 28th the pin in the minimum ther-

---

* The flags on the straightaway were rectangular pieces of cloth about a foot wide. They were dyed orange, and mounted on 24-inch split bamboo sticks. Besides these, of course, were pennants and burgees running out at right angles from the depots.

mometer went to 59° below zero; on Friday, 55° below; and Saturday, 56° below. The film of ice on the walls crept to within three feet of the ceiling, following a zigzag line that reminded me of the charts in schoolbooks showing how the Ice Ages encroached upon the earth.

The last relapse had awakened the original fear that weakness might one day make it impossible for me to bring in fuel. Now, in my stronger moments, I started to build up an emergency supply in the shack, filling all the empty food tins with kerosene. Most of these I stored in the corners of the room; and the overflow, covered with discarded undershirts to keep the snow off, was stored on the veranda, just outside the door. To provide additional containers, I emptied the big tins holding lima beans and rice; as for the beans and rice, they were dumped into a sack—a U. S. mail pouch, of all things. Doubtless the supply officer had thought of that, too.

At midnight, the last hour in the last night of the longest month I have ever known, I started to turn June back behind the other sheets. Then I did a queer thing. I measured the sheet. It was twelve inches high by fourteen inches long. The numerals, white blocks on a blue background, stood one inch high.

ARL. Hislop, Ltd.
Engineers' Supplies
Wellington, N. Z.

said the legend; and down the sides were ranged in neat little frames the other months of the year.

* * *

JUNE III: THE PROPOSAL

Even now I have only to close my eyes to see in complete detail this calendar which confronted me, the first thing in the morning and the last thing at night, for 204 days. A white border ran around the edges. On this I had scrawled marginal notes: Barrels not full of fuel ... Keep ventilator open ... Radio schedule ... The dates I filled the stove tank. But, whereas in April and May each day had been crossed off or blocked out with red pencil, in June fully half the days had passed without similar notice. What was a day in an eternity?

JULY I: COLD

July 1

It is getting cold again—65° below zero today by the minimum thermometer. I have a feeling that it is going to be a very cold month, to make up for June. It was a great piece of luck that June was relatively so warm.* I could not have survived otherwise. Now, when the stove is going, I keep the door cracked as wide as I can stand it; and, when it has been out long enough for the fumes to dissipate, I stuff rags (worn-out shirts and underwear, to be exact) up the engine ventilator in the tunnel and into the intake ventilator, so that the tunnel and shack won't get too cold. As a matter of fact, I do without the stove anywhere from twelve to fourteen hours a day. Believe me, it is a strain on the fortitude. Last night I froze an ear in the sleeping bag.

I'm worried about drift. Ever since I've been unable to attend to it, the drift has been deepening over the

---

* The records show that in June the cold crossed 40° below zero on thirteen days; 50° below on five days, and never once crossed 60° below.

roof. This morning, when I went topside for the observations, I noticed how high the ridges were over the
Escape Tunnel and the tunnels west of the shack. However, I may be able to do something about this before
long. Advancing the radio schedules to the afternoon
has been an immense help in bringing me back to my
feet. With more time to prepare, the drain on me is not
quite so heavy. Today's schedule, though tiring, did not
knock me out as the others did.

There was no news to speak of from Little America.
Hutcheson said that Charlie and John Dyer were out
skiing, and that "Doc" Poulter was with the meteor observers. Lord, how I envy them the multitudinous
diversions of Little America; even, I suppose, as they
must on their side envy the people home with whom
they chat on the radio. . . .

I sent a message approving the meteor journey, subject to its being made with full regard for its hazards.

July 2

. . . I've begun to read again—two chapters from *The
House of Exile*, which I hope to continue with tonight.
It's the best thing imaginable for me—takes me out of
myself for a blessed hour or two. And tonight, also, I
played the phonograph after supper—"In a Monastery
Garden," "Die Fledermaus," "Tales from the Vienna
Woods," and "The Swan." As I listened the hope swept
over me that I have a good chance to pull through,
unless another serious setback comes. Although still

stupidly weak, I have made real progress the past week. The knowledge is exhilarating. . . .

July 3

. . . Cold spell still holding—62° below zero today. The ice is a foot higher on the walls. I have at last managed to get rid of a good deal of the frozen slop which for the most part I've been dumping into the tunnel—just outside the door. Sitting on the rim of the hatch, I've been hauling the stuff topside with a bucket and line, and dumping it a little to leeward. Of course, this meant half a dozen trips up and down the ladder to fill the bucket; and I thought how wonderful it would be if I had a Man Friday topside and had only to shout: "Take a strain, Friday, it's full." As it is, I have to sit down and rest after every trip. However, the job was well worth doing. The tunnels are much tidier.

July 4

I was greatly encouraged over finding myself able to level some of the drifts. Yet, I had to drive myself, for the temperature was in the minus 50's; and, animal-like, I seem to shrink instinctively from anything that hurts. It's odd that I should have changed so much. The cold never used to bother me. I rather liked it for its cleansing, antiseptic action. But now I seem to have very little resistance. This afternoon, for example, I froze my nose rather severely; and, in the minute or two I had my hands out of my gloves to attend to it, I nipped five fingers.

It has been good for me to be outside. I suppose that I was in the air for nearly two hours altogether, though not more than half an hour at a time. The night is still very dark, but at noon the colors on the northern horizon had the hint of sunrise. The sun is now twelve days nearer ... I have always valued life, but never to the degree I do now. It is not within the power of words to describe what it means to have life pulsing through me again. I've been thinking of all the new things I'm going to do and the old things I'm going to do differently, if and when I ever get out of here. I hope that I won't be like the monk in the rhyme which goes something like this:

> The monk when sick a monk would be,
> But the monk when well, the devil a monk was he. . . .

These were days of great beauty, shadowless days. Scarcely a cloud marred the sky. Looking upwards, I seemed to be able to see into depths which at home could scarcely be penetrated by a telescope. Once more I paced my walk, never far nor for long, but enough to take confidence from repossessing the wheeling constellations, the stars, and the opulent inventions of the aurora australis. In the steepening cold the aurora flowered to perfection. For hours on end the Barrier was bathed in the cold white incandescence of its excitation. At times the sky was coursed by a great luminous stream, a hundred times broader than the Mississippi; at other times it was made up of scattered petals of pale light which I liked to think of as wind flowers. And the glow in the ventilator was like the reflection from a forest fire.

Times when the temperature was in the minus fifties or sixties, a wind would come rustling out of the cold, edged with a breath so sharp that it fairly sliced the skin from the face. Turn, twist, and wriggle as I might, I could never elude its numbing clasp. Maybe my toes would first turn cold and then dead. While I was dancing up and down to flex them and restore the circulation, my nose would freeze; and, by the time I had attended to that, my hand would be frozen. The wrists, the throat where the helmet chafed, the back of the neck, and the ankles pulsed and crawled with alternating fire and ice. Freezing to death must be a queer business. Sometimes you feel simply great. The numbness gives way to an utter absence of feeling. You are as lost to pain as a man under opium. But at other times, in the enfolding cold, your anguish is the anguish of a man drowning slowly in fiery chemicals.

The Barrier shrank from the cold. One could almost feel the crustal agony. The snow quakes came with greater violence. Sometimes the sound was like thunder, with one clap breaking upon the other. The shack quivered to the worse concussions, and a few were severe enough to awaken me from sound sleep. I rather had the idea that I was in the equivalent of an earthquake epicenter zone, for the succession of shocks, increasing as the months wore on, meant nothing less than that crevasses were opening up all around Advance Base. Perhaps they were portents. Like the Barrier crust, my reviving security was based upon a doubtful equilibrium—one strong blow could break it in two.

* * *

The blow did in fact fall on Thursday the 5th. That day the gasoline-driven radio generator went out of commission. I had everything in readiness for the schedules, even the engine running. Casually I flipped the switch to test the voltage. Zero, read the dial. A loose connection, probably. But no. When, in tracking down the fault, I arrived at the generator, I found that it was not turning on the shaft. This is bad, very bad, I said to myself; I'd sooner lose an arm than have anything go wrong with this.

Giving up all intention of meeting the schedule, I fell to on the machine. By supper time I had it apart. The fault was fatal. The lug on the generator drive shaft had sheared off. No improvisation of mine would do, although I tried everything that my imagination suggested. Except for a pause to eat or rest, I worked steadily into the night. When midnight came, the table was cluttered with parts and the bunk with tools, but I was no nearer to a solution than at noon. The only possible repair was a new shaft; and where in God's name was I to get that?

Bent over with weariness and despair, I concluded finally that my world was falling to pieces. There remained the emergency hand-powered set, but I doubted that I was strong enough to work it. Ordinarily two men were required to operate these sets, one cranking to supply power to the transmitter, and the other keying. I, who did

233

not possess the strength of half a well man, would have to go it alone. The pity was that the failure had to come at such a critical hour, when the tractor trip was hanging fire. Nor was this all. My imagination was racing. I thought of Dyer calling KFY for hours and becoming worried, perhaps alarmed. No, the failure could not have come at a worse time. All that I had suffered in June to maintain communication was undone by the failure of an inconspicuous bit of steel.

Friday I awakened feeling miserable and uncertain. I unpacked the emergency equipment. Having tested the receiver several weeks before, I knew that it was all right. The transmitter was the doubtful part. It was housed in a steel box about seven inches square which was fixed to a steel tripod, of which one leg had a seat for the operator. Two short crank handles were fitted into the sides of the box; turning these generated "juice." With the help of the instruction book, I finally succeeded in making the right connections. A copper hand switch, clamped to the antenna lead, enabled me to throw either the transmitter or receiver into the antenna. Rigged up and standing hard by my radio table, the set looked workmanlike and simple. But I had a premonition of what it would do to me.

I glanced at my wrist watch. It was nearly 1 o'clock. I had been working with hardly a stop for four hours. I had, of course, missed the 9:30 emergency schedule; but Dyer had said he would also listen in at 2 o'clock in the event of my losing a regular broadcast period. Lunch was a hurried affair of hot milk, soup, and crackers. At 2 o'clock I made the first attempt with the new setup. I threw the

antenna switch on the transmitter side, and planted
Strumpell's *Practice of Medicine* on the key to hold it
down, so that Little America would hear a continuous
signal if they were listening. Then, straddling the seat,
I started to crank with both hands. The strain was even
greater than I had supposed. Just what the magnetic resistance load to overcome was, I do not know; but to me it
was a long, uphill push. As soon as the thing was turning
fast, I knocked the book off the key, and with left hand
still winding, I tried to spell out KFY—KFZ. Have you
ever tried that parlor trick of rubbing your stomach
around and around with one hand, while with the other
hand you pat the top of your head straight up and down?
Well, this was like that; except that the organization of
my movements was infinitely complicated by my weakness
and my unsure handling of the Morse code.

I called for five minutes, then switched to the receiver.
My fingers were trembling as I tuned in on the wave
length Dyer had assigned for this set. I heard only the
scraping of static. I tried the two other frequencies which
Dyer had marked as alternatives. Nothing there, either.
Then I went up and down the dial. Complete silence.
Either my transmitter wasn't on the air, or I hadn't tuned
the receiver properly, or Little America wasn't listening
in. I could have wept from disappointment. After resting
ten minutes or so in the bunk, I called again, although it
was evident that my strength would soon be exhausted at
this rate. When I switched to the receiver, I was almost
too tired to care. Then Dyer's voice welled for a second
out of the silence. I lost it right away. Desperately I ex-

perimented with the tuning dial, trying to find the hair-line paystreak.

"Go ahead, KFY. We heard you. Go ahead, go ahead, please. We heard you." It was Dyer. How wonderful, how perfectly wonderful, I thought.

I switched to the transmitter, and told Dyer in a few words that my engine was "shot" and that I was having a hard time with the emergency set.

"We're sorry to hear that," Dyer said, "and we'll try to keep our messages down."

Murphy came on and read the dispatch he proposed to send to the U. S. in connection with the meteor trip. What he said about me was no longer important. When he finished I simply said, in effect: "OK. Radio uncertain from now on. Don't be alarmed by missed schedules."

Then, speaking slowly and softly, Charlie had this to say: "As you know, the journey to Advance Base may be hard, and it certainly is chancy. We consider it so here. Therefore, the possibilities are being examined; and the preparations are being made with the utmost care. If I were you, I wouldn't count overmuch on the possibility of the tractors before the end of July. There is a good chance it may be considerably later."

For an instant I was taken aback. The thought struck me that they knew the trip was dangerous but were still going ahead with it. Had I somehow given myself away? My heart sank at the thought of having done such a stupid thing. I interrupted with a sharp protest that, if they thought the trip dangerous, they should give it up. There were other things I wanted to say, but I simply couldn't turn the handle any more. I keyed KK, the signal to go ahead, and waited.

In spite of the atrocious sending, they evidently understood, because Murphy, still in the same even tone, said he was sorry I had interpreted his statement that way. He went on: "All I meant to imply was this: that, appreciating how long the last three and a half months must have been, I can also appreciate how disappointing it might be if, after all this talk, the arrival of the tractor were a long time delayed." He talked a long time; but I didn't hear much of it, because my heart was thumping and my head had turned dizzy, and also because the signal, for an unaccountable reason, was fading in and out.

Poulter then gave a quick résumé of the preparations. Much of this, too, I missed; but I did hear him ask if I had any suggestions as to the men who should go.

"No," was my answer.

Beside the key was a long message I had written the morning before, relating to various safety precautions— the need for a big fuel reserve for the tractor, face masks for the men, fur gauntlets, and a suggestion that two complete sets of rations and camping gear be carried, one on the sledges towed behind and one in the tractor cabin, as protection in case one or the other fell down a crevasse. When Poulter finished, I sent what I could of this message before my arms gave out. "Have very thorough drill on trail; also more flags," I concluded, and keyed the signal to repeat it back. If they replied, I did not hear them. Then I spelled the sentence again, and signed off, cursing my weakness as I sagged over the generator head. But, even so, I drew comfort from the fact that Little America, so far as I could tell, had not suspected anything.

The temperature was 60° below zero, but sweat was pouring down my chest. I turned off the stove and stumbled to the sleeping bag. It was the third serious relapse; and, coming on top of five weeks of depleting illness, it very nearly did me in. If it had not been for the week's supply of fuel, plus the three weeks' supply of food, which I had stored squirrel-wise near at hand, I doubt whether I could have lived the period out. Once again I was reduced to doing what had to be done in slow-motion steps, which were ghastly caricatures of my ambitions. The pain came back, as did the vomiting and sleeplessness.

July 7

Everything—myself included—is saturated with cold. For two solid weeks the red thermograph trace has been wandering through the minus 40's, 50's, and 60's. A moment ago, when I turned the flashlight on the inside thermograph, the pen was edging past minus 65°. The ice over the skylight is fanning out to meet the ice on the walls, which has risen level with my eyes. I hope fervently that the cold will let up, for I simply must have more warmth, even at the expense of less ventilation and more fumes.

I am still in wretched condition. My brain seems unspeakably tired and confused. Last night was agony. This morning was one of my worst. The gloom, the cold, and the *evenness* of the Barrier are a drag on the spirits; my poise and equanimity are almost gone. This

new setback reminds me of the one that followed that
attack of typhoid fever which I contracted in England
during the midshipman cruise. For weeks I ran a high
temperature. Then it subsided to normal. The day I
was slated to receive solid food (and I was famished) I
suffered another relapse; so I had the whole siege to
endure again. And now, as then, I am facing another
illness with a weakened body and mind.

Today I missed another radio schedule with L. A.
I called and listened for at least half an hour, which
was as long as I could stand. No luck. Then, on the
chance that they could hear me, I broadcast blind:
"Can't hear anything. Receiver out of order. OK here.
OK, OK, OK." The whole business was disheartening,
and I was teetering on the thin edge of oblivion.

* * *

Wafted in by the prevailing southerlies, the cold
clamped down on the Barrier. From that day to and
through July 17th the minimum daily temperature was
never higher than 54° below zero; much of the time it was
in the minus 60's, and on the 14th reached —71°. Frost
collected inside the instrument shelter like moisture on
the outside of a mint julep. The air at times was alive
with ice crystals, precipitated in a dry, burningly cold
rain. In a sense, I could almost see the cold fall; for,
whenever I opened the trapdoor, a thick fog formed as
the super-chilled air from the Barrier met the warmer
air in the tunnels and the shack. Even when the stove

239

burned fifteen and sixteen hours a day, it did not throw off enough heat to melt the ice crawling up the wall, an inch a day. The ceiling was half covered with crystals that seldom thawed. And meanwhile the glacial film mounted on the walls until at last it met the ceiling on every side except the west, where the heat from the stove stayed the creeping advance. In spite of the fire risk, I left a lantern burning under the register night after night to keep the batteries from freezing.

All this time I lived on the food which was stored under the bunk and on the shelves. It was an uninspired diet— Klim, Eskimo biscuits, tomatoes, canned peas, turnip tops, rice, corn meal, lima beans, chocolate, jelly, preserved figs, and I still had some of my mother's wonderful ham. While these dreary things contained adequate nourishment, I did not concentrate on them for this reason alone. It was simply impossible for me, during this bad time, to prepare anything more complicated. Even after the canned stuff had stood for hours near the stove, I often had to break it out with a hammer and chisel. My fingers were burned raw again from touching cold metal; no matter how much food I forced into my stomach or how much clothing I wore, it seemed impossible to revive the heat-generating apparatus of the body. One night, when I felt up to taking a bath (the first in a week), I was horrified to find how close I was to emaciation. My ribs showed through the flesh, and the skin sagged loosely on my arms. I weighed 180 pounds when I went to Advance Base. I doubt if I weighed more than 125 pounds in July.

July 9

I've been feeling like a joke without a laugh or, more apt, like a tortoise on its back. This damnable evenness is getting me. It has been impossible to read or wind up the phonograph lately. I must pull out of it somehow, and the only way I can do it is by invoking help from my faith, which I depended upon last month. For I have lost almost entirely the inner peace which I had almost achieved then, and which I know pulled me through. I must somehow win this inner harmony back. Somewhere I must have got off the track.

July 10

. . . Because of the continued cold, I have had to keep the stove going so much that I fear I'm getting a heavy dose of fumes. I know the symptoms well by now— aching eyes, head, and back. It's hard to tell which hurts me more—cold or fumes. I've learned a great deal from trial and error, but I'm still uncertain as to what is the sure middle course between the two.

Last night I couldn't get to sleep, and for the first— and I hope the last—time I took one of those sleeping pills, knowing that if I didn't get to sleep somehow, I shouldn't be able to leave the bag in the morning. I've been very weak all day, and the pill must be to blame. . . .

July 11

. . . I was at low ebb last night. My brain was not only tired but confused. The thirst for light was so intense that in spite of my resolve I finally lighted the pressure

241

lantern and drank in its bright light for half an hour.
It was almost like seeing sunlight again, for the gloom
went out of the corner, and there was a respite from the
everlasting dimness and flickering . . .

The trouble with me, I have decided, is that I've been
thinking words without feeling their meaning; that I've
been repeating my convictions about the universe without feeling their significance. That is how I have wandered from the track. If I could feel as well as assert
the truth, I should regain inward peace. . . .

What made it even harder was losing contact with Little
America. Monday the 9th I listened in on the emergency
schedule, but heard nothing; this was also true of Tuesday. I gave up calling; the cranking took too much out
of me. Clearly, the fault lay with my own apparatus. Every
day, hours on end, I fussed with the receiver and transmitter; if I had the set apart once, I had it apart half a
dozen times. I pored over the instruction book and the
handy guide covering minor adjustments which Dyer had
prepared for me. All that I could find wrong with the
transmitter was a loose connection. On Thursday the 12th
I heard Dyer calling, very faintly. I tried to reach him.
"Heard you. Have had radio trouble. Come in," I radioed;
and in my fanatic eagerness I actually spoke the words.
But the code was as futile as the words. I could still hear
Dyer calling KFY and asking me to come in, please. Twice,
at five-minute intervals, I cranked and spelled out: "Can
hear you. All OK here, OK, OK." That was all I could
manage; it never got through. I finished in time to catch

Charlie Murphy's voice. What he said was unintelligible.
Then silence. It was as if I were sinking in quicksand and
calling to a deaf person who did not hear me.

July 14

... Thank heavens, I seem to have found what's wrong
with the radio. I found a loose connection on the antenna lead-in, which was a surprise, since I had examined it the day after the last contact. Ever since then
I've been working steadily, checking all connections in
the receiver and transmitter, and tightening them.

I don't like this unbroken cold. The temperature sank
to 72° by the thermograph, and I had to inject more
glycerin into the ink of all the instruments to prevent
freezing.

July 15

This has been a day of mixed news. I finally made
contact with Little America—which was to the good;
but the cranking has left me exhausted—which is to the
bad. The most comforting fact is the discovery that the
silence has evidently not stirred up Little America.
They are still keeping their heads. Although I was terribly anxious to know how they had interpreted my
silence, I didn't think it prudent to ask. Also, because
I was afraid that Murphy would start cross-examining
me, I plunged at once into the instructions I had written out for Poulter. These said: "Return to Little
America if you lose trail. Have plenty of flags, gas,
food, furs, and tents; but, above all, you must be absolutely certain not to lose trail or run out of fuel."

I could barely hear Dyer say that he got part of it and asking me to repeat, but I simply couldn't. Instead, I finished with a last admonition: "Take no chances with the lives of men."

Charlie came on then and said how glad they were that contact had been restored. He explained that he wasn't going to ask what had happened because of the many important things he had to take up. He went on to say that, in the event that contact was lost again, they would attempt the trip the first good day after July 20th. Then, when he said that, I realized that the radio silence had been taken in the right way. Charlie added that, if they lost contact with me in the future, they would assume that my receiver was working and they would therefore broadcast information to me at 9:30 A.M. and 2:00 P.M. As he finished, I heard him say something about the anemometer pole which was incomprehensible. . . .

When the signal came up, Poulter was talking, carefully and deliberately, as he usually did. The party, he said, would consist of himself, Waite (radio operator), and Skinner (driver), plus Petersen and Fleming—the last two to remain at Advance Base as observers. He expected no great difficulty in navigating the trail but suggested, nevertheless, that at noon, on the days following the start, I fire a can of gasoline which would serve as a beacon.

Harold June talked a little while about the problems of the trip, but I could make out very little of what he said; and when he was done Murphy summed up, repeating himself many times to make sure I understood. What he said, in effect, was that the first attempt was considered experimental; that it was definitely understood no undue risks would be taken; and that if conditions were unfavorable Poulter would return to Little America and wait for better light. "So we'll look for you on Thursday, as usual," he concluded, "and twice a day thereafter, at the given times."

All of which was decidedly reassuring. I tried to frame an acknowledgment, but my strength was drained dry. Dyer was asking me to repeat as I signed off.*

*   *   *

Even now, after four years, the whole business sounds fantastic. I was lying, because there was nothing else for me to do. But at Little America they were lying, too. The difference was that *they* were coming to suspect that I was lying and, even as they divined that I was concocting a fiction to mislead them, so *they* in turn concocted their own brand to mislead me.

It seems that sometime in the last week in June Charlie Murphy began to feel that something was wrong at Advance Base. He had nothing tangible upon which to hang his suspicions—"nothing but my imagination and intuitions and, paradoxically, the absence of news from you," as he put the matter later. But the suspicion was there; and, sitting at the other end of the radio channel, watching

* By the Little America log: ". . . Byrd said then; 'O.K. listen ten minutes every day mhindh dolkng k.' Dyer asked him to repeat. There came a wicked whine of the generator as he cranked; then 'So long.' We called to sign off . . . no answer."

my messages take shape on Dyer's typewriter, he was like a doctor with a finger on a man's pulse. The loss of communications in July gave Murphy's suspicions something tangible to feed upon; and they grew as he noted my floundering with the hand-cranked set, the all but unintelligible code, and the long waits between the words, which to him were not easily explained except by physical weakness.

However, the rest of the men at Little America refused at first to take him seriously. It was argued that he was no psychic and that my deficiencies with the radio were only to be expected. Yet, this notwithstanding, the idea that I was in trouble would not be downed in Murphy's mind.

Although Poulter has always insisted that he was not influenced by Murphy's intuitions when he took up the proposal for the meteor trip to Advance Base, I have my doubts; knowing his gallantry, I have come to suspect increasingly as time has gone on that he told me this to spare my feelings. But I do know that, when he and Murphy started making plans for the meteor trip to Advance Base, they ran into a stone-wall opposition. Under what might be considered the constitutional government which I had set up in Little America, they were obliged to take up all important propositions with the group of sixteen officers who constituted the staff and who had veto power by a two-thirds vote over any act of the executive officers. The struggle was close and, from what I've been told, rather heated. The argument went on for days; the caves at Little America seethed with dissension. The crux of the opposition was the lack of any specific permission from me to come to Advance Base before daylight. It was argued that my original strict instructions had forbidden just such a night journey under any conditions; and it was pointed out that in authorizing the early base-laying trip, I had specifically cautioned Poulter not to start until there was ample light.

But Murphy stood on his intuitions and insisted upon decisive action, even though he admitted before the staff that he had nothing concrete to go on. "I grant you," he told them, "that an intuition is pretty poor stuff to allow men to take risks on; but, if I am right and you are wrong, we'll never forgive ourselves." On his side, Poulter argued earnestly on behalf of the sheer worth of the meteor observations. But, to certain of the men, many of them navy or ex-navy ratings habituated to arbitrary orders, the proposed trip was a deliberate evasion of an explicit command, a reckless dash supported merely by a hunch, and a potential disaster which might bring disgrace upon the leader and themselves. If, as they surmised, this was to be a relief journey, common sense and the leader's instructions required that the man supposedly in need of assistance first be asked directly whether he needed it.

This Murphy would not do, on the ground that the man at Advance Base, if these facts were laid before him, would have no alternative but to veto the journey. His argument was that they could do two things in one throw: provide Poulter with the base line he needed for his observations and, at the same time, find out whether I was all right. It was on this basis that he and Poulter finally persuaded the staff to approve. Thus the field was left clear for them to continue selling the trip to me as purely a meteor project, knowing full well that I should not be apt to stand in the way of one of Poulter's big scientific projects. The instant I gave my consent, hedged in as it was, they felt they had a free hand. If Poulter found me well, so much the better; he would simply set up his meteor equipment, and no one need be the wiser except that Charlie Murphy might never hear the end of his fiasco as a polar medium. On the other hand, if I were actually in trouble, the double purpose would have been served.

During all this uproar and even while I was out of communication, they were assuring me that all was well, preparations for the meteor trip were moving smoothly, no weighty difficulties were anticipated, and they were looking forward to seeing me soon.

All this I know now. I could not know it in July, 1934; and Charlie Murphy took excellent care that I should have no reason to suspect anything. In the four years that have intervened, the story has come to me in fragments; even now I doubt that I know it all. The men who were closest to the crux of affairs have elected to keep their side of the story pretty much to themselves; the others have only a fact or two, plus their own ideas of what happened. But, since these events are as much a part of the story of Advance Base as my own misfortunes, I have felt bound to tell what I now know.

JULY II: THE TRACTORS

Ever so slowly the day was expanding in the northern sky. The varied colors lasted half an hour or so; and the gray dawn-light lingered for an hour on either side of noon. One day, on the hump of drift in the stovepipe's lee, I sat and watched the light wax and wane, telling myself that soon, beyond the Barrier's roll, the yellow blur of a tractor's headlights would show. But I could not bear to think of this for long; I had been through too much to risk fresh disappointment. If they do come, it will be a great thing, I told myself; but, if they turn back, you will certainly be no worse off than you are. When the dawn-light faded, the aurora sprang like an open fan across the sky; for a few minutes the Barrier glistened whitely. I could see for miles; and, though I may have been misled by shadows, I counted three flags, equal to half a mile, on the Little America road.

July 16

Today, for no reason that I can define, my hopes have risen that the tractor party will actually get through.

249

Poulter is a hard man to stop, and I know the men will be safe in his hands. I really think I feel a little better, perhaps because my hopes now have the facts of the preparations at Little America to feed on. Yet, it has been terribly cold; the temperature today has been in the minus fifties. Yesterday it touched − 68°; the day before − 71° and the day before that − 71°, also.

July 17

. . . The thermograph trace touched − 61° today, but is now pushing up into the minus forties. I am praying that this will be the end of this cold spell. Today the kerosene congealed in the drums, and a primus stove left burning in the tunnel had little effect. I therefore had to keep the shack door open all afternoon, and the warmth spreading into the tunnel finally loosened the liquid so that I was able to siphon it off. But all this made the shack almost unbearably cold.

On Wednesday the 18th the cold started to break up. The wind, which had been funneling down through the Queen Mauds with the persistency of a trade wind, worked its way through west into north. In that quarter it freshened; the temperature climbed to − 28°. Next day the wind blew a little harder, shooting the temperature to a maximum of − 23°. I welcomed the change, because the break-up of the cold, though certain to be brief, promised well for the tractor party. However, it was a mixed blessing; for the winds which brought warmth also brought drift, adding to the difficulties of navigation.

Indeed, Little America informed me in the afternoon over the radio schedule that a blizzard was whaling the camp and the visibility was zero. However, the meteorologists were forecasting that it would soon blow itself out. "Weather permitting," Murphy said, "the tractor will put out at 6 o'clock in the morning." He asked me to stand by for a weather report at that time.

"Can you make it that early without an alarm clock?" he asked.

"Think so."

"Is there anything you want them to bring out?"

"Yes, bromide of sodium, cod-liver oil, glucose."

"Well, we'll see how the Southern Mail works out," Charlie said. "Incidentally, Poulter is taking along three months' rations; and he has made for himself a really ingenious searchlight out of scrap metal."

As before, it was difficult to hear. Even with the most delicate adjustment, I was lucky to catch more than two words out of four. The fault, as I discovered long afterwards, lay in a loose connection deep within the maze of wiring of the receiver. Consequently, I had to ask them to repeat many messages, just as they had to ask me to repeat mine. I was fagged out from the cranking. It was all I could do to, pump more than a word or two at a time. I had to ask them to wait while I rested.

"Sorry to make you crank again," Charlie said.

Thrashing around for a plausible explanation, I remembered how I had injured my arm late in March. He knew about that. "Have bad arm, hard to crank," I told him.

"Very bad?" he wanted to know.

"No, but bothersome cranking."

Just before we shut down, a change was made in the future schedules. Commencing at noon next day, Friday the 20th, Little America would broadcast progress bulletins to me every four hours. Although they would listen, it would not be necessary for me to reply unless I had instructions to give. Dyer's closing contribution was a time tick which he had picked up just a few hours before from Arlington.

What with the excitement over the start and the fear that I might not wake up in time for the 6 A.M. schedule, I scarcely slept that night. Before turning in, I filled the thermos jug with water and tucked it and the two remaining heat pads in at the foot of the sleeping bag. The realization that in a few hours men would actually be starting from Little America made me forget the pain. I wrote in the dairy: "... This is such wonderful news that I can't seem to grasp the fact that I am actually about to see people again. For there have been many times when I was convinced that I hadn't the slightest chance of seeing a human being again. And the auspicious fact is that the weather has turned warm. It is a good omen. The red trace has swung up to the minus-thirty-degree line. For once everything seems to be breaking in the right direction. All this makes me feel as if I had had a shot in the arm. But there is no denying that I am still very, very weak...."

Sometime afterwards I fell asleep. It was 5:30 by my wrist watch when I awakened. At that hour I had little will and less strength; but somehow I managed to chivvy myself out of the sleeping bag, into my clothes, and up the hatch. A puffy norther, freezing to the touch, surged across the Barrier; but the sky was marvelously clear. A good omen, which was substantiated by the rising barometer. Nevertheless, my heart sank when I turned the flashlight on the thermograph sheet. The temperature had taken a nose dive, dropping from $-24°$ to $-46.5°$; and the line was still falling steeply. Although the stove was going full blast, it gave off little heat; so, for that matter, did the heat pads, whose chemicals were almost exhausted.

Dyer was on the air almost at the same instant I sat down astride the transmitter's bicycle seat. "Good morning," he said, after I acknowledged the call. "Have you the weather report ready? Haines is waiting for it."

The weather report having been disposed of, Poulter informed me that on Haines's recommendation the start had been postponed until noon, pending another weather report from Advance Base. Although yesterday's blizzard at Little America had from all appearances blown itself out, Haines was reluctant to give an "all clear" ruling until his own upper-air balloon soundings, plus another good report from Advance Base, indicated that conditions were stabilizing. "Still, Bill says to tell you it looks pretty good— good and cold," Poulter concluded.

That extra effort, coming before I had had time to eat or get warm, did me in for a while. In fact, I petered out several times while cranking, and had to ask Dyer to wait while I rested. The hot milk and cereal which I had downed for breakfast came up in a retching spasm before

253

I could reach the tunnel. It made a vile mess. I retreated to the bunk to wait for noon. The hours dragged. By the storm lantern's light I could see the thermograph trace falling, steadily falling. At noon, when I went topside for a look at the weather, the thermometer read 61° below; but the wind was dying; the barometer was still going up; and the sky was clear and, in the north, suffused by a rosy, promising glow.

"Haines is satisfied," Murphy said after I had passed this on. "It's getting cold here, too—only 14° below yesterday, but 40° today. However, clear weather is what Poulter wants; and evidently he's getting it. He says he will shove off in an hour."

"Tell him be careful."

"Yes, indeed. Sorry to be so curt. See you at 4."

* * *

I hesitate to describe the events that followed. No doomed man pacing a cell in the hope of an eleventh-hour reprieve can possibly have endured more than I endured; for, besides my own skin to think about, I had the lives of five other men on my conscience. All the pre-start excitement drained out of me. In its place came remorse over having countenanced the trip in the first place and fear as to the consequences. I could neither lie quiet nor sit still. Once, for no reason at all, I climbed the hatch and stared aloft, as if the sky must in some manner testify to the inception of an heroic act. But there was only the moon, veiled by ice crystals, so cold that it chilled you to look at it.

254

The temperature worked to 62° below. I now prepared for my beacon lights. In the box of navigation gear were eight or nine magnesium flares, fixed to wooden handles, which burn with a vivid light. I counted out six, which I cached in a small box at the foot of the ladder. Rummaging around, I found two spare ventilator-pipe sections, about three feet long. These I hauled to the surface on a line; then I stood them upright on the snow and laid a plank across. This gave me a work bench, and a higher platform for my gasoline pots. My idea was to stand the gasoline in open cans on the bench and fire them one after the other.

I was interrupted in the midst of these preparations by the 4 P.M. schedule. Dyer was too busy for more than a word. Poulter, he said, had put out from Little America at 2:30 o'clock and had just reported that he was four miles out, approaching the edge of Amundsen Arm. Before supper I managed to fill with gasoline four empty tins, none more than a gallon, three of which I hoisted to the surface. At 8 o'clock the thermograph read −65°. Little America advised: "They've crossed Amundsen Arm and are now on high Barrier, about eleven miles south, preparing to square away on the Southern Trail. Evidently they are having trouble picking up the flags. See you at midnight."

Cold. The red trace worked lower. Christmas, is it to be their bad luck to choose the year's bitterest temperatures to come here? I exclaimed to myself. Dyer had told me the wave lengths on which he would exchange hourly reports with the tractor. I tried to overhear; but, while I caught the bustle of traffic, the sending was much too fast for me to handle. Approaching midnight, the wind trace on the register testified that the wind, after dallying briefly in the west, was again haunting the northwest at whisper strength; the barometer was still rising, which was a good sign; but in the last hour the temperature had twitched 5° downward to 75° below zero, the coldest reading of the year, and colder by over 2° than the coldest temperature ever registered at Little America. Although I knew they would have warmer temperatures than these, nonetheless, the thought of five men on the Barrier, trying to keep themselves and a motor alive in such temperatures, drove me frantic.

At midnight Murphy sounded discouraged. "We've just heard from Poulter," he said. "The tractor is now seventeen miles south of us. They've slowed up but are still under way."

I spelled out, "All OK?"

The voice in the earphones seemed to come from very far off as Murphy repeated slowly: "Evidently not. It's snowing hard where they are, though clear here. Poulter says the visibility is zero. Apparently the flags are all snowed under. Only two inches of bunting show above the surface. So they're running on compass courses from flag to flag. When they miss one, they keep circling until they find it. And, because some of the flags have been blown down, leaving gaps in the line, they are necessarily making slow progress."

On account of the faults in my receiver, I had to make Murphy repeat two or three times; but this was the gist of his report. In the face of it I had no right to keep hoping. For I had traveled enough in the polar regions to appreciate what was happening in the oceanic darkness to the north. I could visualize Poulter sitting astride the engine hood, holding the searchlight in his hand, trying to pick up shreds of cloth no bigger than a man's hand, each spaced 293 yards from the next. He knew the courses steered by Innes-Taylor, who had marked the trail nearly five months earlier; but this information was of small help to him in running from flag to flag. Dog teams never travel in a straight line; rather, they make good their direction in short zigzags, first to one side and then to the other. The flags might therefore be twenty yards or more to the right or left of the true course. Hence, this business of circling after the tractor crew had run out their distance by the speedometer without fetching a marker.

"Dick, there's no sense in your staying up all night," Little America advised. "We'll be in touch with Poulter. Suppose we meet you again at 8 o'clock in the morning."

I framed a message to be relayed to Poulter telling him that, if they could fight through, they would find the flags better at this end. There was other advice I wished to give, but I never got it on the air because my arms gave out. That had happened before, and it would happen again, and nothing in life has ever given me such a feeling of utter futility.

When I shut down that night and pitched into the bunk, it was with the knowledge that affairs had indeed passed out of my control. The aches and pains and the nightmares returned to plague me. On Saturday morning, after a dreadful night, I seemed again to be suspended in that queer, truncated borderland between sensibility and unconsciousness. It was all I could do to get up. When I threw the light on the thermograph, I saw that the red trace had twitched past 80° below zero at 3 o'clock in the morning and had not risen. The boric acid which I used for washing out my eyes had burst its bottle. Even the milk in the thermos jar was frozen, and that part of the wall behind the stove which until then had resisted the rise of the ice was now covered with the white film. The skin came off my fingers as I fussed over the stove. I was too weak to stay on my feet; so I slumped into the sleeping bag. When I aroused, the time was nearly noon; I had missed the first radio schedule.

At noon, and again on the 2 o'clock emergency schedule, I tried to regain touch with Little America. All I heard was the scraping of static. The thermograph trace held at 80° below zero, as if rigid in its track. I was beside myself with anxiety. At 4 o'clock, when nothing came out of my third attempt to raise the main base, I broadcast blind: "Poulter, if still on the trail return to Little America. Await warmer weather." Dyer did not hear it, but I had no way of knowing.

My stomach would hold down nothing but hot milk. Most of the time I was screwed up in the sleeping bag, in a kind of daze. There was a fire in the stove all day; yet, the shack was almost unbearably cold. In the evening my senses revived; my eyes were smarting and running water; my head ached, and so did my back; and I realized that the room must be filling with fumes. So I forced myself out of the bunk to do whatever could be done. The outlet ventilator was nearly solid with ice, which I chipped out with the spiked stick. The stovepipe, when I put my hand on it near the top, was cold; so it was clogged as well. And, realizing that I must somehow insulate it, I poked around in the veranda until I found a strip of asbestos. With this in my hand, and a piece of string, I climbed topside. The inside thermograph tracing showed 82° below zero—so cold that, when I opened the hatch, I couldn't breathe on account of the constriction of the breathing passages. The layer of air next to the surface must have been at least 84° below. Anyhow, I had to duck into the shack to catch my breath. Armed this time with the mask and holding my breath until I was out of the hatch, I started again for the stovepipe. Out of the corner of my eye I could see the ventilator spouting like a broken steam line.

I tried not to look northward, knowing that I must only be disappointed; nevertheless, I did, on the chance that the tractor's headlights might be topping a distant rise. A wavering light set my blood pounding, but it was only a star on the horizon. Except for a pale arc of aurora in the northeast quadrant, the sky was absolutely clear. I was glad of that for the sake of the tractor party; at least they could see. But wherever they were, I told myself, nothing mortal could travel for long in such cold. My lungs seemed to contract with each breath; and the spent air exhaled through the vent in the mask pinged and crackled.

A queer thing happened. I was on my knees, crawling. In one hand I had the flashlight, and on my back the asbestos. Halfway to the stovepipe, everything was blotted out. I thought at first the flashlight had gone out from the cold. But, when I looked up, I could not see the aurora. I was blind, all right; the first thought was that my eyeballs were frozen. I groped back in the direction of the hatch, and presently my head collided with one of the steel guys anchoring the anemometer pole. I crouched there to think. I felt no pain. I took my gloves off and massaged the eye sockets gently. Little globules of ice clung to the lashes, freezing them together; when these came off, I could see again. But meanwhile the fingers of my right hand were frozen, and I had to slip the hand down into the crotch to warm them.

I was a longish time wrapping the asbestos around the pipe. My mittened hands were clumsy and unsure. The pipe, I noticed, was choked with ice. The only opening was a little hole not much bigger than my thumb. Before I was done, my eyelashes froze again; this time I nipped two fingers of the left hand. In my hurry to get out of the cold I slid, rather than climbed, down the ladder. When I removed the mask, the skin came off my cheeks, just below the eyes. I was half an hour bringing life back into my fingers; it returned, finally, with hot rushes of excruciating pain.

Weary as I was, I did not dare turn in without trying to get rid of the ice in the stovepipe. To start the thawing, I filled a soup can with meta tablets and played the flame up and down the sides of the pipe, thus supplying additional heat which the asbestos held. After the water started to run, the heat of the stove was enough to keep the flow going. Before it stopped, I collected a pail of water through the hole in the elbow crook. The thermograph trace was crossing 83° below zero, and the water was freezing on the floor as it struck. I hesitated to shut off the stove lest the instruments—not to mention myself—stop from the cold. I lay in the bag, thinking of warm, tropical places; doing this seemed to make me feel warmer. After a little while I got up and turned off the stove.

* * *

Sunday the 22nd I was nearly frantic with anxiety about the tractor men. When I awakened, the head of the sleeping bag was a mass of ice. I had to heat up the feed line from the tank with burning alcohol before the kerosene would flow into the stove. Three times—in the morning, in the afternoon, and in the evening—I tried to raise Little America. Although my hands were in wretched shape, I took the receiver completely apart. But this accomplished nothing. The air was dead. If I raised the trapdoor once to look north, I raised it at least a dozen times. And nearly always I was deceived by tremulous, winking lights which always turned out to be stars. The temperature went up into the minus sixties, but a sixteen-mile wind out of the southeast rose with it. Again the kerosene congealed, and I had to heat up the tunnel, at the expense of the shack.

My hopes died that afternoon; and with them the emotional lift which had been generated by the knowledge that my friends were on their way. I was all hollow inside. Everything that was reasonable had been tried, and it all added up to nothing. The fear grew that Poulter's party had met with tragedy; it was terrible to concede that, but I had no reason to think otherwise. Nevertheless, at 3 o'clock in the afternoon I heaved myself to the surface and fired two cans of gasoline as a signal. Fully a dozen matches went out in the wind in my hand before I managed to bring a flame near the fluid. The gasoline caught fire with a violent uprush of light; and, after the dimness to which my eyes had become accustomed, I was momentarily blinded.

The smoke towered high in the sky, leaning on the wind. No beacon light answered from the north. Later on, I set off a magnesium flare which I lashed to a bamboo pole and held aloft. It was brighter by far than the other, making a tremendous blue hole in the night. It burned for about ten minutes. Then the darkness rushed in, and I was sensible of the ultimate meaning of loneliness.

July 23

No word. I've been to the surface again and again; there is nothing to see—nothing except those deceiving, dancing stars. I knew it was useless; but, nonetheless, I fired two more charges of gasoline late in the afternoon. This is the way to midwinter-night madness. I mustn't give in too easily to senseless hopes. But in spite of my despair I found my spirits lifted by the broadening twilight at noon and the suspicion of color from the sun climbing toward the horizon; all this presages the coming day, now only a month off.

The temperature this morning was 73.5° below zero

by the inside thermograph. For a while I could not lift myself out of the bunk. I may have been close to freezing. My left cheek was frostbitten, and the flaps of the sleeping bag and even my hair were stiff with frost from my breath.

July 24

No word. I wish to God I knew where Poulter is. I'll never forgive myself if anything happens to him. It's blowing and drifting fairly hard from the southeast. But the temperature is easing through the minus fifties and sixties. . . .

July 25

Nothing—nothing but wind and more snow. I've had the radio apart again; yet, I hear nothing. Sometimes I tell myself that this is so because there is nothing to hear; that a disaster has overwhelmed Little America and struck its radio dumb. This *can't* be; I record it only as a reflection of the state of my mind.

On Thursday the 26th it was still snowing and blowing and drifting; but the wind, after being anchored for three days in the southeast, began to let up. One good thing came out of it: the inrush of wind dissipated the cold; and the thermograph trace climbed into the minus teens, which was the warmest level in thirty-two days. Wherever Poulter and his men were, I told myself, they must be grateful for this letup. Twice that morning I listened for Little America. It was no use. I sank down in the bunk,

with two candles burning, watching the drift sift down
the stovepipe, hissing and melting as it touched.

At 2 o'clock in the afternoon I roused myself for another try. Just as I was about to give up, the name Poulter
cleaved through the deadness. With fingers trembling I
adjusted the receiver. Then a mumbo jumbo of words
came through, distorted by static. I recognized Charlie
Murphy's voice. He was evidently speaking with great
deliberation and repeating his sentences two or three
times. I hardly dared to breathe lest I miss something.
From fragments I was able to piece together a picture
of what had happened to the tractor. On the morning
of the third day, Poulter had reached 50-Mile Depot, on
the edge of the Valley of Crevasses; but on the jog eastward, following the detour, he had missed the flags entirely. Unable to proceed, he had finally turned back to
Little America in obedience to my instructions not to
continue if they lost the trail. From the frequent references to wind, I judged that halfway back a terrific blizzard (actually a hurricane, as Poulter described it later)
had caused them to heave to. They waited a day, then
made good the retreat. Nevertheless, Poulter was even then
preparing for a second attempt.

Actually, this was the right of it; but in the confused
state of my mind I couldn't be sure. I tried to break
through and intercept Dyer. I cranked out the call letters,
but my arms gave out after a few turns, and the room
went black. I became sick at my stomach, throwing up
the cereal which I had eaten at breakfast. I gave up then,
for there was nothing left to fall back on. But later on,

brooding in the bunk, I thought of another way to make use of my dwindling strength.

I took the generator head off its tripod and lashed it to a heavy box which was nailed to the floor. In that way, by cranking with my feet while sitting in the chair, I could apply more leverage than was possible with my arms. I tried it out and found it satisfactory. Although the generator wabbled when I cranked, the strain on me seemed somewhat less; and there was an additional advantage, too, in that I would be able to shift from my legs to my arms when I tired. I ended the diary entry for that day with the one solacing thought I had been able to draw from it: "He [Poulter] did a good job in returning safely to Little America—my relief is boundless. The news is most opportune, for I've been very low."

Friday brought an overcast sky; the temperature rose nearly to zero. Now that the weather was softening, I gained in hopefulness; for Poulter now had a real chance. Yet, as I weighed the possibilities, it was clear that with so many flags either blown down or buried, he hadn't even the ghost of a show of reaching Advance Base unless the original order not to leave the trail was abrogated. And this in my desperation I proposed to do. I was to be ashamed of it afterwards, I admit; but at the time I saw no alternative. It was questionable just how much longer I could last, especially in view of the demands made upon me by the radio; the bouts of unmitigated cranking were leaving me as if beaten within an inch of my life.

I puttered around, killing time until the 2 P.M. schedule. Ransacking the Base for more flares, I happened to find out in the tunnel the sections of a seven-foot, T-shaped signal kite, which I had almost forgotten about. It didn't take me long to put the kite together. I also adapted it for serving as an aërial beacon by making a longish tail of antenna wire, to which I bent pieces of paper and cloth. When the time came, I would soak them in gasoline, touch a match, and fly the kite as a signal. I was rather proud of that idea.

At 2 o'clock I heard Dyer dimly calling KFZ. With my chair braced against the wall and my feet pedaling the generator handles bicycle-wise, I started the message. It was to the effect that, if they proposed to make another attempt, better come now during the warm weather, when the moon, the twilight, and the temperature were all in favorable conjunction, and navigate a new trail around the crevasses; I would keep a light burning on the anemometer pole; and at 3 o'clock in the afternoon and at 8 o'clock in the evening I would fly a kite with a light hanging from it. It was a galling chore. I had to stop several times to rest. When it was done, I said I would try to pick up their reply.

Either Dyer or Murphy replied, I'm not sure which. I couldn't make out what was said, except a request to repeat the message. I made five attempts, but finally had to give up in order to preserve my small store of strength. My knees were knocking together, and my feet kept slipping off the handles. Switching to the receiver, I heard somebody talking; but it was all a blur. I let the earphones fall from my hands. Yet, in spite of my inadequacies, I was more successful than I realized.*

Although I had no way of telling, Little America's resolve was already steeled. After consultation with the camp officers, Dr. Poulter decided to make a dash of it to Advance Base. He reduced his party to three men—himself; Demas, chief of the tractor department; and Waite, who was radio operator. With his own tracks to follow to 50-Mile Depot, Poulter expected to make good time over the first half of the journey; and for maneuvering around the Valley of Crevasses he had meanwhile worked out his own patient method. So close to the magnetic pole, he couldn't rely upon ordinary compasses for exact steering—in high latitudes compasses turn sluggish and unreliable. Besides, no one at Little America had been able to figure out an effective way to mount a compass on a tractor, on account of the proximity of metal.† Poulter's idea was to build ten-foot snow beacons every 500 yards or so, mount little lights powered by flashlight batteries on the top, and sight back on them as he moved

---

* This is what was pieced together in the Little America log: "If you hear me cone noudsrimn (come now during) very warm weather. Navigate nertrail around and be cond (beyond) . . . wait." We waited, then in two or three minutes came the whine of the generator. ". . . be cond crevasses near as possible tsald (to old?) kailci (trail?). Will have light outside wait." We waited again, two or three minutes. Then: "sutside anneat (and at?) three pnp delight (and at eight?) P.M. irill (I will?) fly kite kite kite with light. Wait." We waited. Then: ". . . Poulter bring kite and fly at same time. . . ."

† Rawson, however, worked out an ingenious system in time for the spring journeys. The compass was mounted on the sledge towed behind; an observer stretched out there directed the driver by working switches which flashed two lights—one for left and the other for right—that were mounted on the dashboard.

along. Laborious and slow as it promised to be, the method nevertheless was a fairly sure way of laying a straight course past the crevasses in and around the Valley of Crevasses.

* * *

Time was no longer like a river running, but a deep still pool. It was enough to immerse myself in it, quietly and unresentfully, and not struggle any more. The past was done, and the future would adduce its own appropriate liquidation. My one thought was not to endanger further the fragile equilibrium within which my physical being was temporarily balanced and to try to keep my mind calm and stable by the methods I had been using right along. Everything that remained of me was centered upon the radio. I kept up the weather data, made the observations, and wound the clocks; but all this was automatic. Whatever else that was truly alive and reasoning was devoted toward keeping the channel of communication open, not merely on my account, but on account of the men bound for Advance Base. From the beginning I had loathed the radio; now I hated it with a hate that transcended reason. Each day it left me helpless for hours. If I had smashed it with a hammer, as I was more than once tempted to do, I might not have suffered nearly so much. But there was a moral aspect which restrained me. For I had set in motion certain forces which I was powerless to control; and, as long as men were proposing to grope in the darkness between me and Little America, there could be no letup.

On Saturday the 28th the wind flickered into the south and died; and, after falling for three days, the snow stopped. On Sunday the cold again moved in. The temperature pushed down to − 57°. I heard Little America calling, but Dyer could not hear me. At first I thought that Poulter was again on his way; then I decided not, since Dyer made no mention of it, but went on repeating his patient formula. Nonetheless, I set off two signal pots in the afternoon. Weariness took me then. In the tunnels, at the foot of the ladder, was a gallon tin of grain alcohol used in the instruments. I poured myself a stiff hooker, which I mixed with water, and gulped it down. Instead of giving me a temporary lift, it seemed instead to knock me to pieces. I was nearly helpless most of the day, with terrible pains in my stomach, and the top of my head seemed ready to blow off. I decided this one experiment was enough.

July 29

I'm still groggy; but, in spite of the haze in my mind, I've been worrying over my canceling the instructions to Poulter to remain on the trail. . . . It's rotten leadership and, worse than that, a God-damned mess.

On Monday the minimum thermometer in the shelter crept to 64° below zero; the mean for the day was only 6° warmer. The next day was hardly better; I froze an ear while bringing in some corn meal from the tunnel. That day, also, I heard nothing. My heart misgave me. At the schedule time I broadcast a message blind, urging

Poulter not to attempt to force his way through any dangerous crevasses, but to return to Little America if the going turned hard. It went unheard. As best I could, I salved my conscience by setting off two more charges of gasoline, plus a flare, which I tied to a line and threw across the radio antenna, where it burned fifteen feet off the ground. The furious light elicited no response.

* * *

Thus ended July. It ended in cold, as it had been born in cold. I have the meteorological records before me now. Twenty days were 60° below or colder; on six days the temperature crossed − 70°. When I folded the sheet back on the calendar, I said to myself: This is the sixty-first day since the first collapse in the tunnel; nothing has really changed meanwhile; I am still alone. The men at Little America were no nearer. And all around me was the evidence of my ruin. Cans of half-eaten, frozen food were scattered on the deck. The parts of the dismantled generator were heaped up in a corner, where I had scuffed them three weeks before. Books had tumbled out of the shelves, and I had let them lie where they fell. And now the film of ice covered the floor, four walls, and the ceiling. There was nothing left for it to conquer.

And yet, the situation was not simply one of unrelieved disintegration. My life wasn't just moving backwards. Although I was losing on some fronts, I was gaining on others. For the day was coming on; it was heaving ponderously into the north, pushing back the darkness a little bit more every day, firing its own gorgeous signal pots along the horizon to a man who had little else to look for. So there was that on my side: the miraculous expansion and growth of the light, the soundless prelude to the sun which was only twenty-seven days north of me.

AUGUST: THE SEARCHLIGHT

AUGUST BEGAN ON A WEDNESDAY. IT WAS BLACK WITH
threat. I had never seen the barometer drop so low. The
pressure fell to 27.72 inches, and the recording pen ran off
the sheet. Watching it fall, I had the feeling that the air
was being sucked off the Barrier. But the anemometer
cups dawdled on a simpering breeze which was satisfied to
box the compass and presently expire. Nothing else happened. Yet, all day I imagined that the Barrier was holding
its breath, waiting for the swoop of a hurricane.

My mood was infected by the uncertainty in nature. For
the first time I was really on the verge of losing my self-
control; I could not sit still for nervousness. I refilled the
spare kerosene cans just outside the door, which had been
used up during the last setback; and I brought in more
food from the tunnel until I had at least two weeks' reserve
in the shack. The extra effort taxed me, but I would not—
and indeed could not—stop until it was done. Habit and
necessity made me do a number of things automatically;
they were done in spite of myself.

The fact that I had heard nothing from Little America

in five days sharpened my fears. For all I knew, Poulter
might be on his way, might, indeed, be close by. I used up
the last of my strength setting off another can of gasoline.
The surrounding night was empty of signs. So I went to
bed and dreamed fitfully of tractors and crevasses and
strange unfriendly faces crowding the shack, shutting out
something vague which, nevertheless, I ardently desired.

August 2

I have heard nothing today; but, to be on the safe
side, I set off one can of gasoline in the afternoon and
another in the evening. The weather is moderating.
From a minimum of 52° below zero yesterday, the temperature has soared to − 2° at 11 P.M. There's a light
fog, but no wind to speak of.

August 3

Providence has been good to us. Poulter is safe at
Little America, and all my futile tinkering with the
radio seems to have borne fruit. The messages really
made sense today. Poulter hasn't left, but is ready to do
so as soon as Haines gives him a good weather report.
Little America is fogbound, but it is wonderfully clear
here. At noon the northern sky had a fine rosy hue and
a definitely yellow look in the direction of the Ross Sea.
The maximum thermometer read zero this morning,
but it's getting colder again—nearly 40° below zero now
(10 P.M.). The growing light is a factor which each day
lessens Poulter's hazards; but on my side I have almost
ceased to care. A sort of numbness seems to have claimed
me.

Dyer must be having a hell of a time at the other end of the conversations. It is a miserable predicament not to be able to answer Little America's urgent questions. But I must say that Dyer and Hutcheson have been wonderfully patient.

August 4

Poulter has started. This afternoon I was told that he had taken departure five hours earlier with two months' rations aboard and a big reserve of gasoline. The weather looks good, for there's practically no wind, and the temperature is steady in the minus thirties. Also, the fact that Poulter is actually headed south again has pierced my torpor, and hope is once more quickening in my heart.

Sunday was a day I should like to rub from memory. I was in ghastly shape when I awakened—too sick to eat and too tired to lose myself in any passing task. I fussed a bit with the register, but my eyes kept bothering me, and I finally sank into the chair beside the stove to wait for the noon schedule. It brought bad news. Poulter was bogged down in the crevasses on the Little America side of Amundsen Arm. He had missed the passage which had carried him safely through before; in trying to negotiate a new transit, he had lost his way and was even then trying to extricate the car from a pothole crevasse into which it had fallen.

Because the receiver was acting up again, it took me some little time to get these facts straight; and, when I had them in full view after hearing the combined reports of Murphy and Haines, they seemed enormous. If Poulter was in serious trouble, less than ten miles from Little America, why wasn't something being done to help him? My nerves broke. I jerked at the key: "Charlie and Bill, what in God's name is the matter? Won't another tractor help? Use all resources."

Charlie was replying as I adjusted the headphones. The anger was gone, and remorse was flooding in. I would have given anything I possessed to recall those words. My friend spoke deliberately, gently, and even, I thought, a little reproachfully. If I do not remember his exact words, I do remember the sense. In his opinion, he said, Poulter was proceeding cautiously and reasonably. A stand-by tractor was ready, and had been ready from the time Poulter left. They were in constant touch with him. Although Poulter had been offered the full facilities of the camp, he had firmly declined them. So there was no cause for alarm. In all probability the tractor would be under way again within a few hours. Finishing, Charlie said, in the same unemotional tone: "Dick, the truth is that we are more worried about you. Are you ill? Are you hurt?"

I tried to dodge the questions by saying that I understood the whole tractor situation. But at this point first my legs and then my arms gave out on the cranks. The message was left dangling in mid-air. Charlie began to talk. He said that what they had heard was only partly intelligible. And again he asked what was wrong. There was no escape then. The old fiction of the lame arm just wouldn't do any more. Murphy was too insistent. He even mentioned something about sending out a doctor. "Nothing to worry about," I answered finally; "only please don't ask me to crank any more."

All this was duly committed to the Little America log; and with it John Dyer's incidental observation that "Byrd's strength seems to peter out after every few words." My evasions therefore fooled nobody but myself. Murphy's misgivings deepened; yet, he professed to be satisfied. "We appreciate how hard the cranking must be," he said. "Don't worry about us or about Poulter. See you tomorrow."

August 6

At noon today Poulter was only twenty-one miles south. Yesterday he extricated himself from the crevasse, but since then has been crippled by continuous mechanical trouble. The clutch is slipping badly, the fan belts have all been used up, and Charlie was doubtful that Poulter could do much about it. I sent a reassuring message, only to have Charlie say that Dyer couldn't pick up a word; my signal was too weak. He tactfully suggested that I need not exert myself cranking unless I had an important message; otherwise an OK would mean I was all right. I sent two or three OK's, and closed down for the day.

I've suffered for what I said yesterday. I did my friends at Little America a grave injustice in questioning their judgment and efficiency. Of course they know what they are doing, and from this distance I have no right to meddle. Yet, my chagrin goes beyond that. It

maddens me that after sixty-six days I have given myself away in a momentary fit of impatience.

I have no way of telling how much Little America has
guessed. Charlie's casualness may be just a mask. Which
is what torments me. The last thing I want is to see this
trip degenerate into a rescue trip with all the risks and
humiliations which such a trip would involve. And
again I say this in all humility. This business has long
since passed the ephemeral considerations of pride or
face-saving; it is now one of cold calculation. If they are
tempted into recklessness, and something goes wrong,
my chances of ever getting out of here will suffer, too;
for the Barrier is not a fit place for worried, anxious
men. So my solicitude is definitely selfish. Obviously, the
officers at Little America are acting with profound care
as to the risks. They could not act otherwise without be-
traying me and the men under them. . . .

All this notwithstanding, I wish to heaven the matter
were settled, one way or another. I can't go on this way,
raised one minute by hope and dropped the next by
failure. Every day my recuperative resources grow a
little less; and for this I mostly blame the radio. The
steady cranking has raised hell with me. When I finish
a schedule, I am reduced to staggering about in a condition approaching helplessness. One can put up with such
misery only so long, then something has to give. I am
sinking once more to the level of beggary.

I shall go to bed now, supported by the hothouse fiction that tomorrow night will find them here. In my
heart I know this can't possibly happen; not after

Charlie's discouraging report. Worst of all, the cold is steepening: it's close to 60° below zero now.

* * *

Tuesday was heart-breaking. In a matter-of-fact way Murphy informed me that Poulter was once more back in Little America. Twenty-six miles south, or barely half the distance made good on the first attempt, the clutch had given out entirely. Poulter had turned back and was lucky to reach Little America at all. "It's a pity, but these are the facts," Charlie said. "The men are sleeping now. The car is being overhauled and will be ready by midnight."

I replied that what they were doing was sensible. Nothing was to be gained by hurry and push.

"Please repeat; we couldn't get it," Little America said. "John says that your transmitter isn't tuned properly."

Ill fortune seldom comes unattended. My transmitter was failing. Formerly I couldn't hear Little America, but Little America could at least hear me. Now the situation was reversed. I could hear them fairly well, but they could scarcely hear me at all. "Wait," I said. I hurriedly checked the transmitter, made a few adjustments, and started afresh.

"No good, but never mind," said Charlie. "Try to have it fixed by tomorrow. We'll see you at the same time. Don't bother about lights for another two days or so."

That morning I really surrendered. In the diary I wrote: "It appears that aid for me and reasonable safety for the men can't lie in the same bed. . . . It was a mistake to allow my hopes to rise so high. . . . I finally gathered today that three men were in the party, and that one of them was that fine, loyal shipmate of many years—Pete Demas— another was Bud Waite, in whom I have complete confidence. When Poulter and these two men turned back, there must have been good reason for it."

Yet, even with hope gone, the animal tenacity in me, as in every man, would not let me give up. Ever since the first start, I had been preparing flares and firepots. Now, making one trip an hour, I hauled half a dozen more cans of gasoline to the surface. I then had twelve signal pots ready, consisting of tomato cans and a couple of gasoline tins with the tops cut away. Weighted down with snow blocks and covered with paper to keep the drift out, they were racked on the improvised bench on the roof. I stood up the kite in the veranda, at the foot of the ladder, with the line neatly coiled. There, too, I put the last of the magnesium flares, of which I had about half a dozen left. In a sense, I was preparing for a last stand.

Yet, these simple preparations, by taking me out of myself for a while, did me good. And the day itself was almost heartening. It was clear, and not too cold—only 41° below zero at noon. And there was no denying that the daylight was rising with the implacable and irresistible force of the solar system behind it. Between me and Little America the darkness for a little while was broken clearly in two; the pearl dawn-light expanded and turned rosy and yellowish, and it made me think of a rug being laid for the sun. The sun was only three weeks distant now. I tried to imagine what it would be like, but the conception was too vast for me to grasp.

August 8

They started again early this morning for the third try—Poulter, Demas, and Waite. The day was clear, the light good, and the cold only so-so. The air was in the minus fifties early this morning, but it warmed up in the minus thirties around midday and is now holding fairly steady just under the minus-forty-degree line.

Charlie was cheerful. "Keep the lights going, Dick. This time I really think they're going right through," he said. Well, that remains to be seen. I cannot allow myself to hope again; the drop into failure is too abrupt. The great pity is that I am only half in touch with Little America. I can hear them well enough, but they can't get me. I've already had the transmitter apart once, and I shall have another go at it tonight.

Next day was Thursday. I awakened with the unshakable conviction that this trip, like the others, must inevitably end in failure. Better now than then, I understand why I chose to adopt this attitude: it was a defense mechanism for warding off the terrible wrench of another disappointment. Strangely, I had no true sense of despair; rather, I thought I was being downright realistic. My own personal stake in the outcome of the journey was of dwindling importance. No matter how the trip turned out, whether they reached Advance Base or not, I was convinced that I personally had little to gain; my salvage value was next to zero. Only one thing continued to be important: the expedition's prestige and the safety of the three men between me and Little America.

The weather was not exactly auspicious. Although the barometer was flickering upward, the sky was overcast, and the weather vane tentatively fingered the east, which is the storm-breeding quarter. The fear grew in me that either a blizzard or a fresh onslaught of cold would trap the party midway between Little America and Advance Base. I became like a spectator at a play. The dangers massing around the principals were manifest; but, because the resolution lay in the hands of others, I could not shout a warning.

Evidently the same uncertainty permeated Little America. When we met on schedule in the early afternoon, John Dyer sounded hurried and nervous. From what he said, I gathered that Charlie Murphy was off skiing somewhere. Bill Haines reported in his place. All that I could make out was that Poulter was getting along quite well. "How's weather?" I asked. Bill thought it looked none too good. "For God's sake, Bill," I spelled out, "tell them to hurry." If weather were in the making, I wanted the party off the Barrier.

"I understand," Bill answered; "but they'll be all right. They can take care of themselves."

Charlie Murphy took over then. Although his voice was clearer, I lost much of what was said. However, he finally fixed for my benefit the fact that the stand-by tractor was in readiness to go to Poulter's assistance, and that in the event the tractors failed, June and Bowlin could have one of the planes ready to fly within forty-eight hours. Charlie Murphy and I had known each other a long time; we had had a close and deep affection for each other; and, not so much from what he said as from what he left unsaid, I sensed the anxiety in him. "Thanks," I replied, "but you must make no mistakes, nor take chances."

Afterwards I sat beside the fire, with a blanket wrapped around my shoulders. I must have dozed, because the next thing I knew the shack was completely dark. I had neglected to fill the lantern, which had burned itself out. I groped around until I found the flashlight. It was time for the 4 o'clock radio schedule. Sitting in the dark, I heard Charlie telling me that Poulter was forty-odd miles on his way, and evidently moving right along. The rest was barely intelligible. I caught a reference to lights, and then a sentence asking if I needed a doctor. Manifestly, Charlie had his own ideas as to the state of affairs at Advance Base, and no further deception on my part would be apt to mislead him. Nevertheless, I replied, "No, no, no." And on the negative we shut down for the day.

Thereafter the hours fell like chips from a lazy whittler's stick. I paced the shack from the sheer physical necessity of doing something. Once I went topside for a check on the weather. The wind was all but mute in the south, and the sky appeared to be clearing. The cold was coming on again. From a high of 16° below zero around noon, the temperature was again pressing into the minus thirties. I thought: Poulter can put up with that, after what he has been through. Before closing the hatch, I

282

looked north and, I think, said a silent prayer for the three of them.

For supper I had soup, crackers, and potatoes; and, when they were down and promised to stay down, I went to bed. I pondered a long time. The likelihood to which I had blindly closed my mind was virtually a demonstrated fact: namely, Little America had now made up its collective mind that I was in trouble, and Poulter was coming more to help me than to observe meteors. And, if this was truly the case, I knew for a certainty that he must be determined to make a run for it, regardless of the condition of the flags beyond the Valley of Crevasses. This explained all the talk about lights. Once safely around the crevasses, he was evidently of a mind to steer by compass for Advance Base, trusting to find me by a light which could be seen fifteen or twenty miles away.

I could see the risk in that. Suppose I collapsed entirely. Without a light to fetch him in, Poulter might pass within a hundred yards or so of the Base and never see it. That would be easy to do on a dark night. And if in the hurry they should push too far to the south, then it would indeed go hard with them. True, they knew the position, and Poulter could determine his own location within a mile or two by taking star sights. But taking these in the cold is no simple matter; and, indeed, if the sky was overcast, it would be impossible. In that case, Poulter's only recourse would be to block out an area and crisscross it until he ran down the Base. Meanwhile, more hours would be used up, more gasoline; and the danger from crevasses in an untested area would be multiplied by many times.

Clearly, then, I had a task to do. Instead of being merely a passive objective, I must also be an active collaborator. My job was that of lighthouse keeper on a dangerous coast. I simply had to stay on my feet; and, since my reserve strength was almost exhausted, I must husband the little that remained. There was no sense in frittering it away as I had done in the past, setting off my gasoline pots when Poulter was so far away that he couldn't possibly have seen them. So I drew myself up into the bunk, lighted a candle, and calculated his probable arrival time. At 4 o'clock he was some forty miles and thirty-seven hours out of Little America; his average speed, therefore, was one and a fraction miles per hour. He had eighty miles to go. Even with the best of fortune, he wouldn't be apt to travel faster than five miles per hour. Suppose by the grace of God he was able to make that speed. In that case he would arrive about 8 o'clock in the morning.

This seemed too good to be even possible. But I had to be ready for any eventuality. Therefore, I resolved to have the first kite in the air by 7 o'clock in the morning, and to burn gasoline at two-hour intervals during the day. More than that I could not do; and I was doubtful that perhaps even this was within my scope. Anyhow, I reached out for sleep. It was a long time coming; and, when it came, it was haunted with phantasms of crevasses and floundering men and dancing, far-off lights.

* * *

284

In the morning I awakened with a start. Ordinarily the business of waking up was a long-drawn-out inner struggle between resolution and despair, but this time I was pitched headlong into alertness. I dressed as rapidly as I could, lit the stove, and went slowly up to the surface. It was 7:30 o'clock by the wrist watch. The day was dark. Heavy clouds were heaped up in the eastern sky. From habit I glanced north. And this time I swore I saw a light. To be sure, I shut my eyes. When I looked again, the light was gone. Stars had deceived me on many occasions, and one might have misled me then; I did not think so. The conviction brought an access of strength.

The kite was standing at the foot of the ladder. I hauled it up on a string and soaked the long tail in gasoline, leaving a couple of feet of paper dry at the end. This would be the equivalent of a fuse and give me time to haul the kite into the air before the tail burned up. Then I started down wind with it. There was just a whisper of a breeze out of the southeast. To save strength I crept part of the way. Altogether I went about two hundred feet, the longest distance in many a day. I scooped out a little hole, stood the kite upright in it, and piled snow loosely around the vertical strut to hold it erect. Then, after straightening out the tail, I fired the paper. Although I footed it back as fast as I dared, the gasoline was blazing before I reached the other end of the line.

Not having the strength to run, I had to jerk the thing into the air, pulling in the line hand over hand. The first pull was lucky. A gust of wind caught the kite, lifting

285

it cleanly. I yanked hard, and it skated to a height of a hundred feet. The sight of it swaying against the night, dangling a fiery tail, was very satisfying. It was my first creative act in a long time. The light lasted for perhaps five minutes. Then it shrank to a mere incandescent filament, which finally parted and fell. No answer came from the north. I hauled down the kite and turned to the battery of gasoline signals. I fired two charges in quick succession. Nor did this evoke a response. The frenzy passed, and I stumbled from exhaustion. Too weak to go further for a moment, I sat down on the snow to think. My lights must have been visible for at least twenty miles. The fact that Poulter hadn't answered meant that he must be still out of sight. Therefore, I could rest from the signaling for at least four hours more.

Back in the shack I paused at the radio and listened for ten minutes or so on the chance that Little America might be on the air. The air was silent. By then the snow had melted in the water bucket. I made a little hot milk, which refreshed me, then climbed into the sleeping bag, leaving the lantern burning. I dozed intermittently. Several times I thought I heard the scrunch of tractor treads, but it was only creaking noises within the Barrier itself; and several times the singing of the antenna wire in the wind similarly tricked me. At noon I went topside again with my field glasses. The dawn-light was quite strong; I could count at least a dozen flags down the trail, which meant visibility was good for two miles; and a rosy glow suffused the northern quadrant, halfway to the zenith. But nothing moved.

At the regular time I met Little America. Murphy was almost jubilant. Six hours before, Poulter had advised that he was more than halfway around the Valley of Crevasses. Best of all, he had picked up the trail. Indeed, the flags were apparently standing clear. Poulter said that he expected no more trouble; he was over the Hump. "This is the best news in a long time," Charlie said. "We have another schedule with them at 3:45 o'clock. We'll broadcast a report to you then."

An hour later I pulled myself up the hatch, and fired a can of gasoline. No answer came; but, then, I did not expect one so soon. At 4 o'clock Little America was calling in great excitement. Poulter was ninety-three miles south, dead on the trail. "According to the last report," Charlie said, "the generator brushes are giving out, but Poulter is pretty certain that he won't be held up. Good luck to you, Dick. Don't forget to keep the lights burning." I didn't reply, dreading what would happen if I cranked the generator.

When Dyer signed off, saying he would look for me again in four hours, I tried to collect my thoughts. Charlie guessed that with luck Poulter might be at Advance Base in another eight hours—by early morning at the latest. The prospect was too big to visualize. It was like knowing in advance that you would be reborn again, without the intermediate obliteration of death. Moreover, I thought that Charlie was being overly optimistic. Poulter still had about thirty miles to go. In the 61 hours he had been under way, he had averaged 1½ miles per hour; and, in the past 24 hours, less than 2 miles per hour. Even at the latter speed, he was still 15 hours distant from Advance Base. So he wasn't apt to arrive much before 7 o'clock in the morning.

Even so, prudence persuaded me to make ready for an earlier arrival. About 5 o'clock I went up the ladder. The sky had cleared considerably, but the gray dawn-light had gone, and the Barrier had seldom looked so black and empty. I set off another can of gasoline; as before, no answer came, nor did I expect one. I dropped below and rested an hour. I forced myself to read Hergesheimer's *Java Head,* incidentally; but my mind would not follow the words. At 6 o'clock I was again at the trapdoor. And this time I really saw something. Dead in the north a beam of light lifted itself from the Barrier, swept to the vertical, and fell; then it rose again, touched a star, and went out. This was unmistakably Poulter's searchlight, and my first guess was that it wasn't more than ten miles away.

I was inexpressibly happy. With a flare in my hand, I made for the kite, half falling in my eagerness. I made the flare fast to the tail, lit it, and, by repeating what I had done before, I jerked the kite seventy-five feet into the air. The flare burned brilliantly for about five minutes. All the time I watched the north, but in vain. The flare died, and I let the kite fall. For half an hour I sat on the snow, just watching. The darkness deepened perceptibly. I knew that I had seen a light, but after all the disappointments I was ready to mistrust anything. What I had to have was a clear-cut decision, one way or the other. This waiting, this coming and going, this uncertainty, were intolerable.

This was the seventy-first day since the first collapse. I had endured as much as human frailty could bear.

When I moved to rise, my strength was gone. I crawled to the hatch, slipped down the ladder, and made for the bunk. My weariness was infinite. Yet, I could not lie still. Half an hour later I headed topside, halting at every rung of the ladder. You will see their lights close by, I told myself. No lights showed. The Barrier was solid gloom. But they must have seen the kite flare. If they had, then they must have felt no need to make acknowledgment. For I saw nothing, and heard nothing. I fired another can of gasoline; when it burned dry, I ignited another flare, which I planted upright in the snow. Consciousness of my own futility added lead to my feet. The minutes went by. At 7:30 o'clock a few stars struggled clear of the cloud rack. Where are they now? Carefully I lighted another can of gasoline, and waited for it to go out. Maybe they have camped for the night. But I knew they wouldn't do that, having come so close. In my pessimism I imagined the worst: a breakdown, fire, perhaps they had fallen through a crevasse.

The red trace on the thermograph was working through the minus forties. I was unspeakably disheartened when I picked up the earphones. Charlie Murphy was in the midst of a report. As nearly as I could tell, Poulter hadn't been heard from since 4 o'clock. The earphones fell from my hands. It is a pity that I didn't wait to hear more, for Murphy was trying to tell me that this was in all probability a very good sign; that, having drawn so near Advance Base, Poulter had no doubt decided not to waste time broadcasting, but was pushing on as fast as he could. The fact was that I was at the end of my tether. My mind turned vague; and, when I recovered my faculties, I was sprawled half in and half out of the bunk.

The cold roused me. It was then about 8:30 o'clock. I hitched myself to the top of the bunk, pulled the blankets up, and fell asleep. I slept for about an hour and a half. Then, realizing that I simply must tend to the signals, I drove myself to the ladder. The best I could do was to get halfway up. I lunged back into the shack and tried to think what I could do. Obviously, I needed a stimulant. Remembering what alcohol had done to me the last time I had tried it, I ruled that out. The rest is not wholly clear. In the medical chest was a hypophosphate containing strychnine. Around the bottle was a slip of paper listing the ingredients and the dose—one teaspoonful in a glass of water. The fluid was frozen, but I thawed it in the water bucket. I took three teaspoonfuls in a cup of water, and on top of it three cups of the strongest tea I could brew. I felt lightheaded, but my strength seemed to come up.

Armed with another flare and a length of flexible wire, I pulled myself up the hatch. Temporarily, at least, I had strength to spare. I threw the wire over the radio antenna between two of the poles, made the flare fast to one end, fired the fuse, and then hauled it to the top of the antenna. The light was blinding. When it died out, I blinked my eyes and peered into the north. The fingering beam of a searchlight moved slowly up and down against the dark backdrop of the horizon. It might be another hallucination. I sat down, resolutely facing the opposite horizon. When I stood up and looked again, the beam was still fanning up and down. Indeed, I soon made out a second light, fixed and dimmer than the first, evidently a head-light.

This was indeed the world advancing to meet me. In a little while I should see friends and hear voices talking. The escape which for two and a half months had existed only in imagination was now an oncoming reality. It would be hard to describe exactly what that light did to me. In my whole life I can recall but one comparable experience. That was at the fag end of the transatlantic flight. We had crossed the Atlantic in fog and storm, and on the coast of France ran into a succession of line squalls which gave way to rain and more fog. Although we did reach Paris, we were obliged to turn back to the coast, as that was the only place we could land without killing somebody other than ourselves. Our fuel was nearly gone; the four of us were exhausted; and ahead of us, as certain as death, was a crash landing. And then, in the forty-fourth hour, on the coast of France, we saw a revolving light, which was the beacon of the lighthouse at Ver-Sur-Mer. Well, seeing the tractor's lights was something like that, only this time I had waited longer and suffered more. In that miraculous instant all the despair and suffering of June and July fell away, and I felt as if I had just been born again.

Suddenly the lights disappeared. The car had dipped into one of the shallow valleys with which the Barrier abounds, and the intervening ridge had blotted it out.

Therefore the tractor must be some distance off, and I doubted that it would reach me for another two hours. After lighting another can of gasoline—that left only two—and the next to the last flare, I went below, intending to prepare supper for my three guests. I dumped a couple of cans of soup into a pan, and set them on the fire to heat.

When next I peered from the hatch, I saw the searchlight very clearly—so clearly, in fact, that I was able to decide that it was fixed to the side of the cabin. Even then, I decided, they were still about five miles off. It would take them another hour to run out the journey. So I sat down in the snow to await the conclusion of this wonderful event. In a little while I could hear on the clear, vibrant air the rumble of the treads, then the *beep-beep-beep* of the horn. But the car was not appreciably nearer. Feeling cold, I went below and huddled beside the fire for a little while. It was hard to sit still when a miracle was being contrived overhead; yet, I compelled myself to do so lest I collapse completely. I looked around the shack and thought how different it would be in a few minutes. It was a filthy mess, and I remember being ashamed that Poulter and the others should find me in such a state; but, while I did make a few feeble passes at the untidy heaps, I was too weak to do much about them.

A few minutes before midnight I went topside again. They had come very close. I could see the bulking shadow of the tractor. As a greeting I set off the last can of gasoline and the last flare. They were just dying when the car stopped about a hundred yards away. Three men jumped out, with Poulter in the center, looming doubly

big in furs. I stood up, but I did not dare to walk forward.
I remember shaking hands all around, and Waite insists
that I said: "Hello, fellows. Come on below. I have a
bowl of hot soup waiting for you." If that is really so,
then I can only plead that no theatricalism was intended.
The truth is that I could find no words to transport out-
ward what was really in my heart. It is also said that I
collapsed at the foot of the ladder. I have only a muddled
impression of that and a slightly clearer one of trying to
hide my weakness. Nevertheless, I do remember sitting
on the bunk, watching Poulter and Demas and Waite
gulp down the soup and the biscuits; and I do remember
what their voices were like, even if I am not sure of what
they said. And I do remember thinking that much of
what they said was as meaningless as if it were spoken in
an unfamiliar tongue; for they had been together a long
time, occupied with common experiences, and in their
talk they could take a good deal for granted. I was the
stranger.

* * *

All this happened a little after midnight, August 11,
1934. Two months and four days passed before I was able
to return to Little America—which was all to the good,
since it enabled us to extend the meteorological record-
ings that much longer. This second wait was also a long
one, but I was in no shape to leave earlier than I did.
I could not possibly have survived a trip back in the
tractor, and I hesitated to risk an airplane until I had
enough endurance to withstand the rigors of a forced

landing, always a possibility in that part of the world. It is a tribute to Poulter's self-restraint that he never once brought up the question of my returning. Neither, until toward the end, did Charlie Murphy, who continued to act as buffer, relaying only those expedition matters which required my final decision. "We are all happy beyond words over the way things have turned out," he radioed Poulter. "Tell him that he will find an expedition ready to go when he throws the switch."

The two months that followed the tractor's coming were as pleasant as the others had been miserable. True, with four of us in the shack, we couldn't move without getting in each other's way. At night the three of them used to spread their sleeping bags on the deck and sleep shoulder to shoulder like three Musketeers. Demas and Waite took turns at cooking and cleaning house; Poulter looked after the instruments, and observed meteors as long as the darkness lasted. For a long time they wouldn't allow me to do anything; and, to tell the truth, I didn't insist beyond the requirements of simple courtesy. For it was wonderful not to have to do anything for a change. The darkness lifted from my heart, just as it presently did from the Barrier, with a tremendous inrush of white light. I was a long time regaining my strength, but little by little it came back, and with it some of my lost weight.

Yet, for a reason that I can't wholly explain, except in terms of pride, I concealed from these men, as best I could, the true extent of my weakness. I never mentioned and, therefore, never acknowledged it. On their side, the men never pressed me to tell what had happened before they came. They must have had their own ideas when they cleaned up the mess, but whatever they thought they kept to themselves. The self-preservation instinct of leadership and a sense of shame over my flimsiness drove me to wall off the immediate past. I wanted no one to be able to look over the wall; also, something deep inside me demanded that I close my mind to the notion that I had been rescued.

Pride contrives its own special vindications. I was for a long time convinced that whether the tractors had come or not, I could have stuck it out alone. As indeed I might, had it not been for that damnable hand generator. However, that is beside the point. The point is that I needed help badly; and the least that I can do is to express my everlasting gratitude to Poulter and Demas and Waite and Charlie Murphy.

On October 14th Bowlin and Schlossbach arrived from Little America in the Pilgrim. The sun was already high in the sky, and Bowlin told me that the main sledging parties were making ready to start on their three-months' journeys. Poulter said he would fly back with me. Waite and Demas stayed behind to strip the last sheets from the recording drums, and stow the personal gear and the weather records on the tractor. I climbed the hatch and never looked back. Part of me remained forever at Latitude 80° 08′ South: what survived of my youth, my vanity, perhaps, and certainly my skepticism. On the other hand, I did take away something that I had not fully possessed before: appreciation of the sheer beauty and miracle of being alive, and a humble set of values. All this happened four years ago. Civilization has not altered my ideas. I live more simply now, and with more peace.

Before I close this story of Advance Base, I must mention one more thing I learned as a result of what happened to me there. Eager as I was to step directly into the responsibilities of leadership on my return to Little America, I was not long in discovering that a few were beyond me. The medico said that if I flew I should have only myself to blame for the consequences. While I did, in fact, command the first important flight into the unknown—and these flights have been my biggest interest—and another one later on, I had to be satisfied to stay on the ground after that and turn the tricky navigation of the big Condor over to Ken Rawson. Rawson was then only twenty-three years old and, if I remember correctly, had been in the air but once or twice in his life. He performed his job to perfection. No better compliment is possible than the simple statement that the two hard-boiled veteran Navy pilots who sat forward of him never questioned his reckoning. So I say in conclusion: A man doesn't begin to attain wisdom until he recognizes that he is no longer indispensable.